J. R. R. TOLKIEN'S SANCTIFYING MYTH:
UNDERSTANDING MIDDLE-EARTH

J. R. R. Tolkien's

SANCTIFYING MYTH

Understanding Middle-earth

by Bradley J. Birzer

with a foreword by Joseph
Pearce

REGNERY GATEWAY
Washington, D.C.

Regnery Gateway™ is a trademark of Salem Communications Holding Corporation
Regnery® is a registered trademark and its colophon is a trademark of Salem Communications Holding Corporation

Cataloging-in-Publication data on file with the Library of Congress

ISBN: 978-1-68451-535-6
eISBN: 978-1-68451-624-7

Published in the United States by
Regnery Gateway, an Imprint of
Regnery Publishing
A Division of Salem Media Group
Washington, D.C.
www.Regnery.com

Manufactured in the United States of America

10 9 8 7 6 5 4 3 2 1

Interior book design by Kara Björklund

Books are available in quantity for promotional or premium use. For information on discounts and terms, please visit our website: www.Regnery.com.

To Rita, Kevin, and Todd Birzer,
who journeyed with me into the heart of Mordor.
May we all meet in the Blessed Realm someday.

Table of Contents

Foreword

The phenomenal popularity of Tolkien's *Lord of the Rings* continues to be greeted with anger and contempt by many self-styled literary "experts." Rarely has a book caused such controversy and rarely has the vitriol of the critics highlighted to such an extent the cultural schism between the cliquish literary illuminati and the views of the reading public.

It is perhaps noteworthy that most of the self-styled "experts" amongst the literati who have queued up to sneer contemptuously at *The Lord of the Rings* are outspoken champions of cultural deconstruction and moral relativism. Most would treat the claims of Christianity in general, and of the Catholic Church in particular, with the same dismissive disdain with which they have poured scorn upon Tolkien. Indeed, their antagonism could be linked to the fact that Tolkien's myth is enriched throughout with inklings of the truths of the Catholic faith.

According to Tolkien's own "scale of significance," expressed candidly in a letter written shortly after *The Lord of the Rings* was published, his Catholic faith was the most important, or most "significant," influence on the writing of the work. It is, therefore, not merely erroneous but patently perverse to see Tolkien's epic as anything other than a specifically Christian myth. This being so, the present volume emerges as a valuable and timely reiteration of the profoundly Christian dimension in the work of the man who is possibly the most important writer of the twentieth century.

Professor Birzer grapples with the very concept of "myth" and proceeds to a discussion of Tolkien's philosophy of myth, rooted as it is in the relationship between Creator and creature, and, in consequence, the relationship between Creation and sub-creation. In his rigorously researched and richly written study, Professor Birzer helps us to understand the theological basis of the mythological world of Middle-earth and enables us to see that Tolkien's epic goes beyond mere "fantasy" to the deepest realms of metaphysics. Far from being an escapist fantasy, *The Lord of the Rings* is revealed as a theological thriller.

Tolkien's development of the philosophy of myth derives directly from his Christian faith. In fact, to employ a lisping pun, Tolkien is a *mis*understood man precisely because he is a *myth*understood man. He understood the nature and meaning of myth in a manner that has not been grasped by his critics. It is this misapprehension on the part of his detractors that lies at the very root of their failure to appreciate his work. For most modern critics a myth is merely another word for a lie or a falsehood, something which is intrinsically *not* true. For Tolkien, myth had virtually the opposite meaning. It was the only way that certain transcendent truths could be expressed in intelligible form. This paradoxical philosophy was destined to have a decisive and profound influence on C. S. Lewis, facilitating his conversion to Christianity. It is interesting—indeed astonishing—to note that without J. R. R. Tolkien there might not have been a C. S. Lewis, at least not the C. S. Lewis that has come to be known and loved throughout the world as the formidable Christian apologist and author of sublime Christian myths.

Integral to Tolkien's philosophy of myth was the belief that creativity is a mark of God's divine image in Man. God, as Creator, poured forth the gift of creativity to men, the creatures created in his own image. Only God can create in the primary sense, i.e., by bringing something into being out of nothing. Man, however, can sub-create by molding the material of Creation into works of beauty. Music, art, and literature are all acts of sub-creation expressive of the divine essence in man. In this way, men share in the creative power of God.

This sublime vision found (sub)creative expression in the opening pages of *The Silmarillion*, the enigmatic and unfinished work that forms the theological and philosophical foundation upon which, and the mythological framework within which, *The Lord of the Rings* is structured.

The Silmarillion delved deep into the past of Middle-earth, Tolkien's sub-created world, and the landscape of legends recounted in its pages formed the vast womb of myth from which *The Lord of the Rings* was born. Indeed, Tolkien's *magnum opus* would not have been born at all if he had not first created, in *The Silmarillion*, the world, the womb, in which it was conceived.

The most important part of *The Silmarillion* is its account of the creation of Middle-earth by the One. This creation myth is perhaps the most significant, and the most beautiful, of all Tolkien's work. It goes to the very roots of his creative vision and says much about Tolkien himself. Somewhere within the early pages of *The Silmarillion* is to be found both the man behind the myth and the myth behind the man.

The "myth" behind Tolkien was, of course, Catholic Christianity, the "True Myth," and it is scarcely surprising that Tolkien's own version of the creation in *The Silmarillion* bears a remarkable similarity to the creation story in the book of Genesis. In the beginning was Eru, the One, who "made first the Ainur, the Holy Ones, that were the offspring of his thought, and they were with him before aught else was made." This, therefore, is the theological foundation upon which the whole edifice of Middle-earth is erected. Disharmony is brought into the cosmos when Melkor, one of the Holy Ones, or Archangels, decides to defy of the will of the Creator, mirroring the Fall of Satan. This disharmony is the beginning of evil. Again, Tolkien's myth follows the "True Myth" of Christianity with allegorical precision.

Shortly after describing the rebellion of Melkor, Tolkien introduces Sauron, the Dark Lord in *The Lord of the Rings*. Sauron is described as a "spirit" and as the "greatest" of Melkor's, alias Morgoth's, servants: "But in after years he rose like a shadow of Morgoth and a ghost of his malice, and walked behind him on the same ruinous path down into the Void."

Thus, the evil powers in *The Lord of the Rings* are specified as direct descendants of Tolkien's Satan, rendering impossible, or at any rate implausible, anything but a Christian interpretation of the book. In the impenetrable blackness of the Dark Lord and his abysmal servants, the Ringwraiths, we feel the objective reality of Evil. Sauron and his servants confront and affront us with the nauseous presence of the Real Absence of goodness. In his depiction of the potency of evil, Tolkien presents the reader with a metaphysical black hole far more unsettling than Milton's proud vision of Satan as "darkness visible."

Tolkien is, however, equally powerful in his depiction of goodness. In the unassuming humility of the hobbits we see the exaltation of the humble. In their reluctant heroism we see a courage ennobled by modesty. In the immortality of the elves, and the sadness and melancholic wisdom that immortality evokes in them, we receive an inkling that man's mortality is a gift of God, a gift that ends his exile in mortal life's "vale of tears" and enables him, in death, to achieve a mystical union with the Divine beyond the reach of Time.

In Gandalf we see the archetypal prefiguration of a powerful Prophet or Patriarch, a seer who beholds a vision of the Kingdom beyond the understanding of men. At times he is almost Christ-like. He lays down his life for his friends, and his mysterious "resurrection" results in his transfiguration. Before his self-sacrificial "death" he is Gandalf the Grey; after his "resurrection" he reappears as Gandalf the White, armed with greater powers and deeper wisdom.

In the true, though exiled, kingship of Aragorn we see glimmers of the hope for a restoration of truly ordained, i.e., Catholic, authority. The person of Aragorn represents the embodiment of the Arthurian and Jacobite yearning—the visionary desire for the "Return of the King" after eons of exile. The "sword that is broken," the symbol of Aragorn's kingship, is re-forged at the anointed time—a potent reminder of Excalibur's union with the Christendom it is ordained to serve. And, of course, in the desire for the Return of the King we have the desire of all Christians for the Second Coming of Christ, the True King and Lord of All.

Significantly, the role of men in *The Lord of the Rings* reflects their divine, though fallen, nature. They are to be found amongst the Enemy's servants, usually beguiled by deception into the ways of evil but always capable of repentance and, in consequence, redemption. Boromir, who represents Man in the Fellowship of the Ring, succumbs to the temptation to use the Ring, i.e., the forces of evil, in the naïve belief that it could be wielded as a powerful weapon against Sauron. He finally recognizes the error of seeking to use evil against evil. He dies heroically, laying down his life for his friends in a spirit of repentance.

Ultimately, *The Lord of the Rings* is a sublimely mystical Passion Play. The carrying of the Ring—the emblem of Sin—is the Carrying of the Cross. The mythological quest is a veritable Via Dolorosa. Catholic theology, explicitly present in *The Silmarillion* and implicitly present in *The Lord of the Rings*, is omnipresent in both, breathing life into the tales as invisibly but as surely as oxygen. Unfortunately, those who are blind to theology will continue to be blind to that which is most beautiful in *The Lord of the Rings*.

This volume will enable the blind to see, and will help the partially sighted to see more clearly the full beauty of Middle-earth. As a guide for those who would like to know more about the sanctifying power of Middle-earth this volume will prove invaluable. The sheer magnificence of Tolkien's mythological vision, and the Christian mysticism and theology that gives it life, is elucidated with clarity by Professor Birzer in chapters on "Myth and Sub-creation," "The Created Order," "Heroism," "The Nature of Evil," and "The Nature of Grace Proclaimed." There is also an excellent and enthralling chapter on the relationship between Middle-earth and modernity, in which Professor Birzer combines his scholarship as a historian with his grounding in philosophy and theology to place Tolkien's sub-creation into its proper sociopolitical and cultural context.

With Professor Birzer as an eminently able guide, the reader will be taken deep into Tolkien's world, entering into a realm of exciting truths that he might not previously have perceived. As he is led, with the Fellowship of the Ring, into the depths of Mordor and Beyond, he might even come to see that the exciting truths point to the most exciting Truth of all. At its deepest he might finally understand that the Quest is, in fact, a Pilgrimage.

Joseph Pearce
August 2002

Preface

My oldest brother, Kevin, received a first edition of *The Silmarillion* for his birthday in the fall of 1977. I was only ten at the time, but I knew it was a momentous event. The new gift seemed almost biblical. I found the cover, one of Tolkien's own paintings, "The Mountain Path," especially fascinating. Through it I seemed to sense that the Oxford don was inviting me into what he called his "perilous realm." Even at ten, I knew it was a path to a world beyond anything I'd experienced in my central Kansas upbringing.

The present book began, in a sense, during the summer of 1979, as I prepared to enter the sixth grade at Holy Cross Elementary School. That summer I saved up my lawn mowing money, rode my bike downtown to Crossroads Bookstore in Hutchinson, Kansas, and purchased the boxed set of *The Hobbit* and *The Lord of the Rings*. I devoured them. I loved Tolkien and even prayed for him, along with my deceased father, every night before bed. At that age, of course, I got no more deep meaning out of Tolkien than that one should be a good guy and always do the right thing. But nonetheless, Tolkien and his (good) characters very much shaped my thinking as a teenager, and indeed have served as lifelong models of the noble and Christian ideal. I also remember visiting my grandparents in Hays, Kansas, during seventh grade and attempting to read *The Silmarillion*. With the exception of the opening chapter on the creation of Arda, which I thought was intensely and spiritually beautiful (and still do), the book meant little to me. It failed to contain for me the high drama that *The Lord of the Rings* had. I read the opening few chapters of *The Silmarillion* numerous times, but never made it beyond the story of Ilúvatar and the conflict with Melkor.

Eight years later, I wrote a paper on Tolkien's Roman Catholicism for Dr. Kenneth Sayre at the University of Notre Dame. I was struck by how much I had missed as an eleven year old. To be sure, I had captured the essence of Tolkien, but I had missed the important nuances: that the Ring represented sin, the *lembas* the Blessed Sacrament, Galadriel the Blessed Virgin Mary. Of course, in the years between the first reading and the second reading, I had lost, and later regained, my childhood faith. Another nine years passed before my older brother Todd, having just finished the work, talked me into reading it again. I was deep into my dissertation in American frontier and Indian history at the time, and nothing else seemed too important. But as a rule I follow Todd's advice. I picked up the trilogy yet again, and Tolkien struck me like "lightning from a clear sky," as C. S. Lewis had aptly described his own experience of reading Tolkien. I also began to make new connections.

Tolkien, I discovered quickly, fit clearly and neatly into the mold of a number of twentieth-century Christian humanist and antimodernist writers and thinkers, such as Christopher Dawson, Romano Guardini, Etienne Gilson, Eric Voegelin, Russell Kirk, and T. S. Eliot. Each, I believe, wanted to prevent the crumbling twentieth-century Western world from fully entering the Abyss, and I am profoundly thankful to each for their scholarly efforts and courage in the face of extreme secular and ideological opposition.

When I expressed my newly rediscovered enthusiasm for Tolkien to my close friend Winston Elliott, president of the Center for the American Idea in Houston, he encouraged me to deliver a lecture on the topic at the Center's various programs. Another member of the Center, Gleaves Whitney, then finishing his dissertation on Christian humanism at the University of Michigan, advised the same. I followed their advice, and I've been working on Tolkien as an academic project ever since. I owe them each—as well as Winston's wife, Barbara, and his colleague, John Rocha—a great debt for helping me realize that my belief that Tolkien was a serious man and writer worthy of scholarly study was not simply nostalgic. Indeed, I can't imagine my own intellectual development (such as it is, with its many limitations) over the past decade without acknowledging their encouragement—intellectually, morally, and spiritually.

I owe a great thanks to a number of other persons, including: the various members of the Hillsdale College Tolkien Society, especially Dr. Donald Turner, Melinda Dille, Philip Nielsen, Nicholas Brown, James Sherk, and Christopher Neuendorf; friends and family who read drafts and commented on early versions of the chapters: particularly my brother Todd, Melinda Dille (who, along with my wife, proofed the entire text), Kevin McCormick, and Lisa Moreno; David Bratman of Stanford University, who offered me a number of helpful suggestions on chapter 2; my many friends at ISI, especially Jeremy Beer, Jason Duke, Jeff Nelson, Jeff Cain, and Admiral Mike Ratliff; Philip Nielsen and Nicholas Brown for assisting me in research; Judy Leising of Hillsdale College Library for finding a plethora of useful sources via interlibrary loan; Christopher Mitchell and the staff of the Wade Center at Wheaton College, Wheaton, Illinois; Matt Blessing, head archivist for the Tolkien Papers at the Marquette University Library; and a number of others for offering their help in a variety of ways, including Bill Ratliff, John Dichtl, Annette Kirk, Michal Semin, Patrick Curry, Tom Shippey, Joseph and Susannah Pearce, Bud Macfarlane Jr., and Pieter Vree. I owe special thanks to Hillsdale College Provost Bob Blackstock and my division dean, Tom Conner, for providing a summer research grant in 2001, materials, and time to allow me to research and write this book. Finally, I need to recognize a debt to several scholars who have greatly influenced my own thinking on Tolkien: Jane Chance, Patrick Curry, Verlyn Flieger, Clyde Kilby, Joseph Pearce, and Tom Shippey.

My greatest thanks are to my wife, Dedra, and my children, Nathaniel and Gretchen. Dedra never realized what a Tolkienite she married, though she's quickly becoming one herself. And Nathaniel, age three as of March 2002, knows the *very* important difference between Gandalf and Dumbledore. Gretchen, age one as of January

2002, is more interested in the VeggieTales, and, for now, her father is fine with that. Each, however, gave up considerable playtime and space to allow me to research, think, and write, though of course I cherish any and all distractions they provided and always will.

Bradley J. Birzer
Fayette Township, Michigan
Feast of St. Finan, 2002

Introduction to the New Edition

I was spiritually and mentally exhausted.

Don't get me wrong. I was glad to have earned the degree. Indeed, rather proud to have done so. But I had just spent several years in graduate school, a relatively dehumanizing process of narrowing and narrowing and still more narrowing when it comes to intellectual thought. Unlike the liberal arts experience I had so thoroughly and richly enjoyed in my undergraduate years and which had opened realms upon realms of diverse thought, graduate school demanded an intense focus, digging ever deeper and deeper into one small aspect of American history. My own dissertation—which, admittedly, I loved researching and writing—dealt in depth (of course!) with the American Revolution and the War of 1812 on the frontier. But by 1999, having finished the Ph.D., I was tired of it and ready to get back to exploring broader themes of philosophy, theology, and literature. At the time, I felt like I couldn't give my dissertation another glance.

I had published several articles in academic journals, and I still very much wanted to be a professional writer, but I just didn't have it in me to rework the dissertation. When I explained all this to my very close friend Winston Elliott, he challenged me. If I could write on anything at all, what would I write about? That was easy, I told him without hesitation. If I had all the options in the world, I would readily write a book about J. R. R. Tolkien, my hero since childhood. Additionally, I had just read Joseph Pearce's outstanding *Tolkien: Man and Myth*, and I was fascinated, in particular, by the intersection of the moral imagination and Roman

Catholicism. As beautifully as Pearce had delved into that subject, I thought there was still more to be done.

Winston's response was brilliant. Then do it, he said, and he promised to use every resource and contact possible to get the book published. As it turns out, Winston and I reached out to Jeff Nelson and Jeremy Beer at ISI Books, and these two amazing editors graciously agreed to my book proposal. I was off and running. Indeed, I was alive. Really alive.

Unlike with my dissertation, Tolkien never bored me. In fact, quite the opposite. The two and a half years I spent researching and writing *Tolkien's Sanctifying Myth* were two of the best years of my professional career. Every day witnessed a new revelation, a new inspiration, a new thought as I typed away.

Looking back over two decades now, I can state with confidence that I will never tire of Tolkien and all things Tolkienian. He is, as a man and as a creator, endlessly fascinating. To dig deep into Tolkien is to dig deep into all that matters in this whirligig of a world and to touch upon all things eternal. Tolkien matters.

Since *Tolkien's Sanctifying Myth* first came out in 2002, the Tolkien estate has released and published a whole host of original works by the great man. Through these books, I have been utterly entranced by the comprehensiveness of Tolkien's understanding not just of Northern mythology but, frankly, of all mythology, as these many volumes reveal. Reading them, I began to see not just how Tolkien sanctified parts of Norse, Anglo-Saxon, Germanic, and Finnish myth, but how he incorporated the Arthurian and other myths and took them to levels before unimagined. At least unimagined by me. Indeed, for those of us who want to study Tolkien as seriously as possible, the most important books to come out over the last two decades are those written but not finished by Tolkien. Instead, his genius son Christopher Tolkien continued his father's work well after his death in 1973. Christopher, who passed away in 2020, had worked so hard on his father's publications over the last forty-plus years that it had become increasingly impossible to know when it was J. R. R. Tolkien writing and recording and when it was his son. From a broad perspective, this means that Tolkien's legendarium is so vast and so deep that it has taken the lives of not one but two men to bring to it to completion.

Additionally, since 2002, several excellent scholars—Carl Hostetter, Holly Ordway, Father Michael Ward, Stratford Caldecott (R.I.P.), Jonathan McIntosh, Michael Drout, Matthew Dickerson, Father Dwight Longenecker, Michael Jahosky, Carol and Philip Zaleski, Jay Richards, Jonathan Witt, Fleming Rutledge, and John Garth, to name a few—have come onto the scene as well, each adding brilliantly to the ever-growing corpus of great works on Tolkien. They join the ranks of classic Tolkien scholars such as Pearce, Clyde Kilby, Humphrey Carpenter, Jane Chance, R. J. Reilly, Robert Foster, Verlyn Flieger, Richard Purtill, Tom Shippey, Colin Duriez, and Randel Helms. And then, there are stalwarts such as Christina Scull and Wayne G. Hammond. We all owe each a great deal.

Though much of this book's scholarship is rooted in the early 2000s, I am thrilled that Tom Spence and Regnery have chosen to give *Tolkien's Sanctifying Myth* a new life. It was my first intellectual child, so to speak, and I still remember the day the first box of author's copies showed up at my home. It was one of the greatest moments of my life. I still love this book. It also opened a million doors for me, including a now lifelong friendship with John J. Miller, who originally reviewed it for the *Wall Street Journal*.

Since I have your attention, though, I must make two corrections, one small and one large. In the original version of the book, I told a story—taking it from John Lawlor's excellent memoirs of his time at Oxford, and conflating it with a story from Carpenter's biography of Tolkien—of how Tolkien and Lewis dressed up as Russian bears at a faculty party. Crazily enough, I have even seen this story repeated as a popular meme on social media. Here I must officially correct myself and apologize for mis-telling the story. As it turns out, the two Russian bears were J. R. R. Tolkien and C. L. Wrenn, not Tolkien and Lewis. Still, I think this incident speaks volumes about the genius, the whimsy, and the wit of a personal hero. I'm just sorry that I was wrong about Lewis, another personal hero. He, too, would've made an excellent Russian bear.

As a second, much larger correction, I must note that I argued that Tolkien was a poor soldier in World War I. That is, after all, what he said about himself. Intriguing me greatly, Sir Martin Gilbert, who was just beginning at Merton College when Tolkien was retiring, and who knew Tolkien well personally, corrected me in person. "Bradley," he told me over lunch one day in 2006, "every soldier who survived the Great War thought he was a poor soldier." It seems that Tolkien, suffering from survivor's guilt, thought only the dead were true heroes.

Bradley J. Birzer
Hillsdale, Michigan
St. George's Day, 2023

Introduction

To enter faerie—that is, a sacramental and liturgical understanding of creation—is to open oneself to the gradual discovery of beauty, truth, and excellence.[1] One arrives in faerie only by invitation and, even then, only at one's peril. The truths to be found within faerie are greater than those that can be obtained through mere human understanding; and one finds within faerie that even the greatest works of man are as nothing compared with the majesty of creation. To enter faerie is, paradoxically, both a humbling and exhilarating experience. This is what the Oxford don and scholar J. R. R. Tolkien firmly believed.

The last story Tolkien published prior to his death, "Smith of Wootton Major," follows a normal but charitably inclined man who has been graced with the ability to make extraordinarily beautiful things while metal smithing. Smith, as he is known, discovered the gift of grace on his tenth birthday, when the dawn engulfed him and "passed on like a wave of music into the West, as the sun rose above the rim of the world."[2] Like the earth at the end of Eliot's "Wasteland," Tolkien's Smith had been baptized, and through this gift he receives an invitation to faerie. While visiting that world, he discovers that in it he is the least of beings. Its beauty, however, entices him, and he spends entire days "looking only at one tree or one flower."[3] The depth of each thing astounds him. "Wonders and mysteries," many of them terrifying in their overwhelming beauty and truth, abound in faerie, Smith discovers, and he dwells on such wonders even when he is no longer in faerie.[4] Nevertheless, some encounters terrify him:

> He stood beside the Sea of Windless Storm where the blue waves like snow-clad hills roll silently out of Unlight to the long strand, bearing the white ships that return from battles on the Dark Marches of which men know nothing. He saw a great ship cast high upon the land, and the waters fell back in foam without a sound. The elven mariners were tall and terrible; their swords shone and their spears glinted and a piercing light was in their eye. Suddenly they lifted up their voices in a song of triumph, and his heart was shaken with fear, and he fell upon his face, and they passed over him and went away into the echoing hills.[5]

And yet, despite the fact that he portrayed the man Smith in prostration before such grand visions, the rest of the story reveals that it was not Tolkien's intention to denigrate Smith's importance, but only to emphasize his place—and therefore the place of humanity in general—in the economy of creation. The English Roman Catholic G. K. Chesterton, who served as a significant source of inspiration to Tolkien when he was a young man, once wrote that "[h]e not only felt freer when he bent; he actually felt taller when he bowed."[6] Likewise, Tolkien shows in "Smith of Wootton Major" that it is an understanding of the transcendent that allows Smith to fully become a man. This was a teaching to which Tolkien ascribed his entire life.

For Tolkien, one of the best ways to understand the gift of grace was through faerie, which offered a glimpse of the way in which sacrament and liturgy infuse the natural law and the natural order. Faerie connects a person to his past and helps order his understanding of the moral universe. In an essay describing the greatness of the medieval poem, "Sir Gawain and the Green Knight," Tolkien wrote:

> Behind our poem stalk the figures of elder myth, and through the lines are heard the echoes of ancient cults, beliefs and symbols remote from the consciousness of an educated moralist (but also a poet) of the late fourteenth century. His story is not about those old

things, but it received part of its life, its vividness, its tension from them. That is the way with the greater fairy-stories—of which this is one. There is indeed no better medium for moral teaching than the good fairy-story (by which I mean a real deep-rooted tale, told as a tale, and not a thinly disguised moral allegory).[7]

Not only does faerie teach us higher truths; it also bonds us together in communities, of which there are two kinds: the one which is of this time and place, and the one which transcends all time and all places. As Chesterton wrote, "[B]eauty and terror are very real things," but they are also "related to a real spiritual world; and to touch them at all, even in doubt or fancy, is to stir the deep things of the soul."[8]

Certainly myth, of which faerie is one kind, holds an estranged place in the modern world, as Tolkien well knew.[9] But, he believed, so much the worse for the modern world. Indeed, myth might just be the thing needed to save the modern world from itself, as Tolkien suggested in his famous poem, "Mythopoeia," which echoes the Beatitudes:

> Blessed are the legend-makers with their rhyme
> of things not found within recorded time.
> It is not they that have forgot the Night,
> or bid us flee to organized delight,
> in lotus-isles of economic bliss
> forswearing souls to gain a Circe-kiss
> (and counterfeit at that, machine-produced,
> bogus seduction of the twice-seduced).[10]

Myth, Tolkien thought, can convey the sort of profound truth that was intransigent to description or analysis in terms of facts and figures, and is therefore a more powerful weapon for cultural renewal than is modern rationalist science and technology.[11] Myth can emphasize the beauty of God's creation as well as the sacramental nature of life.[12] "Our time, sick nigh unto death of utilitarianism and literalness, cries out for myth and parable," American novelist and political philosopher Russell Kirk explained. "Great myths are not merely susceptible of rational interpretation: they are truth, transcendent truth."[13] Tolkien believed that myth can teach men and women how to be fully and truly men and women, not mere cogs in the vast machine of modern technological society.

In his inimitable way, Chesterton once wrote that

> imaginative does not mean imaginary. It does not follow that it is all what the moderns call subjective, when they mean false. Every true artist does feel, consciously or unconsciously, that he is touching transcendental truths; that his images are shadows of things seen through the veil. In other words, the natural mystic does not know that there is something there; something behind the clouds or within the trees; but he believes that the pursuit of beauty is the way to find it; that imagination is a sort of incantation that can call it up.[14]

Besides offering an essential path to the highest truths, myth plays a vital role in any culture because it binds together members of communities. "It is quite easy to see why a legend is treated, and ought to be treated, more respectfully than a book of history. The legend is generally made by a majority of the people in the village, who are sane. The book is generally written by the one man in the village who is mad," Chesterton wrote in *Orthodoxy*.[15] Communities "share symbols and myths that provide meaning in their existence as a people and link them to some transcendent order," political theorist Donald Lutz explains. "The shared meaning and a shared link to some transcendent order allow them to act as a people."[16] The man "who has no sympathy with myths," Chesterton concluded, "has no sympathy with men."[17] One cannot, it seems, separate men from their myths.

Yet many of our contemporaries—a bizarre combination of those who have embraced secular modernity as well as those who abhor it, the Christian fundamentalists—have rejected the importance of myth. For the modernist, imbued with the doctrines of Jamesian and Deweyite pragmatism, myth is a lie. One cannot, after all, see, feel, smell, taste, or hear myth. Myth remains just beyond our material and physical senses, and we most certainly cannot scientifically verify it. Though myth is essential to man qua man, as Chesterton rightly contended, one of modernity's chief characteristics is the watering down

of richly felt and imagined reality, and the substitution of cheap coun-
terfeits and thin shadows for the mythic vision. "In this new sphere,"
wrote theologian Romano Guardini in the mid-1920s, "things are no
longer directly detected, seen, grasped, formed, or enjoyed; rather, they
are mediated by signs and substitutes."[18] To the modernist, "myth,"
like religion, merely signifies a comfortable and entrenched lie. For the
postmodernist, myth simply represents one story, one narrative among
many; it is purely subjective, certainly signifying nothing of transcendent or any other kind of importance.

For religious fundamentalists, myths also represent lies. Myths,
the argument runs, constitute dangerous rivals to Christian truth and
may lead the unwary astray, even into the very grip of hell. Why study
The Volsunga or Homer, for example, when the Christian Gospels tell
us all we need for salvation? It is likely, the fundamentalist concludes,
that all myth comes from the devil and is an attempt to distract us
from the truth of Christ. The ancient gods and demigods of Greece,
Rome, and northern Europe, after all, must have been nothing more
than demons in disguise.

For Tolkien, however, even pagan myths attempted to express
God's greater truths. True myth has the power to revive us, to serve
as an *anamnesis*, or way of bringing to conscious experience ancient
experiences with transcendence. But, Tolkien admitted, myth could be
dangerous, or "perilous," as he usually stated it, if it remained pagan.
Therefore, Tolkien thought, one must sanctify it, that is, make it Christian and put it in God's service. Medieval believers had the same idea,
and the story told of the early-medieval saint Boniface of Crediton
exemplifies one such attempt. The story (a non-factual myth, certainly!) of Boniface claims that while evangelizing the pagan Germanic tribes in north-central Europe, he encountered a tribe that
worshiped a large oak tree. To demonstrate the power of Christ as
the True God, Boniface cut down the tree, much to the dismay of the
tribe. But rather than seeing Boniface struck down by their gods, the
pagan tribe saw an evergreen instantaneously spring up on the same
spot. So that Boniface could continue preaching to the astounded
pagans, the story continues, his followers placed candles on the newly

grown evergreen, which eventually became the first Christmas tree. This motif of "sanctifying the pagan" has been repeated throughout history by Christians in a multitude of ways, and was instrumental in contributing to the wildly successful spread of the faith. Christmas and Easter, for example, were placed on high pagan holidays; St. Paul attempted to convert the Athenians with reference to their statue of the "Unknown God"; St. Augustine re-read the works of Plato and Cicero in a Christian light in his *City of God*; St. Aquinas uncovered the synchronies between Aristotelian and Christian thought; and on our own continent, we see that Catholic monks built a monastery on top of the highest mound-temple in Cahokia, Illinois, former site of the priest-king of a vast Native American empire. Indeed, churches throughout Europe and North America sit on formerly sacred pagan sites. In building churches in such places Christians sought, in essence, to baptize the corrupt ground, just as Sts. Augustine and Aquinas baptized pagan ideas.

It was Tolkien's understanding that man's role in the sanctification of the world is a cooperative and limited one. Given the constraints of his materiality, man ultimately only catches a glimpse of the highest things, and his attempts to emulate them in their truth, beauty, and excellence are but meager. When Smith of Wootton Major discovers to his embarrassment that a doll of a beautiful woman his village has revered is horribly shabby and trite when compared to its transcendent model, the Faery Lady, whom he has just met, she calms his fears: "Do not be grieved for me. . . Nor too much ashamed of your own folk. Better a little doll, maybe, than no memory of Faery at all. For some the only glimpse. For some the awakening."[19] As an artist, a scholar, and a mythmaker, Tolkien gave us a glimpse of the truth, beauty, and excellence that lies beyond and behind our tangible world. That glimpse, which leads to real joy, Tolkien labeled the *euchatastrophe*.

Throughout his entire mythology—*The Silmarillion*, *The Lord of the Rings*, and the other works on Middle-earth—Tolkien stubbornly affirmed that the hope of the modern world lay in a return to some form of the *Christiana Res Publica*. "Someday Christendom may come/Westward/Evening sun recedent/Set my resting vow/Hold in open heart," cries the poet Mark Hollis.[20] What form such a transfigured world would take, of course, is unclear. After all, Tolkien believed, man's job is not to plan the universe, but to use the gifts God has given him for the betterment of all. "The awful Author of our being," one of Tolkien's favorite thinkers, Edmund Burke, wrote, "is the author of our place in the order of existence." He, "having disposed and marshalled us by a divine tactic, not according to our will, but according to His, He has, in and by that disposition, virtually subjected us to act the part which belongs to the part assigned to us."[21]

In his thinking about truth, reason, science, art, and myth, and in his hope for a renewal of Christendom and an end to the ideologically inspired terror of the twentieth century, Tolkien fits in nicely with a group of twentieth-century scholars and artists which we might collectively label as "The Christian humanists."[22] The Christian humanist asks two fundamental questions: (1) what is the role of the human person within God's creation? and (2) how does man order himself within God's creation? Christian, or theocentric, humanism, as opposed to anthropocentric, secular, Renaissance, or Enlightenment humanism, argues that one cannot understand man's position in the world until one first acknowledges that man is created in the image of God and lives under the natural law as well as the divine law.[23] The ranks of the Christian humanists include such poets and scholars as T. S. Eliot, C. S. Lewis, Christopher Dawson, Eric Voegelin, Russell Kirk, and Romano Guardini. As will become readily apparent in the following chapters, Tolkien should be counted as one of their foremost thinkers and spokesmen.

Each of the seven chapters of this book examines a different aspect of Tolkien and his mythology. Chapter 1 considers Tolkien himself; in essence, it is a mini-biography. Chapter 2 describes the nature of myth and the realm of faerie; specifically, it explores Tolkien's academic ideas on myth and language, as well as his broader goal for his own mythology, which was, in short, to revive the northern spirit of courage by infusing it with the Christian doctrine of grace. Tolkien thought such a coupling necessary in order to bring back a genuine and effective Christendom. Chapter 3 considers Tolkien's conceptions of the Good and the created order. It looks at the role of God/Ilúvatar in Tolkien's mythology, as well as the various sacramental symbolisms and parallels found within the legendarium (Tolkien's word for his entire mythology). Chapter 4 follows chapter 3 in theme. It attempts to show, at least from Tolkien's perspective, what man's duty is within God's created order by focusing on five characters from *The Lord of the Rings*—Gandalf, Aragorn, Faramir, Frodo, and Sam—as representative archetypes of Western heroes. Chapter 5 delves into Tolkien's conception of evil and its role within the created order. Chapter 6 looks at Tolkien's political philosophy, with special attention to his views regarding modernity and the perverse ideologies of the twentieth century. Finally, the conclusion evaluates Tolkien's legacy and considers the future of his mythology and its power to revive the world's understanding of right reason.

Chapter I

The Life and Work of J. R. R. Tolkien

When Denis and Charlotte Plimmer interviewed J. R. R. Tolkien in 1968, they met with him in his garage-turned-study. "Not that the garage itself is any cave of wonders," the Plimmers admitted. "Jammed between the Professor's own house and the one next door, in an undistinguished Oxford suburb, it would be no more than a banal little room, filled with files and a clutter of garden chairs, if it were not for the man."[1] A normal man in a normal world, but with something profoundly and almost indescribably different. For the Plimmers, Tolkien's very being transformed the drab office into something and somewhere else. As he did with his family, his classroom, and his fiction, Tolkien turned his normal, middle-class setting into the enchanted world of Middle-earth. Those who met Tolkien often noted that graces seemed to follow and flow from him, lifting up the lives of all those they touched. That same grace reached his readers, as raw numbers alone demonstrate. By one estimate, *The Lord of the Rings* has sold over 150 million copies since its publication in the mid-1950s.[2] More than any other author of the twentieth century, Tolkien resuscitated the notion that the fantastic may tell us more about reality than do scientific facts. When the army asked Michael Tolkien to list his father's profession, it should surprise no one that he answered "wizard."[3]

John Ronald Reuel was born to Mabel and Arthur Tolkien in Bloemfontein, South Africa, on January 3, 1892. When the climate caused Ronald to become ill in 1895, his mother moved him and his brother Hilary back to England. A year later, his father died. With aid from her family, Mabel raised the two children as a single parent. When she joined the Roman Catholic Church in June 1900, her family withdrew its financial support, leaving Mabel to fend for herself. Four years later, in November 1904, Mabel died of a form of diabetes, leaving Ronald and Hilary in the care of Father Francis Morgan, a Roman Catholic priest at the Birmingham Oratory, which had originally been founded by John Henry Newman.[4]

In 1908, Tolkien met his future wife, Edith Bratt. Father Morgan forbade Tolkien's relationship with Edith, but the two became engaged when the priest's legal status as guardian ended when Tolkien turned twenty-one in 1913. With the strong encouragement of Tolkien, Edith joined the Roman Catholic Church in 1914, and the two married on March 22, 1916. They would have four children: John (b. 1917); Michael (b. 1920); Christopher (b. 1924); and Priscilla (b. 1929).[5]

In 1915, after taking his degree from Exeter College, Oxford, Tolkien joined the 11th Lancashire Fusiliers, one of the most decorated English regiments of World War I.[6] A year later, he saw battle at the Somme, one of the bloodiest of the war. On the first day alone, Germans slaughtered over 20,000 French and British soldiers. "One didn't expect to survive, you know. Junior officers were being killed off, a dozen a minute," Tolkien told an interviewer nearly sixty years after the war. "Parting from my wife then—we were only just married—it was like a death."[7] After several months on the front lines, Tolkien contracted what was generally referred to as "trench fever" and returned permanently to England.[8] Though he spent less than a year in the war, it affected him deeply. Tolkien had lost several of his closest friends, and their loss, he believed, gave him an even greater duty to carry on their jointly conceived project, which was to do God's will in the world.[9] It was also during the war that Tolkien began to combine his conception of faerie—i.e., fairyland, that realm of magical beauty and charm that for Tolkien served as an analogue for a sacramental understanding of the world—with the urgent need for new myths to reinvigorate the twentieth century.[10] "The war made me poignantly aware of the beauty of the world I remember," Tolkien said in 1968. "I remember miles and miles of seething, tortured earth, perhaps best described in the chapters about the approaches to Mordor. It was a searing experience."[11]

Upon returning to civilian life, Tolkien first took a job on the *Oxford English Dictionary*, where he took great pride in his work.[12] Two years later, in 1920, he accepted his first teaching position at Leeds University. Though Leeds awarded him the prestigious title of "Professor of English Language" in 1924, Tolkien accepted an even more eminent position as Rawlinson and Bosworth Professor of Anglo-Saxon at Oxford University in 1925. His academic sub-speciality was the literature and language of Mercian, an Anglo-Saxon dialect.[13] He remained at Oxford for the rest of his academic career. The only significant change in his position there came in 1945, when he was named Merton Professor of English Language. In 1959, Oxford awarded him emeritus status.[14]

Most of his students thought Tolkien a mumbling lecturer. "The first professor to harrow me with the syntax and morphology of Old English had a speech impediment," Guy Davenport wrote in reference to Tolkien in 1979, and "wandered in his remarks."[15] Tolkien had mumbled for a long time, and it had often caused him problems. As an interviewer from the American Library Association told him in 1957, "I do appreciate your coming up from Oxford so that I might record you Professor Tolkien, but I can't understand a word you say." In typically self-deprecating fashion, Tolkien responded, "A friend of mine tells me that I talk in shorthand and then smudge it."[16] When invited to give a guest lecture at Marquette University in Milwaukee, Tolkien responded, "I should not, of course, object to lecturing several times. I am quite hardened by it, and even enjoy it—more than my audience."[17] Students reported that he spoke too quickly, hurrying through parts Tolkien himself found boring.[18] Lewis, Tolkien's closest friend, could be blunt when describing Tolkien's speaking abilities.

> He is scholarly, and he can be brilliant though perhaps rather recondite for most undergraduates. But unfortunately you may not be able to hear what he says. He is a ba lecturer d. All the same I advise you to go. If you do, arrive early, sit near the front and pay particular

attention to the extempore remarks and comments he often makes. These are usually the best things in the lecture. In fact one could call him an inspired speaker of footnotes.[19]

As Lewis conceded, though, if Tolkien often mumbled, moments of brilliance and clarity revealed themselves equally often, especially when he recited poetry. "I remember one [lecture I] attended, delivered by Professor Tolkien," poet W. H. Auden wrote. "I do not remember a single word he said but at a certain point he recited, and magnificently, a long passage of *Beowulf*. I was spellbound."[20] A student in a 1926 class was equally enthralled with Tolkien's reading of *Beowulf*: "He came in lightly and gracefully, I always remember that, his gown flowing, his fair hair shining, and he read *Beowulf* aloud. We did not know the language he was reading, yet the sound of Tolkien made sense of the unknown tongue and the terrors and the dangers that he recounted—how I do not know—made our hair stand on end. He read like no one else I have ever heard."[21]

Students most remembered Tolkien's kindness and his endless efforts to make them learn. He always approached his subject with "appealing jollity."[22] Anthony Curtis contrasted Tolkien and Lewis's teaching styles:

> At the end of the hour with Lewis I always felt a complete ignoramus; no doubt an accurate impression but also a rather painful one; and if you did venture to challenge one of his theories the ground was cut away from beneath your feet with lightning speed. It was a fool's mate in three moves with Lewis smiling at you from the other side of the board in unmalicious glee at his victory. By contrast Tolkien was the soul of affability. He did all the talking, but he made you feel you were his intellectual equal. Yet his views beneath the deep paternal charm were passionately held.[23]

Other students compared Tolkien to his medieval counterparts. "With Tolkien you were in the meadhall in which he was the bard and we were the drinking, listening guests," detective writer Michael Innes said.[24] Oxford professors rarely received standing ovations, but Tolkien frequently did, despite his speech impediments.[25] Another student, now a famous lexicographer, remembered, "He made acute observations. I followed them all up. He beamed when I made some discoveries."[26]

Tolkien's habit of treating his students as his equals was a trait that socially conscious Oxford students must have found appealing. Female students especially appreciated Tolkien, since he treated them just as he did the men.[27] Indeed, while he certainly had his angry moments, Tolkien seems to have treated nearly everyone well. John Lawlor wrote that his "first and abiding impression [of Tolkien] was of immediate kindness."[28] Walter Hooper labeled Tolkien a "deeply sympathetic man." "I resemble a hobbit," Tolkien wrote George Sayer, "at any rate in being moderately and cheerfully domesticated."[29] His children have said similar things. Michael wrote that his father always talked to, rather than at, him. "I have simply looked upon my father as a far more interesting, far more kindly, and even far more humble man than any other I knew, and whose intimate friendship I was privileged to enjoy." Michael noted that his father especially listened intently to his children, and he took what they said to heart.[30] Despite his harried schedule, Tolkien rarely put his work above his family. "Our father's study at home was in some ways the hub of the house," Priscilla remembered. "It was never forbidden territory to us, except when he was teaching." When Tolkien needed to work to make deadlines, he usually did so late at night, after his children were asleep.[31]

Tolkien's jovial personality led him to thoroughly enjoy playing pranks. With C. S. Lewis, he once dressed as a polar bear for a non-costume party, wearing "an Icelandic sheepskin hearthrug" and painting "his face white."[32] As Tolkien and Lewis walked home heavily covered in fur, they claimed convincingly, according to another Inkling, "to be two Russian bears."[33] At a lecture in the 1930s, Tolkien told his audience that leprechauns really existed and pulled out a green, four-inch long shoe to prove it.[34] Tolkien's biographer Humphrey Carpenter notes that Tolkien would chase neighbors away dressed as "an Anglo-Saxon warrior complete with axe." As an elderly man, Tolkien often included his false teeth when paying store clerks.[35] And he loved the slapstick humor of the Marx Brothers.[36]

It would be difficult to overemphasize the importance to Tolkien of C. S. Lewis and the "Inklings," the professor-student literary group they helped make famous. In turn, it would be equally wrong to suggest that the relationship was not reciprocal, as Tolkien also greatly influenced Lewis and the Inklings. It was with the Inklings that Tolkien read his own works and criticized those read by others. The Inklings also served as an extrafamilial social outlet. "He was a man of 'cronies' rather than of general society," Lewis wrote of him, "and was always best after midnight (he had a Johnsonian horror of going to bed) and in some small circle of intimates where the tone was at once Bohemian, literary, and Christian (for he was profoundly religious)."[37]

Tolkien first met Lewis at Oxford in 1926. After a faculty tea, Lewis approached Tolkien to discuss the latter's ideas on a revised English curriculum. After the meeting, Lewis offered a mixed reaction in his diary. "No harm in him," Lewis recorded, he "only needs a smack or two."[38] Soon, though, Lewis joined Tolkien's academic club, the Kolbitár, which was dedicated to reading the Icelandic Sagas in Old Norse.[39] The two remained merely academic colleagues until the autumn of 1929, when they realized that their love for Old Norse and the sagas represented more than mere academic subjects to each of them. For Tolkien and Lewis, the northern myths contained within the sagas revealed much about lost truths in the world. "One week I was up till 2.30 on Monday talking to the Anglo Saxon professor Tolkien," Lewis wrote to his friend Arthur Greeves, "who came back with me to College from a society and sat discoursing on the gods & giants & Asgard for three hours."[40] It proved a major moment for both of them, the real beginning of their long-lasting friendship. Tolkien must have especially regarded the late-night discussion as important, for he afterwards lent to Lewis parts of *The Silmarillion*, a work he regarded as intensely personal. In what must have been a great relief to Tolkien, Lewis responded positively to Tolkien's work.[41] After that, Tolkien read other parts of *The Silmarillion* to Lewis, and Lewis continued to critique these pieces favorably.[42] Their friendship grew almost unabated from 1929 to 1940.[43]

Lewis, who would become the greatest Christian apologist of the twentieth century, was a magnetic figure. As numerous people have testified, he served as the heart and soul of Oxford during his years there. Lewis had his eccentricities: he drank frequently and heavily and smoked up to sixty cigarettes a day, in addition to smoking a pipe regularly.[44] One of his students, John Wain, wrote: "The thick-set body, the red face with its domed forehead, the dense clouds of smoke from a rapidly puffed cigarette or pipe, the brisk argumentative manner, and the love of debate kept the conversation going at the pace of some breathless game." Lewis had, according to Wain and most other students who knew him, a "dramatic personality."[45] Anthony Curtis recorded an interesting incident with Lewis: "I arrived [as a student to a class with C. S. Lewis] before the others and he was staring out of the window at the deer. 'A deer has only two concepts,' he told me, 'the concept of food which they approach and the concept of danger from which they retreat. Now what interests me is how a deer would react to the idea of poison . . . which is both food and dangerous.'"[46] Unlike their more moderate responses to Tolkien, students either loved the rather intense Lewis or they hated him.[47]

Religion proved both a major unifier and a point of contention between Lewis and Tolkien. Lewis had been raised as a strong Irish Protestant Ulsterman. From an early age, he had heard much from his relatives about the wickedness of Roman Catholics. His maternal grandfather, a preacher, stressed frequently that Roman Catholics were the "devil's own children."[48] As a young child, Lewis had taken his faith very seriously, chastising those who flirted with Catholicism. During his teenage years, however, Lewis had lost his faith, substituting for it a pure rationalism.

Tolkien played a fundamental role in bringing Lewis back to Christianity. On September 19, 1931, Tolkien, Lewis, and another friend, Hugo Dyson, talked until three in the morning about the meaning of Christianity. "We began," Lewis noted, "on metaphor and myth—interrupted by a rush of wind which came so suddenly on the still, warm evening and sent so many leaves pattering down that we thought it was raining. We all held our breath, the other two appreciating the ecstasy of such a thing."[49] Tolkien used arguments regarding the truth of myth to discuss the story of Christ as the true myth. "Pagan stories are God expressing Himself through the minds of poets, using such images as He found there," Lewis explained a month later, "while Christianity is God expressing Himself through what we call 'real things.'"[50] In the fall of 1931, Lewis found himself a Christian.[51]

In addition to their participation in the Kolbitár, Lewis and Tolkien also belonged to the Inklings, which had been founded and named by an Oxford undergraduate. When that student graduated in 1933, Tolkien and Lewis remained the club's only two original members. Unintentionally combining the Kolbitár and the Inklings, Tolkien and Lewis formed a new group but maintained the Inklings name. As Tolkien explained, the Inklings really consisted of "the undetermined and unelected circle of friends who gathered about [Lewis], and met in his rooms in Magdalen."[52] By the end of 1933, the Inklings still consisted only of the Lewis brothers and Tolkien. Humphrey Havard (a.k.a., "the Useless Quack") and Hugo Dyson both joined in 1934. Charles Williams became a member in 1940, and Charles Wrenn, Nevill Coghill, and Owen Barfield attended irregularly beginning in the 1930s.[53] Other irregular members and attendees included Christopher Tolkien, John Tolkien, Lord David Cecil, J. A. W. Bennett, James Dundas-Grant, Adam Fox, Colin Hardie, Gervase Mathew, R. B. McCallum, Tom Stevens, and John Wain.[54]

Rarely did women attend meetings of the Inklings. Dorothy Sayers visited once, though Tolkien, by chance, was not at the meeting.[55] In the late 1950s, Lewis brought his wife Joy to the meetings.[56] This must have grated on Tolkien, for as a bachelor Lewis had "on occasion chide[d] him for having to return him" to his own wife. Indeed, while a bachelor, Lewis had trouble understanding Tolkien's dedication and commitment to his wife, once complaining to George Sayer that Tolkien was "the most married man he knew."[57] Tolkien often grew frustrated with his bachelor friends as well. "The ever-clamant society" of the pub where the Inklings met, "no less than the sometimes tumultuous exchanges of the Inklings, were decidedly not to Tolkien's taste," reported John Lawlor.[58]

Meetings of the Inklings became increasingly frequent in the late 1930s. Tolkien and Lewis met each other every Monday morning for a drink before the week began. "This is one of the pleasantest spots in the week," Lewis wrote. "Sometimes we talk English school politics: sometimes we criticize one another's poems: other days we drift into theology or 'the state of the nation': rarely we fly no higher than bawdy and 'puns.'"[59] The Inklings formally met on Thursday evenings in Lewis's rooms at Magdalen, and informally met on Tuesdays for lunch and drinks at a local pub, "The Eagle and Child," more affectionately known as "The Bird and Baby."[60] On Tuesdays, more persons than just the formal Inklings, including the publican, joined in the discussions. "We sat in a small back room with a fine coal fire in winter," one of Lewis's students, James Dundas-Grant, remembered: "Back and forth the conversation would flow. Latin tags flying around. Homer quoted in original to make a point. And, Tolkien, jumping up and down, declaiming in Anglo-Saxon."[61]

The Thursday evening sessions were more formal and unvarying. John Wain remembered the Thursday nights: "I can see that room so clearly now, the electric fire pumping heat into the dank air, the faded screen that broke some of the keener draughts, the enamel beer-jug on the table, the well-worn sofa and armchairs, and the men drifting in (those from distant colleges would be later), leaving overcoats and hats in any corner and coming over to warm their hands before finding a chair."[62] C. S. Lewis described it as a group of "literary friends. [Williams] read us his manuscripts and we read him ours: we smoked, talked, argued, and drank together."[63] Lewis asked a Benedictine friend, "Is any pleasure on earth as great as a circle of Christian friends by a fire?"[64] Visitors, too, viewed the Inklings as essentially Lewis's group.[65] Typically, Lewis led the group and the discussion, but he throughly enjoyed having others read to him.[66] "Warnie," as Lewis's brother was called, described the meetings as follows:

> The ritual of an Inklings was unvarying. When half a dozen or so had arrived, tea would be produced, after which when pipes were

alight Jack would say, 'well has nobody got anything to read us?' Out
would come a manuscript and we would settle down to sit in judgement upon it. Real, unbiased judgement too, for about the Inklings
there was nothing of a mutual admiration society; with us, praise for
good work was unstinted but censure for bad, or even not so good,
was often brutally frank. To read to the Inklings was a formidable
ordeal.[67]

Certainly, the Inklings could be rough with one another, and they
rarely pulled punches. Though Tolkien probably dealt his share of
blows, he received a number of them as well, especially from Dyson.
As Tolkien read *The Lord of the Rings* chapter by chapter, Dyson usually commented negatively or sighed loudly. One night, he went as far
as to say, "Oh f—k, not another elf."[68] After Tolkien achieved immense
popularity with *The Lord of the Rings*, Dyson told a reporter, "'Dear
Ronald writing all those silly books with three introductions and 10
appendixes. His was not a true imagination, you know: He made it
all up."[69] For a man as sensitive as Tolkien, such comments must have
been quite painful. However, as C. S. Lewis noted, Tolkien had "only
two reactions to criticism: either he begins the whole work over again
from the beginning or else takes no notice at all."[70] Tolkien himself
seemed proud that he was hard to influence. Lewis, he said, "used to
insist on my reading passages aloud as I finished them, and then he
made suggestions. He was furious when I didn't accept them. Once he
said, 'It's no use trying to influence you, you're uninfluenceable!' But
that wasn't quite true. Whenever he said, 'You can do better than that.
Better, Tolkien, please!' I used to try."[71] When a scholar, Charles Moorman, wrote of the Inklings as a collective entity, Warnie recorded in his
diary, "I smiled at the thought of Tollers being under the influence of
Moorman's group mind."[72]

The Inklings did more than criticize each other's writings; their
meetings were also occasions of sophisticated—and heated—conversation and academic discourse. Unfortunately, only brief glimpses of
Inklings discussions remain, but topics included the Nuremberg Trials,
the Blessed Eucharist as a form of cannibalism, and child mortality, to

name only a few.[73] "The Inklings is now really v[ery] well provided, with Fox as chaplain, you as army, Barfield as lawyer, Havard as doctor—almost all the estates," Lewis joked in 1940, "except, of course, anyone who could actually produce a single necessity of life, a loaf, a boot, or a hut."[74]

Visitors and shorter-term Inklings rarely found the group as intellectually diverse as did the long-time members of the group. Lewis's student John Wain, for example, confirmed Moorman's thesis about a corporate mind. Coming from a modernist and leftist perspective, Wain viewed the Inklings as politically very conservative, religiously very Catholic (either Anglo or Roman), and artistically very antimodernist.[75] They were, Wain writes, "a circle of investigators, almost of incendiaries, meeting to urge one another on in the task of redirecting the whole current of contemporary art and life."[76] In Wain's view, C. S. Lewis led the group as a pro-Christian political cell, working with fellow travelers such as Dorothy Sayers, Roger Lancelyn Green, and Roy Campbell. The only open leftist among the more permanent Inklings was Coghill.[77] Ultimately, Wain concludes, the Inklings failed to remake the world in a traditionalist image; "Jack didn't kill the giant, but the bout was a good one, and worth watching."[78]

The rise and fall of the Inklings reflected the ups and downs of Tolkien and Lewis's friendship. After the autumn of 1949, the Inklings began to meet less frequently, though they never officially broke up until Lewis's death in 1963. The same could be said for the friendship of the two men, which suffered under the strain of several factors. As will be discussed more fully in chapter 3, their theological differences played the most significant role in the decline of their mutual affection. Other issues intruded as well. Tolkien resented Lewis's strong and quick friendship with Charles Williams, which began in 1940.[79] Tolkien also seemed perturbed by Lewis's significant borrowing of Tolkien's ideas and private mythology for his novels.[80] In the late 1950s, Tolkien regretted Lewis's secret decision to marry a divorced woman, Joy Gresham, which would have been forbidden in the Roman Catholic Church.[81] Finally, Tolkien openly rejected Lewis's children's fiction, especially the Narnia tales.[82] "I hear you've been reading Jack's children's story.

It really won't do, you know!" Tolkien said to Lewis's friend and future biographer, Roger Lancelyn Green. "'Nymphs and their Ways, The Love-Life of a Faun.' Doesn't he know what he's talking about?"[83]

Lewis noticed the strain as well. Sometime in the late 1950s or the early 1960s, Lewis asked Christopher Tolkien, over a drink, why his father "had allowed their friendship to lapse." Christopher, most likely embarrassed at the highly personal question, offered no explanation.[84] Lewis biographer A. N. Wilson suggests that Lewis and Tolkien only saw each other a few times in the last few years prior to Lewis's death, and, even then, he writes, the meetings were intensely awkward.[85]

Still, it is possible to exaggerate too much the differences between Tolkien and Lewis after 1940. Tolkien, for example, worked vehemently and successfully to secure Lewis a prestigious chair at Cambridge.[86] Tolkien's wife Edith and Lewis's wife Joy became good friends in the late 1950s.[87] Walter Hooper asserts that Tolkien visited "Lewis several times . . . before Lewis died that autumn, and he certainly didn't abandon him in his last days."[88] Douglas Gresham, Joy's son, confirms Hooper's claim, further noting that Tolkien offered to help Douglas in any way he could.[89] Wheaton English professor Clyde Kilby, who knew both men in the early 1960s, said in an interview: "C. S. Lewis had a pure love for Tolkien with never any hitch; he would criticize Tolkien straight off the cuff."[90] Lewis's death hit Tolkien hard. "This feels like an axe-blow near the roots," Tolkien wrote his daughter. "Very sad that we should have been so separated in the last years; but our time of close communion endured in memory for both of us."[91]

Tolkien knew that his writings would never have seen publication had it not been for the constant encouragement of Lewis. It was Lewis who first showed real excitement regarding *The Silmarillion*, it was Lewis who first encouraged Tolkien's publisher to accept *The Hobbit*, and it was Lewis who encouraged the writing and publication of *The Lord of the Rings* from the very long years of its beginning in late 1938 until its publication in 1954, 1955, and 1956.[92] After its publication, Lewis reviewed it and praised it publicly as well as privately. In his own published writings, Lewis referred to Tolkien's works as indispensable. Indeed, it would have been impossible for Tolkien to have found a better or more enthusiastic promoter of his works. Tolkien admitted as much in 1965 in a letter to Clyde Kilby: "But for the encouragement of C.S.L. I do not think that I should ever have completed or offered for publication *The Lord of the Rings*."[93] Tolkien once even admitted that he "wrote *The Lord of the Rings* to make Lewis a story out of *The Silmarillion*."[94]

Although Tolkien wrote prolifically, he published very few of his works during his lifetime. In 1937, roughly four years after he had completed it, Tolkien published *The Hobbit*.[95] The *New York Herald-Tribune* awarded it best children's story of the year in 1938.[96] With the success of *The Hobbit*, the publishers asked for a sequel. Tolkien, however, wanted to revise and complete *The Silmarillion*. But his publishers rejected it, or so he thought, and he therefore proceeded with the sequel.[97] (In fact, the reviewer for the publisher had never even delved into *The Silmarillion*, but Tolkien believed he had and had rejected it.)[98] When a being Tolkien called a Ringwraith introduced itself to Tolkien's imagination, however, the "New Hobbit" quickly become a much darker and more adult story than its predecessor. Tolkien haltingly wrote *The Lord of the Rings* through 1949, sending much of it in serialized form to Christopher, stationed in South Africa during World War II. Tolkien's insistence that *The Silmarillion* and *The Lord of the Rings* be published together, along with a shortage of paper during the postwar period, prevented the latter's publication prior to 1954. Publishers Allen and Unwin considered it as merely a prestige book, and they decided to publish it as a trilogy, distributing the costs over three books rather than one.[99] His American publisher, Houghton Mifflin, loved the books, but was unsure how the public would respond. "I would say that the general reaction around Houghton Mifflin was one of astonishment, perhaps even bewilderment, as to what the public's reaction to such a book would be," Houghton Mifflin editor Austen Olney stated.[100]

The reviews of *The Lord of the Rings* tended toward the extremes. W. H. Auden, a former student of Tolkien's, came down decidedly in its favor, even declaring that one's opinion of the trilogy served as a litmus test for one's fitness as a reviewer.[101] But many of Tolkien's academic colleagues were appalled at the Oxford professor's creation. "He ought to have been teaching!" complained one don.[102] The most prominent and devastating dismissal from among the professional literary critics came from Edmund Wilson. "How is it that these long-winded volumes of what looks to this reviewer like balderdash have elicited such tributes?" Wilson asked rhetorically. "The answer, I believe, is that certain people, especially, perhaps, in Britain, have a lifelong appetite for juvenile trash."[103] An anonymous reviewer for the *New Yorker* labeled *The Two Towers* "tedious a good deal of the time."[104] Mark Roberts, an English professor at the University of Sheffield, thought the trilogy merely a "matter of contrivance." Because it lacks "a serious controlling principle, the work sprawls," he concluded.[105] A Benedictine priest despised *The Fellowship of the Ring*, labeling it "pretentious snobbery." He continued: "To dress up an elongated fairy tale and sell it with overtones of greatness is a fraud."[106]

Nevertheless, a number of reviewers greatly admired the work. Auden wrote that the author "is fortunate in possessing an amazing gift for naming and a wonderfully exact eye for description; by the time one has finished his book one knows the histories of hobbits, elves, dwarves, and the landscape they inhabit as well as one knows one's own childhood."[107] An English professor at Columbia, Donald Barr, wrote: "It is an extraordinary work—pure excitement, unencumbered narrative, moral warmth, barefaced rejoicing in beauty, but excitement most of all; yet a serious and scrupulous fiction, nothing cozy, no little visits to one's childhood."[108] Another English professor, William Blissett, noted that when reading *The Lord of the Rings*, "We are under a spell from the beginning."[109] In perhaps one of the most complimentary reviews, Louis J. Halle in the *Saturday Review* treated *The Fellowship of the Ring* as a serious history of a real time and a real place. The reviewer found himself "incapable of putting it down at any point; and when he finished it late at night he immediately turned to the first pages to read them over again."[110] Patricia Meyer Spacks of Wellesley College predicted the trilogy would "assume . . . a central position in the canon of serious supernatural literature."[111] The reviewer for the *New Republic* called the trilogy one of the "very few works of genius in recent literature."[112] And Edward Wagenknecht of the *Chicago Sunday Tribune* labeled *The Fellowship of the Ring* "a literary creation of enduring beauty."[113]

Tolkien was not above taking a few jabs at his critics. In the foreword to the second edition of *The Fellowship of the Ring*, Tolkien wrote: "Some who have read the book, or at any rate have reviewed it, have found it boring, absurd, or contemptible; and I have no cause to complain, since I have similar opinions of their works, or of the kinds of writing that they evidently prefer."[114] Tolkien's biographer Humphrey Carpenter writes that the harsh critiques of *The Lord of the Rings* "amused" Tolkien.[115] Tolkien even wrote a short poem about it: "*The Lord of the Rings*/is one of those things:/if you like you do:/if you don't, then you boo!"[116]

Despite its mixed critical reception, Tolkien's trilogy developed an ardent following in England and the United States. Unlike the horde of student followers that was to appear in the mid-1960s, Tolkien's most devoted admirers during this first decade after the trilogy's publication were mostly academics.[117] Daphne Castell recalled that the science faculty at Oxford were enthralled with *The Lord of the Rings* when the first volume came out in 1954. They quoted it often and even wrote messages to one another in Quenya, one of Tolkien's many invented languages.[118] In America, Anglophiles at Harvard and Yale initiated a cult following of the English author. From there, Tolkien's popularity seems to have spread to Cornell, via its math department, to a black magic group at the University of Virginia, and then to "the very nicest people" at Bryn Mawr, a writer for *Esquire* reported.[119] By 1959, though still available only in hardback, over 156,000 copies of *The Lord of the Rings* had been sold.[120] By the mid-1960s, Tolkien had reached the status of a popular icon.[121] This proved especially true in America, where in the first ten months of the paperback's appearance in 1965, *The Lord of the Rings* sold 250,000 copies.[122] Indeed, *The Lord of the Rings* sold briskly on almost every campus. College and university bookstores rarely met the demand with adequate supply.[123]

Hippies and the political Left embraced the trilogy in the mid- to late-1960s. It was, purportedly, one of drug guru Timothy Leary's favorite books, and headshops throughout the United States sold all manner of Tolkien paraphernalia.[124] As Beatles biographer Philip Norman has reported, *The Lord of the Rings* became a vital part of hippie culture, finding admirers among the devotees of "Indian religion, cannabis, and free love."[125] Said the Berkeley campus bookstore manager in 1966, "This is more than a campus craze; it's like a drug dream."[126]

The Lord of the Rings found followers far beyond the borders of the drug world, though. "Going to college without Tolkien is like going without sneakers," a mother of a college student told a *Time* magazine reporter.[127] "Housewives write him from Winnipeg, rocket-men from Woomera, pop-singers from Las Vegas," the Plimmers wrote in 1968. "Ad-men discuss him in London pubs. Germans, Spaniards, Portuguese, Poles, Japanese, Israelies, Swedes, Dutch, and Danes read him in their own language."[128] Fan clubs arose all over the United States, using the greeting, "May the hair on your toes grow ever longer," a reference to hobbits' feet, which are covered with woolly, curly hair.[129] When Wheaton College English professor Clyde Kilby helped Tolkien organize for publication *The Silmarillion* in the summer of 1966, some friends wrote to him: "We're all saying prayers and lighting votive candles for the early appearance of the *Silmarillion*. Tell JRRT his following is no longer a cult. It is a zeitgeist. He is determining the frame of mind of a whole university generation."[130]

His iconic status overwhelmed the elderly Tolkien. He complained that many saw him as a "gargoyle to be gaped at."[131] American fans "are involved in the stories in a way that I am not," Tolkien told a reporter in 1966.[132] He referred to the American fans as "my deplorable cultus."[133] The conservative Catholic author especially despised the hippies.[134] Neither his lifestyle nor his worldview fit theirs. "I suppose I'm a reactionary," he stated in 1966.[135] (Ironically, as the conclusion to this volume explores in more detail, Tolkien's reactionary anti-mechanistic, pro-environmental themes were precisely what his hippie readers identified with.) In a letter written in 1971, Tolkien implied that America must provide a "soil in which the fungus-growth of cults" can easily arise.[136] Tolkien, according to a friend, hated "the cult, and people who have absolutely nothing in common with him cashing in."[137] Still, he concluded that there was very little he could do about it. "I reflect that one must endeavour to do one's work in one's own way and not be deflected," Tolkien wrote to an American scholar. "No one who publishes anything can control the effects it may have or the uses it may be put to in other minds."[138]

Fans from all over the world, but especially from America, bothered Tolkien in every way imaginable. They would show up at his home unannounced and uninvited. They telephoned at all hours. They begged him for autographs, maps, manuscript pages, hair, and other memorabilia. They sent him letters and other items, which arrived "three times a day six days a week, they have been arriving for years and they are still coming; the trickle has become a stream, a river, a flood," Tolkien's secretary Joy Hill reported.[139] Fans sent numerous gifts: paintings, tapestries, tapes, a silver chalice, and even food, which rarely survived the transatlantic flight.[140] Tolkien labeled them "Hoopers, Snoopers, Goopers, press-gangs, phone-bugs, and trans-Atlantic lion hunters and gargoyle fanciers."[141]

With the incredible success of *The Lord of the Rings*, Tolkien's publishers demanded *The Silmarillion*. Tolkien had long wanted to publish it, and now he was getting his chance. As he told a reporter, he was "working like Hell! A pen is to me as a beak is to a hen."[142] Still, Tolkien expressed some bitterness toward his publisher, Allen & Unwin. "Most of [*The Silmarillion*] is written, of course," he said in a telephone interview, "but when I offered it to the publishers first [before *The Lord of the Rings*] . . . they turned it down [as] they were too high and mighty."[143]

Several things worked against the completion of *The Silmarillion*. In a letter to Kilby, Tolkien revealed many of his frustrations:

> [W]hen your letter came to me I was rather burdened and distracted. My wife's health for more than a month has given me much anxiety (it necessitated my going twice to the South-coast in the autumn with much loss of time, but became worse with the sudden early onset of winter). A competent part-time secretary, after giving me much assistance with Ballantine business, departed. And I was suddenly presented with the necessity of revising, and correcting the proofs of, *The Hobbit*, for new editions. Each day I thought it would be done, but I only got off the last material a few days ago.[144]

Tolkien's perfectionism also got the best of him.[145] He wanted *The Silmarillion* totally consistent with *The Lord of the Rings*. Considering the complexity of each, this proved no easy task. It is remarkable, in fact, that Tolkien achieved the cohesion that he did. But even more importantly, given the growing pop-icon status of his works, Tolkien wanted *The Silmarillion* to be as consistent internally regarding theology and philosophy as possible.[146] He most adamantly did not want to be the originator of a religious cult. Insecurities also plagued Tolkien. The same fears that led him to write the autobiographical "Leaf by Niggle"—in which a painter continues to "niggle" at perfecting his painting of individual leaves while fearing that the grand picture of the tree will eventually elude him—resurfaced as he attempted to finish *The Silmarillion*.[147] He also feared, in the words of his son Christopher, that many readers of *The Lord of the Rings* had "delight[ed] in the sensation of 'depth' without wishing to explore the deep places."[148] Finally, Tolkien was in his seventies and physically slowing down. George Sayer visited him often in his last decade and recalled that Tolkien rarely seemed to be working on his mythology.[149]

Tolkien died without completing *The Silmarillion*, but before he passed away he made Christopher his literary heir. The choice made perfect sense. While all of Tolkien's children played some role in his legendarium, Christopher was the most intimately involved. Tolkien had sent large pieces of *The Lord of the Rings* to Christopher in serialized form during World War II. Christopher had made the maps of Middle-earth for his father, had joined the Inklings in 1946, and had earned his degree in medieval literature and taught at Oxford. He also loved detail.[150] He was famous at Oxford for his brilliant lectures, and, as A. N. Wilson has stated, "Christopher is a man of extraordinary intelligence."[151] John and Priscilla Tolkien remembered Christopher correcting his father on details of the Middle-earth stories, with Tolkien exclaiming "damn the boy," but quickly taking notes on what his son had told him.[152]

To complete *The Silmarillion*, Christopher left his position at Oxford, where he had become a successful academic.[153] Completion, though, proved no simple task. He had to go through sixty years of his father's work, wading through multiple versions of the same stories and dealing with primitive versions of others. In addition, there was intense pressure from Tolkien's fans for *The Silmarillion* to appear. Just one day after Tolkien's death, for example, the *New York Times* had assured fans that *The Silmarillion* would still be released.[154] To assist him, Christopher hired Canadian Guy Gavriel Kay, then fresh out of college, but now a famous fantasy writer. Kay worked for Christopher from October 1974 to June 1975. In Christopher's barn, they organized, analyzed, and discussed Tolkien's multiple files, stories, poems, and letters. Kay remembers "the barn as an island, a sanctuary of light amidst the darkness." He and Christopher "felt like medieval monks."[155] Cloistered, they attempted to reconstruct *The Silmarillion*. The dilemma: whether to make it a comprehensive narrative or a scholarly collection of disparate writings.[156] Tolkien himself had once toyed with the idea of Bilbo simply finding the manuscript of *The Silmarillion* in Rivendell. In that case the novel would have appeared as a series of stories and histories.[157] But, in the end, Tolkien's frustration over failing to find an organizing scheme for the book helped lead to its non-completion.[158] Christopher and Kay settled on a coherent narrative.

> *The Silmarillion* is emphatically my father's book and in no sense mine. Here and there I had to develop the narrative out of notes and rough drafts; I had to make many choices between competing versions and to make many changes of detail; and in the last few chapters (which had been left almost untouched for many years) I had in

places to modify the narrative to make it coherent. But essentially what I have done has been a work of organization, not of completion.[159]

"When I finished, I felt an enormous relief that I had survived," Christopher stated. "I had been afraid that, for some reason, I wouldn't be able to complete it. It had been a great responsibility."[160] The twelve-volume *History of Middle-earth* (1983–1996) and *Unfinished Tales of Númenor and Middle-earth* (1980), edited by Christopher Tolkien, served as the scholarly version of *The Silmarillion*.

Though the demand for *The Silmarillion* set publishing and sales records when it first appeared in September 1977, only one reviewer gave it unqualified praise.[161] "It is a work of power, eloquence, and noble vision that would be notable even if 'The Hobbit' and 'The Lord of the Rings' had never been," wrote Edmund Fuller of the *Wall Street Journal*.[162] Of the first reviews to appear, only three others gave it qualified praise. Joseph McLellan of the *Washington Post* contended that *The Silmarillion* was uneven, but that "its best parts stand up well under . . . comparisons" to Hesiod, *Paradise Lost*, and *Genesis*.[163] Even *National Review*, which had unwaveringly supported Tolkien since the early 1960s, gave *The Silmarillion* but guarded praise. There "are gaps and bulges in the narrative," Richard Brookhiser complained. Still, Brookhiser compared Tolkien to Dante and concluded that the book "is a worthy prequel to *The Lord of the Rings*, and no discredit to the man who devoted so much time to it."[164] After a strange and lengthy explanation of how schizophrenics hide in their imaginary languages and worlds, *Harper's* reviewer Charles Nicol concluded his assessment: "A curious, difficult production, not really for the general reader, but absolutely required for Tolkien's serious admirers, *The Silmarillion* is the greatest, strangest monument in Middle-earth."[165] Readers of this odd review must have wondered if J. R. R. Tolkien himself had suffered from schizophrenia.

Negative reviews came from every direction and, in terms of quantity, overwhelmed the aforementioned positive reviews. Strangely, *Christianity Today* complained that the prequel was too Christian.

Whereas *The Lord of the Rings* had been original, *The Silmarillion* seemed too much a copy of the Bible.[166] Several other reviews also faulted the book for its mock-biblical style and structure. *Time* complained that it read as though Tolkien "were writing a parody of Edgar Rice Burroughs in the style of the *Book of Revelations*."[167] In the cover story of its October 1, 1977 issue, the *New Republic* compared it to *The Book of Mormon*, a "cross between Joseph Smith and L. Ron Hubbard." In addition, the reviewer stated, Melkor ends up being more of a John D. Rockefeller than Satan figure. The angelic Valar, the heroes of the book, are simply "trust-busters."[168] *America* (a Jesuit magazine), the *Economist*, and *Newsweek* each complained that *The Silmarillion's* language was ponderous, pretentious, or a "patter of begattery."[169] "Unreadable" was the judgment of the *London Times Literary Supplement*.[170] The *New York Review of Books*, the *Christian Science Monitor*, and the *Atlantic Monthly* referred to the book as pompous, dull, and wearying.[171] Although he noted that it had a few strong elements, the famous literary critic John Gardner complained that *The Silmarillion* was "reminiscent of Walt Disney's 'Fantasia'" and the "language is . . . the phony Prince Valiant language."[172] (Had he been alive, Tolkien would have been rankled by the comparison. He despised Walt Disney, claiming him "simply a cheat—willing and even eager to defraud the less experienced by trickery sufficiently 'legal' to keep him out of jail.")[173] Finally, Peter Conrad of the English leftist *New Statesmen* thought Tolkien deficient in imagination and unable to write properly. Though no hobbits appear in *The Silmarillion*, Conrad wrote that "Tolkien pleases not because he is arcane and outlandish but because he is an unadventurous defender of mediocrity. Middle-Earth is a suburb; its hobbits are Babbits, homespun, humdrum shopkeepers."[174]

Tolkien, of course, was four years dead when the reviews came out. Christopher has never published his reactions to the reviews.[175]

———

Despite his failure to complete *The Silmarillion*, the last decade of Tolkien's life was a productive one. Freed of academic obligations, and unexpectedly finding himself financially secure for the first time in his life, Tolkien found time to publish the autobiographical *Tree and Leaf*, *The Adventures of Tom Bombadil*, several poems, "Smith of Wootton Major," and *The Road Goes Ever On*.[176] Tolkien knew his time was getting short, and he was determined to finish as much work as possible.

With fame, however, came constant interruptions. "We were discussing elves, the professor and I, and there was an alarm clock ticking beside us as a reminder to be brief," wrote one interviewer.[177] The hordes of fans became so great that Tolkien and Edith had to move out of their Oxford home. "I wonder how things are with you. And I daresay you think I have been rather churlish in my silence," Tolkien wrote to his friend and fellow Inkling, the Useless Quack. "But this 'move' has been disastrously disordered by all kinds of mishaps, minor and major, and I am still not able to live in my own house, while all my books, documents, and files remain piled in confusion."[178] Still, Tolkien never wanted to leave England, even to escape high taxes and the annoyance of fame. Like Socrates, Tolkien complained that a move would simply mean that he would live in a place where no one would understand his jokes.[179]

During the 1960s, Edith's health declined rapidly. She passed away in November 1971. Two months later, Queen Elizabeth awarded Tolkien the prestigious C.B.E., or "Commander of the British Empire."[180] That same year, Oxford awarded Tolkien an honorary doctorate for his work in philology. On September 2, 1973, at the age of eighty-one, Tolkien, suffering from a bleeding ulcer and chest infection, died.

Chapter 2

Myth and Sub-creation

In the summer of 1972, a little more than a year before his death, Tolkien requested that his recently deceased wife's gravestone read: "Edith Mary Tolkien, 1889–1971, Lúthien." His gravestone would bear the name of "Beren." One of the central figures of *The Silmarillion* and much of the *History of Middle-earth*, Lúthien is a beautiful Elven woman who renounces her earthly immortality to spend a "heavenly" eternity with her true love, and who devotes her intellect and even her physical prowess to helping her beloved. She and her lover, Beren, work as a perfect team, resisting her skeptical and taunting father as well as Morgoth, the mythological equivalent of Lucifer.[1] Tellingly, as his wife's gravestone suggests, Tolkien viewed his wife in both historical and mythological terms. Indeed, the Edith of her teens and twenties had served as the inspiration for Lúthien. Tolkien mythologized nearly everything in his life. "I shall never write any ordered biography," Tolkien explained to his son Christopher, for "it is against my nature, which expresses itself about things deepest felt in tales and myths."[2] For Tolkien, mystery surrounds us. But modernity has deformed our perception of this reality. His mythologizing of the world, Tolkien believed, increased our ability to see the beauty and sacramentality of creation. It also allowed ideas and loves to transcend time and space. In essence, Tolkien's mind remained complexly medieval and oriented toward myth and mystery.

Tolkien wrestled with the concept, meaning, and execution of myth throughout his adult life, as well as for a significant number of years during his childhood. More than anything else, his love of myth provided a bridge between his academic and fictional work. "I am a philologist and all my work is philological. I avoid hobbies because I am a very serious person and cannot distinguish between private amusement and duty," Tolkien wrote Harvey Breit of the *New York Times Book Review*. "I only work for private amusement, since I find my duties privately amusing."[3] One of Tolkien's students, Anthony Curtis, noted that Tolkien "spoke without any self-consciousness of a set of events which in his mind seemed to exist with as much reality as the French Revolution or the Second World War."[4]

Indeed, for Tolkien, myths expressed far greater truths than did historical facts or events. Sanctified myths, inspired by grace, served as an *anamnesis*, or a way for a people to recall encounters with transcendence that had helped to order their souls and their society. Myth, inherited or created, could also offer a "sudden glimpse of Truth," that is, a brief view of heaven. At the very least, sanctified myth revealed the life humans were meant to have prior to the Fall.[5]

Two fundamental aspects of Tolkien's mythology must be stated from the outset. First, as every reader of Tolkien has found—either to his delight or to his chagrin—Tolkien created a world vastly complex and nuanced. For those who enjoy it, the mythology is invitingly real and awesomely complete. For Tolkien, *The Silmarillion*, *The Hobbit*, and *The Lord of the Rings* represent manifestations or fragments from the mythological world of Middle-earth. These stories by no means exhaust the history of Middle-earth. When Tolkien's popularity within mainstream culture hit a high mark in the mid-1960s, interviewers and reporters incredulously commented that the elderly author believed the most troublesome problem with the 1,000-plus page *Lord of the Rings* was that it was too short![6] As Christopher Tolkien has demonstrated with the twelve-volume *History of Middle-earth*, his father's creativity was immense, if not overwhelming.

Tolkien believed his legendarium to be a single entity revealed to him over time.[7] To him, *The Silmarillion* and *The Lord of the Rings* were a continuation of the same story, inseparable, and, when divided, incomprehensible. In fact, as Clyde Kilby has noted, there are over 600 references to *The Silmarillion* in *The Lord of the Rings*.[8] "Beren now, he never thought he was going to get that Silmaril from the iron Crown in Thangorodrim, and yet he did, and that was a worse place and a blacker danger than ours," Sam says in *The Lord of the Rings*, as Frodo and Sam reluctantly follow Gollum to the stairs of Cirith Ungol, entering Mordor. Sam, looking at the light of the Phial from Galadriel, realizes that the quest to destroy the Ring is a continuation of the story of *The Silmarillion*. "You've got some of the light of it in that star-glass that the Lady gave you! Why, to think of it, we're in the same tale still! It's still going."[9] When a rider from Rohan encounters Aragorn, the future king, for the first time, a similar conversation ensues. After a mention of a Halfling, the rider exclaims: "Halflings! But they are only a little people in old songs and children's tales out of the North. Do we walk in legends or on the green earth in the daylight?" Unmoved, Aragorn responds: "A man may do both. For not we but those who come after will make the legends of our time. The green earth, say you? That is a mighty matter of legend, though you tread it under the light of day!"[10] Little difference, Tolkien's characters state, exists between history and myth, or between the historian and the minstrel. Indeed, the minstrel may understand the complexities of life far more than the historian, trapped in his archives and specialized, cramped world.

While these passages nicely tie together the two major tales (or "manifestations" as Tolkien preferred) of Middle-earth, they also warn the reader that the fight against evil must continue until the end of time. When Sam asks if "the great tales never end?" Frodo replies no, "but the people in them come, and go when their part's ended. Our part will end later—or sooner."[11] Tolkien's world of myth comes before our world of history, and his tale—because it is linked with our tale, the tale of a fallen world—never truly ends, until the Apocalypse.[12]

The second aspect of Tolkien's mythology that must be understood is his firm conviction that God authored the history of Middle-earth, in all its manifestations. Tolkien thought that he merely served as a scrivener of God's myth.[13] "I have long ceased to invent," Tolkien wrote in 1956. "I wait till I seem to know what really happened. Or till it writes itself."[14] A British Member of Parliament once told Tolkien, "*You* did not write *The Lord of the Rings*," implying that the story had a divine source.[15] Tolkien agreed. "The Other Power then took over: the Writer of the Story (by which I do not mean myself), 'that one ever-present Person who is never absent and never named.'"[16] Usually, this presented no great burden to Tolkien. His task to record was, he knew, a supreme gift. After all, both Tolkien and Lewis argued, God spoke through the minds of poets. "[T]he story of Christ is simply a true myth," Lewis wrote to his friend Arthur Greeves. "One must be content to accept it in the same way, remember that it is God's myth where the others are men's myths, i.e. the Pagan stories are God expressing Himself through the minds of poets, using such images as He found there."[17] G. K. Chesterton had argued something similar in 1925: "Mythology . . . sought God through the imagination; or sought truth by means of beauty."[18] Similarly, Tolkien believed that he served as a poet-recipient of God's secondary myths, that he was a recorder rather than an inventor.

The word "hobbit" illustrates the way in which Tolkien was often inspired: "I was doing the dull work of correcting exam papers when I came upon a blank page someone had turned in—a boon to all exam markers," he told an interviewer in 1972. "I turned it over and wrote on the back, 'In a hole in the ground there lived a hobbit.' I'd never heard or used the word before."[19] Bilbo Baggins, Tolkien noted several times, simply wandered into his larger mythology.[20] "I didn't do much choosing. . . . I wrote *The Hobbit* you see. . . . [A]ll I was trying to do [with *The Lord of the Rings*] was carry on from the point where *The Hobbit* left off. I'd got hobbits on my hands hadn't I?"[21]

Tolkien frequently found his own stories and mythology puzzling, and he always sought to dig deeper into Middle-earth to find the answers to questions presented him.[22] One of the most troubling manifestations of Tolkien's "recording" developed at the very beginning of *The Lord of the Rings* with the unexpected arrival of the

Ringwraith. "[S]tories tend to get out of hand, and this has taken an unpremeditated turn," he confided to his publisher in 1938.[23] The Ringwraith's appearance, Tolkien noted, disturbed him as much as it did the frightened hobbits in the story.[24] Thus, the new story was rapidly transformed from a delightful and whimsical children's sequel to *The Hobbit* into an adult story that wrestled with questions of enormous theological and philosophical import and subtlety.

Besides Ringwraiths and hobbits, other characters presented themselves to Tolkien, and he did not always have time to discuss them in detail.[25] One of the most intriguing omissions from the tales is the story of Berúthiel, briefly mentioned by Aragorn during the harrowing journey of the Fellowship of the Ring through Moria.[26] "There's one exception that puzzles me—Berúthiel," Tolkien told an interviewer. "I really don't know anything of her. . . . She just popped up, and obviously called for attention, but I don't really know anything certain about her." He proceeded to take a spontaneous and rather long guess at who she might be, and why she despised cats. The interviewer, a former student of Tolkien's, writes nothing of what must have been a bewildering and surreal discussion except that she enjoyed being in the presence of such a fine storyteller.[27] Tolkien also regretted leaving Círdan, the keeper of the Grey Havens, as a minor and poorly developed character in *The Lord of the Rings*. *The Silmarillion* and the twelfth volume of the *History of Middle-earth* gives him a satisfactory and interesting context, but the reader never really learns about Círdan as a person. Finally, Tolkien seemed genuinely puzzled over the names, whereabouts, and fate of the two unnamed wizards (members of the Istari) who arrived at roughly the same time as Gandalf, Saruman, and Radagast. Known only as the "Blue Wizards," they simply fade from the legendarium, never to be seen by any of the characters who populate Middle-earth. Tolkien predicted that either Sauron corrupted them to evil, or they had become the founders of Eastern mystery religions and gnostic cults.[28] Considering that Tolkien created such a complex and believable world with what he called an "inner consistency of reality," complete with its own culture, religion, politics, law, peoples, languages, topography, and climate, it is astounding that there are not more loose ends in Tolkien's mythology.

===

What was it that shaped Tolkien's immensely fertile imagination? He insisted that it was his love of language.

> The seed [of the myth] is linguistic, of course. I'm a linguist and everything is linguistic—that's why I take such pains with names. The real seed was starting when I was quite a child by inventing languages, largely to try to capture the esthetic mode of the languages I was learning, and I eventually made the discovery that language can't exist in a void and if you invent a language yourself you can't cut it in half. It has to come alive—so really the languages came first and the country after."[29]

Since early childhood, Tolkien had loved and excelled at languages. But rarely did he embrace the language that he was supposed to be studying. "When I was supposed to be studying Latin and Greek, I studied Welsh and English," he told an interviewer. "When I was supposed to be concentrating on English, I took up Finnish."[30] He continued formally and informally on his own as a teenager to study Spanish, French, Anglo-Saxon, Old Norse, Gothic, and Welsh.[31] Tolkien worked on the *Oxford English Dictionary* after World War I. His superior at the dictionary, Dr. Henry Bradley, offered high praise of his abilities. "His work gives evidence of an unusually thorough mastery of Anglo-Saxon and of the facts and principles of the comparative grammar of the Germanic languages," Bradley reported. "Indeed, I have no hesitation in saying that I have never known a man of his age who was in these respects his equal."[32]

In addition to mastering contemporary and historical languages, Tolkien created his own languages beginning at the age of thirteen, the most detailed and complex of which would become Elvish (two languages, actually, Sindarin and Quenya).[33] "This was no arbitrary gibberish but a really possible tongue with consistent roots, sound laws, and inflexions, into which he poured all his imaginative and philological powers; and strange as the exercise may seem it was undoubtedly the source of that unparalleled richness and concreteness which later distinguished him from all other philologists," Tolkien's obituarist wrote. "He had been inside language."[34] To invent Elvish, Tolkien studied the manner in which Welsh, one of his favorite languages, had developed out of old Celtic. He separated its actual linguistic permutations from its possibilities, and then patterned Elvish on what the Celtic language might have become, had it evolved differently.[35] "You start with p, t and k, then you introduce b, d and g followed by the nasals," Tolkien told an interviewer in 1972. "I still remember seeing the name 'Ebbw' on a railway journey to Wales as a small child and never quite getting over the fascination of the name."[36] Tolkien's other invented languages follow a similar trajectory of creation, developing what might have been in the real, historical world.[37] Within each of Tolkien's languages, then, many paths diverge yet again, just as languages did historically. None remain static. Instead, Tolkien posited "a basic and phonetic structure of Primitive Elvish, and then modif[ied] this by [a] series of changes (such as actually do occur in known languages) so that the two end results would each have a consistent structure and character, but be quite different." In the mythology, for example, "the hymn to Elbereth is an entirely different mode and prosody from that of Galadriel's lament."[38]

Tolkien, though, quickly grew bored of his invented languages, even when evolving them along their possible divergent lines of development. Without anything additional to them, something to give them weight, significance, and depth, they became mere mental games, little more than complex abstractions.

> [T]o give your language an individual flavour, it must have woven into it the threads of an individual mythology, individual while working within the scheme of natural human mythopoeia, as your word-form may be individual while working within the hackneyed limits of human, even European, phonetics. The converse indeed is true, your language construction will breed a mythology.[39]

Language without history means little, and, Tolkien adamantly
argued, one cannot abstract language from a culture or a people.[40]

Another Inkling, Owen Barfield, voiced what Tolkien wanted to
argue regarding myth and language but as of the mid-1920s had failed
to put together on an intellectual level. Barfield contended that language derived from mythology, not vice versa, as was generally thought.
His pathbreaking 1928 work, *Poetic Diction*, significantly influenced
both Lewis and Tolkien.[41] In a letter to Barfield, Lewis wrote: "You
might like to know that when Tolkien dined with me the other night
he said *à propos* of something quite different that your conception of
the ancient semantic unity had modified his whole outlook and that he
was always just going to say something in a lecture when your conception stopped him in time." Barfield felt a strong affinity with Tolkien's
notions on myth as well.[42]

It is impossible for the historian to reconstruct or discover the
moment at which Tolkien realized that this revelation that language
derived from myth was true in his own life, his academic work, and
his legendarium. His views on when he had formed the basis of the
Middle-earth mythology changed over time. As he grew older, Tolkien
placed the origins of the myth at increasingly earlier dates. Indeed, he
found it very difficult to distance himself from Middle-earth. All that
he read or absorbed throughout his life became a part of him, and,
hence, a part of his grand mythology. To paraphrase a trite truism,
he was what he read. In the mid-1960s, he told an interviewer: "Of
course, the images we retain are usually combinations. We remember
the same scene in different circumstances, sometimes with one set of
people, sometimes with another. We put all our impressions together
and believe that our image is what the place we're remembering was
really like. Of course, it isn't."[43]

Clyde Kilby, who spent the summer of 1966 helping Tolkien organize his papers to rewrite *The Silmarillion*, has argued that Tolkien
may have developed Middle-earth as early as the age of fourteen.[44]
Tolkien wrote to Kilby that a line from Cynewulf's medieval poem,
"Crist," greatly affected him as a young man. "*Ëalä Eärendel engla
beorhtast ofer middengeard monnum sended* (Here Eärendel, bright-

est of angels, sent from God to men)." "Rapturous words," Tolkien wrote, "from which ultimately sprang the whole of my mythology."[45] "Years later," Tolkien wrote, "I felt a curious thrill as if something had stirred in me, half wakened from sleep. There was something very remote and strange and beautiful behind those words, if I could grasp it, far beyond ancient English."[46] Tolkien first attempted to grasp the meaning of Cynewulf's Anglo-Saxon line when he presented a composition titled "Earendel" (Tolkien's spelling of the name was inconsistent) at the Oxford Essay Club in 1914.[47] He later incorporated an Elvish version of Eärendil, "Of the Voyage of Eärendil and the War of Wrath," into his larger mythology.[48]

Although its origins are unclear, it does seem that Tolkien constructed much of his initial mythology, and committed it to paper, during World War I. Distraught by the mechanized, dehumanized warfare of the trenches, and admittedly a poor, undisciplined officer, Tolkien conceived *The Silmarillion* in "grimy canteens, at lectures in cold fogs, in huts full of blasphemy and smut, or by candle light in bell-tents, even some down in dugouts under shell fire."[49] Outlining it provided a sense of relief, and the budding mythology served as a catharsis. "I sense amongst all your pains (some merely physical) the desire to express your feeling about good, evil, fair, foul in some way: to rationalize it, and prevent it just festering," he wrote Christopher, then serving as an R.A.F. pilot during World War II. "In my case it generated Morgoth" and *The Silmarillion.*[50] In his famous academic essay, "On Fairy Stories," Tolkien admitted that war "quickened to full life" his love of fairy stories.[51] Christopher Tolkien confirms that extant pieces of *The Silmarillion* and the larger mythology appear on the back of official army documents dating from the war.[52]

Tolkien wrote in 1964 that the parameters of his mythology had been set by 1926. To him, the writings that followed constituted further understandings, revelations, and manifestations of the mythology as Tolkien began to understand it better,[53] including the tales of Arda and Middle-earth.[54] "They arose in my mind as 'given' things, and as they came, separately, so too the links grew," Tolkien wrote. "An absorbing, though continually interrupted labour (especially, even apart from the necessities of life, since the mind would wing to the other pole and spread itself on the linguistics): yet always I had the sense of recording what was already 'there', somewhere: not of 'inventing.'"[55] In his fascinating study of Tolkien, *The Road to Middle-earth*, T. A. Shippey notes that "invention" originally derives from Latin, meaning "to discover."[56] Philologists, then, according to Shippey, often see themselves as true historians, uncovering the deepest meanings of a culture.[57] Still, Tolkien implied in interviews and letters that his "discovery" was as much theological as it was linguistic.

Even if one accepts the premise that Tolkien "received" his mythology as a form of revelation, Tolkien's own vast knowledge of Germanic, Roman, Greek, and even North American mythology greatly informed it. Tolkien had a profound grasp of the literature of northern European mythology in particular. The Icelandic *Poetic Edda*, the Finnish *Kalevala*, various Anglo-Saxon poetry, George MacDonald, and G. K. Chesterton served as the most obvious influences, directly or indirectly, on Tolkien's legendarium.[58] But there were other influences, some not so immediately obvious. "[H]e used to have the most extraordinary interest in the people here in Kentucky," Allen Barnett, a Kentuckian and former Oxford classmate of Tolkien's said. "He could never get enough of my tales of Kentucky folk. He used to make me repeat family names like Barefoot and Boffin and Baggins and good country names like that."[59] The New York frontier also may have influenced the Oxford philologist; Shippey argues that Tolkien borrowed much from James Fenimore Cooper's *Leatherstocking Tales*: "The Journey of the Fellowship from Lorien to Tol Brandir," for instance, "with its canoes and portages, often recalls *The Last of the Mohicans*, and as the travelers move from forest to prairie, like the American pioneers, Aragorn and Éomer for a moment preserve faint traces of 'The Deerslayer' and the Sioux."[60]

Tolkien kept his mythology private until he met C. S. Lewis in the mid-1920s. Only his family and a research assistant knew anything about it.[61] As we saw in chapter 1, Lewis responded enthusiastically to his colleague's private world. "I sat up late last night and have read the Geste as far as to where Beren and his gnomish allies defeat the patrol of orcs above the sources of the Narog and disguise themselves," Lewis wrote to Tolkien in 1929. "I can quite honestly say that it is ages since I have had an evening of such delight."[62] According to a friend, Lewis "was aghast. This was the sort of writing which he would not have dared to believe could exist."[63] By 1930, Tolkien had shared much of his mythology—the poems, prose stories, and maps—with Lewis.[64] Once Lewis converted to Christianity, in no small part due to Tolkien's influence, he specifically admired Tolkien's mythology for its Christian essence.[65] Much to Tolkien's chagrin, Lewis even used the Middle-earth mythology as a background for several of his own stories, including the Space Trilogy and even parts of the Chronicles of Narnia.[66] Throughout his life, Lewis played a prominent role in the development of Tolkien's mythology, always showing enthusiasm for the project and encouraging Tolkien to publish it. Indeed, Lewis never understood Tolkien's reluctance to see his mythology in print and blamed it on his colleague's perfectionism.[67] Tolkien admitted as much. "Only from [Lewis] did I ever get the idea that my 'stuff' could be more than a private hobby," Tolkien acknowledged in 1965, two years after his friend's death. "But for his interest and unceasing eagerness for more I should never have brought *The L. of the R.* to a conclusion."[68]

Two of Tolkien's academic essays, "The Monsters and the Critics" and "On Fairy-Stories," shed much light on Tolkien's view of mythology in general as well as on his own particular mythology. Tolkien viewed these essays as two parts of the same argument.[69] He delivered the first to the British Academy as the Sir Israel Gollancz Memorial Lecture on November 25, 1936.[70] The second, "On Fairy-Stories," he presented at the University of St. Andrews in Scotland as the Andrew Lang Lecture on March 8, 1939.[71] He considered this essay especially explicative of his own thinking and analysis on a range of subjects.[72] In fact, he later claimed that he had written *The Lord of the Rings* to demonstrate much of the argument presented in "On Fairy-Stories."[73]

Tolkien's examination of *Beowulf*, the subject of the first essay, has become a standard in the field of Beowulf criticism, and Anglo-Saxon scholars and critics typically either agree with it or abhor it.[74] For Tolkien, who had committed to memory almost the entire poem, *Beowulf* represented one of the great moments in western history.[75] Shippey claims that Tolkien believed he understood the *Beowulf* poet intimately, that they were kindred spirits separated only by time.[76] Perhaps they were, for numerous scholars give Tolkien high praise for his analysis of the medieval poem. In the introduction to his translation of *Beowulf*, for example, poet Seamus Heaney contends that Tolkien's essay is the "one publication that stands out. . . . Tolkien's brilliant literary treatment changed the way the poem was valued and initiated a new era— and new terms—of appreciation."[77] *Beowulf*, Tolkien had argued, is as important for the historian and the theologian as for the English teacher. Two things should immediately prove this, he thought. First, the story contains a dragon. Rarely in literature does one find them. Contrary to our popular memory of legends, no "wilderness of dragons" abounded in medieval literature. Instead, when such a bestial worm does present itself, the critic should take its significance to the story and its symbolism seriously.[78] Indeed, the appearance of a dragon signifies a number of things—most of them evil. A dragon personifies "malice, greed, destruction."[79] Second, Tolkien noted that few authors would devote over 3,000 lines of high poetry to something "not worth serious attention."[80] Instead, the "high tone, the sense of dignity, alone is evidence in *Beowulf* of the presence of a mind lofty and thoughtful."[81]

Beowulf's greatest strength, Tolkien believed, lay in the author's understanding that the theme should be implicit rather than explicit. According to Tolkien, the *Beowulf* poet wisely avoided a formal allegory and created his setting as "incarnate in the world of history and geography." Unless highly cautious, Tolkien continued, the author could have easily destroyed the poetry and significance by making the meaning too explicit.[82] The anonymous author bravely set the mortal hero in the "hostile world" to be destroyed within time, thereby intermixing legend and history.[83] Indeed, mortality in the fallen state of sin represents one of the most important themes of *Beowulf*.

For Tolkien, the Beowulf poet beautifully intertwined pagan virtues with Christian theology. The anonymous author most likely lived at the time Christianity was slowly spreading throughout England. Most certainly a Christian, the author used the poem to demonstrate that not all pagan things should be dismissed by the new culture. Instead, the Christian should embrace and sanctify the most noble virtues to come out of the northern pagan mind: courage and raw will.[84] "It is the strength of the northern mythological imagination that it faced this problem, put the monsters in the centre, gave them victory but no honour, and found a potent but terrible solution in naked will and courage," Tolkien wrote. "The northern [imagination] has power, as it were, to revive its spirit even in our own times."[85] Tolkien thought that a vigorous Christianity stood in need of the mythologically oriented, northern pagan spirit.[86] The German-Italian theologian Romano Guardini argued along the same lines.

> Deeply significant for the new religious outlook of medieval man was the influx of the Germanic spirit. The religious bent of the Nordic myths, the restlessness of the migrating peoples and the armed marches of the Germanic tribes revealed a new spirit which burst everywhere into history like a spear thrust into the infinite. This mobile and nervous soul worked itself into the Christian affirmation. There it grew mightily. In its fullness it produced that immense medieval drive which aimed at cracking the boundaries of the world.[87]

Tolkien's belief that the best of the pagan world should be sanctified reflects St. Augustine's thinking. In his "On Christian Duty," St. Augustine wrote, "[If philosophers] have said aught that is true and in harmony with our faith, we are not only not to shrink from it, but to claim it for our own use from those who have unlawful possession of it." In much of the *City of God*, St. Augustine uses Cicero and Plato to support his argument that a thriving Christianity was compatible with a stable post-Roman world. Clement of Alexandria, living in the late second and early third centuries, presaged Augustine's argument. Pre-Christian faiths, he argued in *Miscellanies*, served as a "preparatory teaching for those who [would] later embrace the faith." Additionally, he speculated that philosophy was given to the Greeks as an introduction to Christianity. For philosophy, Clement concluded, "acted as a schoolmaster to the Greeks, preparing them for Christ, as the laws of the Jews prepared them for Christ."[88] That is, Plato and Aristotle served to prepare the way for Christianity in a manner similar to the way Abraham and Moses had.

For Tolkien, the anonymous author of *Beowulf* followed Clement's and Augustine's advice, appropriating the best of pagan culture and sanctifying it as Christian. And with the Beowulf poet, Tolkien believed that the sanctification of the pagan was an essential Christian project. He once found a celandine flower while on a walk in the woods with George Sayer. "Did you know that when picking celandine various combinations of Aves and Paternosters have to be said?" Tolkien asked. "This was one of the many cases of Christian prayers supplanting pagan ones, for in ancient times there were runes to be spoken before it was picked."[89]

With the arrival and acceptance of Christianity, Tolkien asserted, the understanding of the nature of "the good" changes, but the nature of evil remains the same:

> For the monsters do not depart, whether the gods go or come. A Christian was (and is) still like his forefathers a mortal hemmed in a hostile world. The monsters remained the enemies of mankind, the infantry of the old war, and became inevitably the enemies of the one God.[90]

The true battle remains, as always throughout time and space, the struggle between "the soul and its adversaries."[91] As Beowulf discovers, Tolkien wrote, "the wages of heroism [Christian or Pagan] is death."[92] Such is God's will for good men. Christ provided the ultimate example of this, as did his followers, the martyrs of pagan Rome.

Three years later, in 1939, Tolkien delivered his seminal "On Fairy-Stories" lecture in Scotland. At the beginning of the essay, Tolkien introduces a significant caveat to what follows:

> The realm of fairy-story is wide and deep and high and filled with many things: all manner of beasts and birds are found there; shoreless seas and stars uncounted; beauty that is an enchantment, and an ever-present peril; both joy and sorrow as sharp as swords. In that realm a man may, perhaps, count himself fortunate to have wandered, but its very richness and strangeness tie the tongue of a traveler who would report them. And while he is there it is dangerous for him to ask too many questions, lest the gates should shut and the keys be lost.[93]

That is, a scholar presents an analysis of faerie only at the peril of the story itself. Like tradition, myth and fairy stories are fragile things.

Only an accident of recent history, Tolkien claimed, made fairy stories seem as if they were for children. "It is true that in recent times fairy-stories have usually been written or 'adapted' for children. But so may music, or verse, or novels, or history, or scientific manuals."[94] In Tolkien's view, the adult relegation of fairy stories to the nursery has been dangerous for both adults and children. Fairy stories demand the attention of a mind that can separate fact from fantasy, and children remain children because of their inability to do just that. "Children's knowledge of the world is often so small that they cannot judge, off-hand and without help, between the fantastic, the strange (that is rare or remote facts), the nonsensical, and the merely 'grown-up.'"[95] Instead of fairy stories, children demand knowledge of reality, especially because they desire to know what is dangerous and what is safe, what is good and what is bad. "I desired dragons with a profound desire," Tolkien admitted of his childhood. "Of course, I in my timid body did not wish to have them in the neighborhood, intruding into my relatively safe world, in which it was, for instance, possible to read stories in peace of mind, free from fear. But the world that contained even the imagination of Fáfnir was richer and more beautiful, at whatever cost of peril."[96]

In addition to believing that fairy stories do not belong to children, Tolkien dismissed the notion that fantasy belongs to the same categories as day-dreaming or mental disorders. Rather, it takes the highest quality of mind, and ultimately character, to create good fantasy.

> Fantasy is a natural human activity. It certainly does not destroy or even insult Reason; and it does not either blunt the appetite for, nor obscure the perception of, scientific veracity. On the contrary. The keener and the clearer is the reason, the better fantasy will it make. If men were ever in a state in which they did not want to know or could not perceive truth (facts or evidence), then Fantasy would languish until they were cured. If they ever get into that state (it would not seem at all impossible), Fantasy will perish, and become Morbid Delusion.[97]

Tolkien warned that fallen man can pervert fairy stories, fantasy, and myth, making them something for the promulgation of evil. Therefore, Tolkien concluded, one should leave fantasy to the mental imagination and to the written word. To take fantasy to the animated visual arts, such as with motion pictures or the theater, must result in either "silliness or morbidity."[98]

Despite its many perils and the great possibilities of misunderstanding in the modern world, the effort of entering faerie, at least for Tolkien, is worth exploring and may even prove necessary for the survival of modern man. Indeed, as high art forms, fairy stories and fantasy offer much to human existence. First, fairy stories illuminate the vast inheritance our ancestors have bequeathed to us. Second, fairy stories give us a new sense of wonder about things we have taken for granted or which have become commonplace. "It was in fairy-stories that I first divined the potency of words," Tolkien wrote, "and the wonder of all things, such as stone, and wood, and iron; tree and grass; house and fire; bread and wine."[99] Fairy stories and fantasy allow one to see "things as we are (or were) meant to see them."[100] Considering Tolkien's Roman Catholic faith, one may infer that he was referring to the significance of the Eucharist and transubstantiation with his reference to "bread and wine." Third, fairy stories provide humans with a means to escape the drabness, conformity, and mechanization of modernity. Tolkien warned that this is not the same thing as escaping from reality. We still deal with life and death, comfort and discomfort. We merely escape progressivism and the progressive dream, which reduces all of complex reality to a mere shadow of creation's true wonders.[101]

Most importantly, fairy stories and fantasy allow the writer to act as a sub-creator, an artist made and making in the image of the ultimate creator, God. The artist should "create as lavishly as possible," Lewis wrote. "The romancer, who invents a whole world, is worshipping God more effectively than the mere realist."[102] Yet, because we are fallen, restless, and susceptible to pride, Tolkien argued, even the well-intentioned can pervert the high calling and gift of creativity. In such perversions, man turns art into power; adulterated by sin the prideful man uses his gifts not to exalt creation and the creator, but to serve himself.[103] The Elves, especially Fëanor, exemplify this in *The Silmarillion*. Endowed by Ilúvatar with the "Spirit of Fire," Fëanor, the greatest of all Elves, creates the three Silmarils, unequaled gems capturing the light of the Two Trees, Telperion and Laurelin. When Morgoth destroys the trees, the angelic powers are left without light. Fëanor's Silmarils, though, may hold the key, as they contain the holy light. Possessive of his sub-creation, even though they contain a light beyond his ability to create, Fëanor refuses to give the Silmarils to the angelic regents of earth.

With such religious implications and significance in its artistry, Tolkien concluded, the best fairy story and sub-creation provides the reader with what he labeled the *euchatastrophe*, the unexpected joy. In fantasy, one gains a "fleeting glimpse of Joy, Joy beyond the walls of the world."[104] Such evangelium rarely happens in our world. When it does, one must be content with it, for it will most likely not occur again in one's lifetime. The ultimate fairy story, or true myth, then, is the incarnation, crucifixion, and resurrection of Christ. "The Christian joy, the Gloria, is of the same kind; but it is pre-eminently (infinitely, if our capacity were not finite) high and joyous,"[105] Tolkien wrote. "The heart of Christianity is a myth which is also a fact," C. S. Lewis argued along Tolkienian lines. "The old myth of the Dying God, without ceasing to be myth, comes down from the heaven of legend and imagination to the earth of history."[106] With the Incarnation of Christ, "art has been verified," Tolkien claimed. "God is the Lord, of angels, and of men—and of elves. Legend and History have met and fused" with the arrival of God in Time, and man has been blessed beyond earthly comprehension.[107] Tolkien made a similar argument about the Holy Spirit in the *History of Middle-earth*. God's ability to enter into his story without becoming incarnate occurs when he sends his Spirit. The relationship between these two persons of the Blessed Trinity reveals "the mystery of 'authorship,' by which the author, while remaining 'outside' and independent of his work, also 'indwells' in it, on its derivative plane, below that of his own being, as the source and guarantee of its being."[108]

═══════════════

One of the trickier issues for Tolkien scholars is the question of allegory. Is there a specific allegory or a number of allegories contained within Tolkien's mythology? When *The Lord of the Rings* first appeared, reviewers quickly propagated several erroneous assumptions. For example, some argued that Sauron represented Hitler or Stalin.[109] More commonly, critics claimed that the Ring and its ultimate power represented the relatively new and fearsome atomic weaponry that was shaping the postwar world. Still others argued that *The Lord of the Rings* represented World War II.[110]

Tolkien adamantly rejected the notion that his mythology served as an allegory.[111] In his preface to *The Fellowship of the Ring*, Tolkien wrote, "As for any inner meaning or 'message,' it has in the intention of the author none." Furthermore, he explained, "It is neither allegorical nor topical."[112] Indeed, Tolkien utterly rejected the use of allegory altogether and noted his dislike of it wherever he could detect it. In "The Monsters and the Critics" Tolkien expressed his fear that in making his meaning too explicit an author risks destroying the art and deeper significance of his work. As Lewis claimed, "the essence of a myth [is] that it should have no taint of allegory to the maker and yet should suggest incipient allegories to the reader."[113]

But Tolkien's stories did contain explicit and implicit moral judgments. The world seemed to be descending into chaos, into a new dark age, he believed, and needed sound moral judgment more than ever. Thus, as Tolkien frankly admitted, he communicated his beliefs and worldview under the cover of "mythical and legendary dress."[114] Each person is "an allegory," Tolkien conceded to his former student, W. H. Auden, "each embodying in a particular tale and clothed in the garments of time and place, universal truth and everlasting life."[115]

At other times, Tolkien confessed that Middle-earth represented Europe in the long distant past, prior to the recording of history. The term Middle-earth, after all, was merely Anglo-Saxon for the land between the oceans—Christian Europe.[116] "Rhun is the Elvish word for 'east.' Asia, China, Japan, and all the things which people in the west regard as far away," Tolkien noted in an interview in 1966, referring to his invented world's geography. "And south of Harad is Africa, the hot countries."[117] England, by such logic, would be the Shire, Tolkien stated.[118] Indeed, Tolkien originally had hoped that his legendarium would serve as a mythology for England, a land devoid of all but the Arthurian myth (which was really Welsh, not English). Even *Beowulf*, written in Anglo-Saxon, dealt with the history of the Danes and the Geats as opposed to the Anglo-Saxons. And, to Tolkien's tastes, Christianity and Welshness (the Britons) too blatantly pervaded the Arthurian legends, diminishing their potential to revive the spirit of the modern world.[119] "I was distressed that almost all the myths were Welsh or Scots or Irish, French or German. All we English seemed to have were a few things like Jack the Giant-Killer," Tolkien once admitted to an interviewer. "So I thought I'd make one myself."[120] Tolkien had further hoped to inscribe *The Silmarillion* to Queen Elizabeth II with the words, "The only thing in which your country is not rich is mythology."[121]

Tolkien's hobbits represented the best of the pre–Norman invasion Anglo-Saxons.[122] Like the English (made up of Jutes, Angles, and

Saxons), the hobbits (made up of Harfoots, Stoors, and Fallohides) migrated from the east.[123] Additionally, the hobbits lived on land that was originally not theirs but had once belonged to a greater, and now long-gone, power. There were other specifically Anglo-Saxon elements as well. Tom Shippey speculates that the Rohirrim are Anglo-Saxons as they might have developed had they had a mounted horse culture. Much of the ceremony, for example, of Gandalf entering the Golden Hall mirrors Beowulf's entrance into the Great Hall. Additionally, the Riders call their own land, "The Mark." The old translation for Mercia (an Anglo-Saxon medieval kingdom) was "The Mark." Indeed, as we have seen, Shippey believes that Tolkien mixed his affection for the Anglo-Saxons with his regard for the warrior culture of North American Indians found in James Fenimore Cooper's *Leatherstocking Tales*.[124] And in "On Fairy-Stories," Tolkien remarked that he liked "Red Indians" better than *Alice in Wonderland* or *Treasure Island*, as they offered him "glimpses of an archaic mode of life, and, above all, forests."[125]

Many of Tolkien's pro-English (not British!) feelings stemmed from his childhood move from South Africa to England:

> [My] earliest memories are of Africa, but it was alien to me, and when I came home, therefore, I had for the countryside of England both the native feeling and the personal wonder of somebody who comes to it. I came to the English countryside when I was about 3 ½ or 4—it seemed to me wonderful. If you really want to know what Middle-earth is based on, it's my wonder and delight in the earth as it is, particularly with the natural earth.[126]

But from its original conception as a myth for England, Tolkien's legendarium grew much larger in scope and significance. The story, especially *The Lord of the Rings*, became much more than a myth for any one people or any one nation. It, instead, became a myth for the restoration of Christendom itself. The intrepid Anglo-Saxon missionaries, in particular St. Boniface of Crediton, created medieval, Christian Europe by carrying classical and Christian traditions into the heart of pagan, barbarian Europe. St. Boniface converted innumerable barbarians to Christianity, unifying them under Rome. St. Boniface even crowned Pepin, son of Charles Martel, an action that would eventually lead to the papal recognition of Charlemagne as the revived Holy Roman Emperor in 800 A.D.[127] With the return of the king Aragorn to his rightful throne, Tolkien argued, the "progress of the tales ends in what is far more like the re-establishment of an effective Holy Roman Empire with its seat in Rome."[128] In his own private writings, Tolkien equated numerous parts of Italy with various geographical aspects of Gondor.[129] In his diary, for example, Tolkien recorded that with his trip to Italy, he had "come to the head of Christendom: an exile from the borders and far provinces returning home, or at least to the home of his fathers."[130] In a letter to a friend, Tolkien stated that he had holidayed "in Gondor, or in modern parlance, Venice."[131] That Tolkien should place a mythologized Italy, and ultimately Rome, at the center of his legendarium is not surprising, since he viewed the Reformation as ultimately responsible for the modern, secularized world.

As will be further explored in chapter 6, Tolkien also saw his myth as a means to attenuate the re-emergence of nationalism. The Roman Catholic Whig historian Lord Acton had stressed that the end of Christendom would mean the rise of nationalism. "Christianity rejoices at the mixture of races," he wrote in his famed essay, "Nationalism." Paganism, however, "identifies itself with their differences, because truth is universal, errors various and particular." "By making the State and the nation commensurate with each other in theory," Acton continued, those deemed inferior will be "exterminated, or reduced to servitude, or outlawed, or put in a condition of dependence."[132]

For Tolkien, mythology was a profound tool for shaping the goals, worldviews, and actions of men. "A man who disbelieved the Christian story as fact but continually fed on it as myth would, perhaps," Lewis explained, "be more spiritually alive than one who assented and did not think much about it."[133] Or, as Tolkien wrote of the myth makers:

They have seen Death and ultimate defeat,
and yet they would not in despair retreat,
but oft to victory have turned the lyre
and kindled hearts with legendary fire,
illuminating Now and dark Hath-been
with light of suns as yet by no man seen.[134]

Chapter 3

The Created Order

"Of course God is in *The Lord of the Rings*. The period was pre-Christian, but it was a monotheistic world," Tolkien responded defensively when asked by interviewers in 1968 why he had ignored God in his trilogy. When the interviewers pushed him further, asking who the God was, Tolkien responded: "*The* one, of course! The book is about the world that God created—the actual world of this planet."[1]

As a subcreator, Tolkien desired to recreate the truth, laws, and beauty of God's created order. As he told a Jesuit friend, *The Lord of the Rings* is "a fundamentally religious and Catholic work; unconsciously so at first, but consciously in the revision."[2] To American evangelical Clyde Kilby, Tolkien wrote: "I am a Christian and of course what I write will be from that essential viewpoint."[3] In an interview in 1997, Tolkien's close friend George Sayer stated that *The Lord of the Rings* "would have been very different, and the writing of it very difficult, if Tolkien hadn't been a Christian. He thought it a profoundly Christian book."[4] According to his son Michael, Roman Catholicism "pervaded all [Tolkien's] thinking, beliefs and everything else."[5] In fact, that only a few Catholic magazines and periodicals initially reviewed *The Lord of the Rings* proved deeply disappointing to Tolkien.[6]

Tolkien's Roman Catholicism shaped—or so he hoped and desired—almost every aspect of his life. He viewed life as "part of a cosmic conflict between the forces of good and evil, God and the devil,"[7] wrote Sayer, and Kilby remarked that he never once visited

Tolkien without Tolkien bringing up the topic of Christianity.[8] But Tolkien's faith was not merely intellectual; in Sayer's words, Tolkien was "a devout and strict old-fashioned Catholic"[9] who was devoted to the sacraments, which he believed "freed one from enthralment [sic] to Sauron."[10] Once, while resting from a hike at a "simple little Church" in the hamlet of Welford, "Tollers [the Inkling name for Tolkien] said a prayer," much to Warnie Lewis's surprise.[11] Tolkien believed that God answered prayers directly, even miraculously healing sicknesses.[12] This disarmingly earnest faith wavered only once, a time that Tolkien later remembered with much self-directed bitterness, accusing himself of "wickedness and sloth."[13]

Even when in front of largely agnostic or atheistic academic audiences, Tolkien would openly admit that he rarely held "strong views" about his major subject of scholarship, philology, as he deemed it "[un]necessary to salvation."[14] To his literary friends, Tolkien often expressed his fondness for scripture.[15] He was committed, however, to seeking truth, unhindered by fundamentalist zealotry. When an overly eager Roman Catholic sought to discover a Catholic heritage to a particular place in England, Tolkien objected to the man's method. "With reference to the letter of 'H. D.' on the subject of COVENTRY I am at a loss to know how the etymology of any place-name can be pursued 'in keeping with Catholic tradition,' except by seeking the truth without bias, whether one ends up in a convent or not."[16]

Tolkien believed that God had given him the mythology of Middle-earth along with the task of recording it.[17] In addition, he saw his legendarium as a monument to his friends who had died in the Great War: his mythology, he hoped, would help restore knowledge of the old truths in the ravaged postwar world. One of his three closest friends, G. B. Smith, wrote to Tolkien from the trenches in 1916:

> Death can make us loathsome and helpless as individuals, but it cannot put an end to the immortal four! . . . Yes, publish. . . . You I am sure are chosen, like Saul among the Children of Israel. Make haste, before you come out to this orgy of death and cruelty. . . . May God

bless you, my dear John Ronald, and may you say the things I have tried to say long after I am not there to say them, if such be my lot.[18]

A German shell would end Smith's life shortly thereafter.

Even more keenly than the burdens of fulfilling God's purpose for him and honoring his fallen friends, Tolkien felt the difficulty of creating an internally consistent and believable secondary world that was still theologically in line with orthodox Christianity.[19] The success of *The Lord of the Rings* only increased his determination to mesh the mythological world of Middle-earth with Christian theology. As Christopher Tolkien has noted, his father spent the year prior to his death wrestling with the theological implications of Elvish immortality.[20] Tolkien feared, rightly, that many readers would interpret the moral and spiritual elements of his mythology as pagan or, worse, as the heralds of a new religion.

As quick as Tolkien was to claim that God created the myth and he was merely the recorder of it, he was equally quick to note that God's grace had touched him directly through the premature death of his mother, a convert to Roman Catholicism. "I have consciously planned very little; and should chiefly be grateful for having been brought up (since I was eight) in a Faith that has nourished me and taught me all the little that I know," Tolkien wrote to his friend, Father Robert Murray. That faith "I owe to my mother, who clung to her conversion and died young, largely through the hardships of poverty resulting from it."[21] Lewis claimed that Tolkien's mother, Mabel, was probably the single most influential person in Tolkien's life.[22] "He was taught by his mother," Lewis wrote, "from whom he derived all his bents and early knowledge, linguistic, romantic, and naturalist."[23]

Throughout his life, Tolkien considered his mother a martyr for Roman Catholicism.[24] As a convert to the faith, she suffered intense anti-Catholic bigotry from her immediate and extended family. After her conversion in 1900, they cut off their financial support to her and the two Tolkien boys, J. R. R. and his brother Hilary, which only com-

pounded the financial burden the family had felt since the death of
Tolkien's father four years earlier. His mother's death profoundly shaped
Tolkien's rather negative view of Protestants, as well as his own sense
of obligation to raise his children in the Catholic faith. "When I think
of my mother's death," Tolkien wrote to his son Michael, "worn out
with persecution, poverty, and, largely consequent, disease, in the effort
to hand on to us small boys the Faith . . . I find it very hard and bitter,
when my children stray away" from Catholicism.[25] (No details exist on
the possibly errant religious ways of Tolkien's children.)

The other great Catholic influence in Tolkien's life was Father Francis Morgan, who became Tolkien's legal guardian when his mother
died in 1904. A man of Welsh and Spanish ancestry, Morgan had studied under John Henry Cardinal Newman and was a member of his
Oratory in Birmingham.[26] Tolkien and Hilary lived as "junior inmates"
at the strict Oratory House, which was still filled primarily with those
who had converted to Roman Catholicism under Newman's influence.[27]
Tolkien credited Father Morgan with much in his own intellectual and
moral development. If his mother had instilled in him his faith, Father
Morgan had taught him the nature and essence of that faith. The reign-
ing progressive, anti-Catholic environment of early-twentieth-century
England only added to Morgan's burden.[28] "I first learned charity and
forgiveness from him; and in the light of it pierced even the 'liberal'
darkness out of which I came, knowing more about 'Bloody Mary'
than the Mother of Jesus."[29] Tolkien considered Father Morgan equal
in importance to his biological father.[30]

Father Morgan imbued Tolkien with a doctrinally traditional
Roman Catholicism. Like all Catholics, Tolkien believed that the
Church stood upon scripture, tradition, and the teaching authority of
the Magisterium. The Protestant fascination with the early, primitive
Christian church, Tolkien wrote, simply resulted in a morbid fascina-
tion with ignorance; the Church had needed time to grow.[31] To trap the
Church in one era, as Tolkien believed the Protestants had attempted
to do, meant the retardation of the Church's doctrinal development.
In essence, by denying tradition, Protestants paradoxically forced the
Church into a state of stasis or regress.

Thanks to his mother's and Father Morgan's example, Tolkien strove to perform the good works necessary for sanctification within the Roman Catholic tradition. He taught his son Christopher, for example, to memorize a variety of prayers as well as the entirety of the mass in Latin. "If you have these by heart you never need for words of joy," he commented.[32] Tolkien kept a rosary by his bed, even during the nights he spent on watch for Nazi bombings of Oxford during World War II.[33] In addition to his strong devotion to Mary, Tolkien frequently prayed to various saints for their intercession.[34]

Not surprisingly, given his strongly traditional views, Tolkien failed to understand the necessity of the Second Vatican Council of the mid-1960s, especially its acceptance of the use of the vernacular in the mass.[35] After a summer spent with Tolkien, Kilby described Tolkien's anxiety over changes imposed by the council:

> The Church, [Tolkien] said, "which once felt like a refuge now feels like a trap." He was appalled that even the sacred Eucharist might be attended by "dirty youths, women in trousers and often with their hair unkempt and uncovered" and, what was worse, the grievous suffering given by "stupid, tired, dimmed, and even bad priests." An anecdote I have heard involved his attendance at mass not long after Vatican II. An expert in Latin, he had reluctantly composed himself to its abolishment in favor of English. But when he arrived next time at services and seated himself in the middle of a bench, he began to notice other changes than the language, one a diminution of genuflection. His disappointment was such that he rose up and made his way awkwardly to the aisle and there made three very low bows, then stomped out of the church.[36]

Despite his disappointment with what he viewed as the liberalization of the Church, Tolkien remained a loyal and practicing Catholic.

For better or worse, one can learn as much about Tolkien's Christianity from his deprecatory remarks regarding Protestantism as from his appreciative statements regarding Catholicism. Indeed, Tolkien's own dislike of Protestantism surfaced frequently. The true foundation of the Anglican church, Tolkien once wrote to his son Christopher, was nothing but a deep hatred of Roman Catholicism, coupled with sheer "cockiness."[37] He thought Anglicanism "a pathetic and shadowy medley of half-remembered traditions and mutilated beliefs."[38] For Tolkien, the entire Reformation had been nothing but a blasphemous farce. He labeled the Reformation the "W[estern] European revolt," in reality little more than an evil attack on the sanctity of the Blessed Sacrament, with "faith/works a mere red herring."[39]

The anger Tolkien felt toward the Church of England and other manifestations of Protestantism most obviously revealed itself in his occasionally testy relationship with C. S. Lewis after 1939. Lewis's everyman "Mere Christianity" theology was a source of annoyance to Tolkien. Worse was Lewis's apparent indifference to the persecution of Catholics. When Roman Catholic poet Roy Campbell visited the Inklings in the autumn of 1944 and discussed the communist atrocities against the Church in Spain, Tolkien noticed that the martyrdom of Roman Catholic priests seemed not to affect Lewis. "I daresay [he] really thinks they asked for it," Tolkien commented. Lewis was ready to go to war over a jailed Protestant, wrote Tolkien, but he all too readily dismissed the murder of Catholics perpetrated by similarly corrupt regimes.[40]

Lewis's anti-Catholic tendencies have been confirmed by others. He and his brother Warnie often referred to Catholics as "Bog-trotters" or "Bog-rats," a term of extreme abuse.[41] Warnie once recorded that Lewis "considers himself a broad-minded man on the ground that he once talked civilly with a Roman priest and also listened without interrupting to a Socialist."[42] John Lawlor, a student of Lewis's, remembers Lewis arguing that a particular Roman Catholic priest "knew as much about theology as a pig." Lawlor waited for the punch-line, smile, or laugh, but the deadly serious Lewis offered none.[43]

Though he became increasingly Roman Catholic in practice if not in his intellectual sympathies, Lewis understood his own prejudices well. As a young boy, he resented any semblance of high-church liturgy "infecting" what he considered the true Protestant faith. Warnie dismissed much of Lewis's anti-Catholicism as simple Ulster nationalism.

> We went to church regularly in our youth, but even then one sensed the fact that church going was not so much a religious as a political right, the weekly assertion of the fact that you were not a Roman Catholic Nationalist. Our butcher and our grocer attended one suspected primarily to draw customers' attention to the fact that at their shops could be bought decent Protestant food untainted by the damnable heresies of Rome.[44]

In his justly famous memoirs, *Surprised by Joy*, Lewis admitted, probably only half in jest: "At my first coming into the world I had been (implicitly) warned never to trust a Papist, and at my first coming to the English Faculty (explicitly) never to trust a philologist. Tolkien was both."[45] Nevertheless, in addition to his strong friendship with Tolkien, Lewis correspondended and formed friendships with numerous Roman Catholics throughout his life. Beginning in 1940, he attended Anglo-Catholic confession on a weekly basis.[46] And in a moving letter written in the 1940s or 1950s, Lewis asked a Jesuit priest to pray that God would give him "the light and grace to make the final gesture" and for his prayers "that the prejudices instilled in me by an Ulster nurse might be overcome."[47]

Tolkien knew little, if any, of Lewis's internal struggles regarding a possible move to the Roman Catholic Church, and his most scathing attack on Lewis, "The Ulsterior Motive," remains unpublished and unavailable to the general or academic public. Tolkien wrote it within a year of Lewis's death in 1963. He nominally wrote it as a response to Lewis's posthumous *Letters to Malcolm*, a work Tolkien considered "distressing and in parts horrifying."[48] Only a few people have read the entire manuscript, and from the few available glimpses of it, "The Ulsterior Motive" seems to digress into a serious analysis of Tolkien and Lewis's friendship. In it, for example, Tolkien remembers a conversation with Lewis in which Tolkien noted that St. John served as his patron saint. "Lewis stiffened," Tolkien wrote.

[H]is head went back, and he said in the brusque harsh tones which
I was later to hear him use again when dismissing something he
disapproved of: 'I can't imagine any two persons more dissimilar.'
We stumped along the cloisters, and I followed feeling like a shabby little Catholic caught by the eye of an 'Evangelical clergyman of
good family' taking holy water at the door of a church.[49]

Lewis's personality was such that he most likely forgot this comment
a moment after making it.[50] Like his character Treebeard, though,
Tolkien forgot very little, and Lewis's dig remained strong in his
memory for several decades. Tolkien further argues in "The Ulsterior
Motive" that Lewis was "keen-witted rather than clear-sighted."[51] In
the margins of his own copy of *Letters to Malcolm*, Tolkien wrote
that far more than being about prayer, the book was really about
how Lewis prayed. It was according to Tolkien autobiographical,
which he thought was the case with all of Lewis's works.[52] On the
whole, "The Ulsterior Motive" provides strong evidence that Tolkien, one of the two men most instrumental in Lewis's conversion to
Christianity, resented that Lewis never became Roman Catholic but
instead re-awoke to "the prejudices so sedulously planted in childhood and boyhood."[53]

Tolkien's serious theological differences with Lewis seem to have
begun when Charles Williams became an Inkling in 1939.[54] "[W]e saw
less and less of one another after [Lewis] came under the dominant
influence of Charles Williams," Tolkien wrote nearly a year after
Lewis's death.[55] From the moment he arrived in London, Williams and
Lewis became fast friends.[56] As John Patrick has argued, Williams provided Lewis with a companion whose intellect was equal to Tolkien's,
but who did not carry the embarrassing baggage of Tolkien's Roman
Catholicism.[57]

Many authors and friends have attributed the strain between
Lewis and Tolkien's friendship that became more evident at this time
to the jealousy Williams's intrusion inspired in Tolkien.[58] But while
Tolkien does seem to have been very sensitive—in the best and worst
senses of that word—the breach with Lewis runs more deeply than

that. For though Tolkien enjoyed Williams as an acquaintance, he deeply distrusted his theological views. Whereas Lewis described Williams as an "angel," Tolkien labeled him a "witch doctor" and an "apparition."[59] When Lewis became fascinated with Williams, who, as a young man, had been a self-professed gnostic, it must have frightened Tolkien profoundly.[60] Tolkien believed strongly in the devil, fearing his powerful ability to tempt and further corrupt fallen man, and he therefore especially feared knowledge of or flirtation with any form of evil, something Williams seemed to do constantly, possibly influencing Lewis to do the same. As Elrond says, explaining why Saruman had turned to evil, "It is perilous to study too deeply the arts of the enemy."[61]

In contrast, or so he thought, to Lewis's *Screwtape Letters* and most of Williams's fiction, Tolkien was careful to make his own mythology as Christian as possible. He specifically wanted to affirm his own devoutly Catholic worldview, especially its emphasis on the salvific efficacy of free will in response to God's grace.

In the beginning of Tolkien's mythology, Ilúvatar, also known as Eru, the All-God or All-Father, created the Ainur, the archangels. He gave to each of them a piece of his wisdom and knowledge, and together they sang the universe into existence. Ilúvatar declared a theme and commanded: "I will now that ye make in harmony together a Great Music. And since I have kindled you with the Flame Imperishable [the mythological equivalent of the Holy Spirit], ye shall show forth your powers in adorning this theme, each with his own thoughts and devices, if he will."[62] This creating song was to be the greatest of all music until the "end of days" when God would create an even greater theme.[63]

Soon, though, discord arose, as Melkor, the greatest of the Ainur, desired to make his own theme, to create as though equal to Ilúvatar. Rather than subcreate to glorify God, Melkor wanted to become God and praise himself. His discord ended the beauty and harmony of the first theme. Undaunted and patient, Ilúvatar finished the first theme and began a second. Melkor (or Morgoth, as the Elves would later name him) again corrupted it with his own theme, and, this time with some sternness, Ilúvatar silenced it and began a third theme. Melkor countered this divine theme with noise so grating and violent it drowned out the other Ainur. With great anger, Ilúvatar reprimanded and embarrassed Melkor, who in his pride would never forgive his creator. Ilúvatar then presented to the Ainur the world that their music had created, the world of Middle-earth, known as Arda. Within the third theme, Ilúvatar had secretly and uniquely created his children, the Elves and the Men; the music of the Ainur "had no part" in their making.[64]

Full of spite against Ilúvatar and the Ainur, Melkor desired to rule the beings created in the third theme and so descended to Arda. Under the regency of the greatest angelic voice of the second theme, Manwë, numerous Ainur also went to Arda, hoping to rule not as gods but to live as Ilúvatar's servants and serve as his regents. Once in Arda, others referred to them as "The Valar," and they warred with Melkor until the end of the First Age, when they finally captured and chained him. The holy war, though, disrupted life on Arda severely.

Whether in legend, when angels and devils visibly walked the earth, or in history, when the angels and devils no longer assumed a visible form, "the whole of Middle-earth was 'Morgoth's Ring,'" as we will see in chapter 5.[65] His lies "sowed in the hearts of Elves and Men are a seed that does not die and cannot be destroyed; and ever and anon it sprouts anew, and will bear dark fruit even until the latest days."[66] Only when Ilúvatar issues the final theme will Morgoth and his influences finally be utterly destroyed. In the few accounts of the "Last Battle" that appear in the *History of Middle-earth*—a very Tolkienesque mixing of the Old Norse legends of Ragnagrök and the Christian "Apocalypse of St. John"—the Valar under the stewardship of Manwë defeat Morgoth once and for all. Arda becomes unbroken, and the recovered Silmarils are used to resurrect the Two Trees.[67]

Throughout the mythology, Ilúvatar remains indisputably sovereign, but he distributes his gifts and the responsibility to govern his creation through a complex system of subsidiarity. Throughout *The Silmarillion* as well as the *History of Middle-earth*, the reader comes to understand that while the stories focus on various falls from grace, grace also is given to right wrongs, although this is accomplished through the angels rather than by Ilúvatar directly. As Tolkien explained, Ilúvatar commanded the Valar to act only as governors, to aid in the war against Morgoth, but never to appear as gods themselves or to demand that lesser beings worship them. Though Manwë held the title of king in Arda, Manwë's king was Ilúvatar.[68]

Equally important, Ilúvatar reshapes the corruptions of evil to make his plan not only ultimately work out, but also to create something entirely better than the original. At each of the vital moments of the legendarium—the creation, the end of the First Age, the end of the Second Age, the end of the Third Age, and the Last Battle—Ilúvatar intrudes directly. When Melkor sang his own tune during creation, Ilúvatar incorporated it into the larger design and began anew. When Morgoth became too powerful in Middle-earth, Ilúvatar ended his reign, as he will do again at the Last Battle, an event foreshadowed by Ilúvatar's destruction of Númenor.[69] When the Sauron-allied Númenoreans attempted to invade the Blessed Realm at the end of the Second Age and become gods themselves, Ilúvatar destroyed their island and made Arda round, preventing further contact with the Blessed Realm. As Tolkien once told Lewis, "the Earth might owe its importance in the eyes of God solely to the principle of the one lost sheep as against the ninety nine."[70] In other words, no matter how foul the vast majority of humanity might become, God still protects his faithful.

Though Tolkien beautifully described the fall of Satan, that is, Morgoth, or Melkor, he found it far more difficult to describe the fall of man. Clybe Kilby recorded:

> Tolkien described to me his problem in depicting the fall of mankind near the beginning of THE SILMARILLION. 'How far we have fallen!' he exclaimed—so far, he felt, that it is impossible even to think in the right pattern about it or how to imagine the contrast between Eden and the world which followed.[71]

Tolkien wrote a "Job-like conversation," as Kilby described it, in which he explained the reason for evil and the fall. Entitled "Athrabeth Finrod Ah Andreth," Tolkien's conversation considers the relation of Elves and Men in Ilúvatar's created order and the role of Ilúvatar in remaking the marred and fallen earth. It is possibly Tolkien's most theological and profound writing in the entire legendarium, and it is essential to one's understanding of Tolkien's mythological vision. In *Morgoth's Ring*, editor Christopher Tolkien labeled the previously unpublished essay a "major and finished work." Tolkien had originally wanted it to appear as an appendix to any completed form of *The Silmarillion*.[72]

"Athrabeth Finrod Ah Andreth" is a dense and complex discussion between the Elven king Finrod and the human wise-woman Andreth. Finrod desires to know why men are fallen and have short-lived lives, while Elves remain unfallen and nearly immortal. Why is it, Finrod asks, that while men and Elves are almost identical biologically, they have different natures. Andreth incorrectly believes that Melkor marred the real nature of men, shortening their lives. Finrod disagrees, noting that while Melkor may influence and corrupt individuals, he could never corrupt an entire race. Only Ilúvatar would have the power to do such a thing, and he would never do it. Finrod fears even to consider Melkor as wielding such immense power. "The Lord of this World is not [Melkor], but the One who made him, and his Vice[reg]ent is Manwë, the Elder King of Arda who is blessed," Finrod notes.[73] Andreth admits that many men believe they are *"born to life everlasting,"* but she misinterprets it to mean the life of the body.

Finrod notes the tension within men regarding the conflict of the body and the soul; men are both flesh and spirit, but they often remember one at the exclusion of the other. This conflict, he argues in Platonic fashion, results in men looking "at nothing for itself. . . . [I]f they study it, it is to discover something else."[74] This unrest existed in men prior to Melkor's corruption, thinks Finrod. Ilúvatar gave it to them so that they would desire a return to their true home, heaven. The restlessness prevented men from becoming too attached to the earth. Wickedly, Melkor precipitated the restlessness, lying that death was a punishment, not a gift. Men believed Melkor, and they grew to resent Ilúvatar.

Still, as Finrod notes, Ilúvatar will not suffer the victory of Melkor. Rather than undoing the past, he will use the errors of Melkor and the men who aligned themselves with him to make something better. In a letter to Christopher, Tolkien explained: "evil labours with vast power and perpetual success—in vain: preparing always only the soil for unexpected good to sprout in."[75] As its creator-author, Ilúvatar will remake the world into a "third thing and a greater, and yet the same."[76] Finrod concludes that

> a master in the telling of tales [may] keep hidden the greatest moment until it comes in due course. It may be guessed at indeed, in some measure, by those of us who have listened with full heart and mind; but so the teller would wish. In no wise is the surprise and wonder of his art thus diminished, for thus we share, as it were, in his authorship.[77]

While Finrod does not know what Ilúvatar has in store for the remaking of the earth and the undoing of Melkor's wickedness, he knows that he must trust Ilúvatar completely. Trust, indeed, becomes the essence of the relationship between the children of Ilúvatar and their creator. From such trust, all blessings flow.

Andreth offers a radical possibility that she refuses to believe but has heard other men say: "The One will himself enter into Arda." She argues that this seems impossible. As creator, he is simply too great to enter his own creation. "Would it not shatter Arda?" she worries.[78] Putting forth a mythological version of what a Christian would consider incarnational theology, Finrod speculates that "even if He in Himself were to enter in, He must still remain also as He is: the Author without."[79] In other words, in Tolkien's tale the very wise understand that Ilúvatar can remain Ilúvatar while simultaneously entering into time and space, his own creation.

While Tolkien feared many readers would see this chapter as a "parody of Christianity," his son thought otherwise. "[T]his surely

is not parody, nor even parallel," Christopher wrote, "but the exten-
sion—if only represented as vision, hope or prophecy—of the 'theology' of Arda into specifically, and of course centrally, Christian
belief." One should regard this as *the* central explanatory text of the
theology of Tolkien's mythological world. As Kilby wrote approvingly
after first seeing the text in 1966, in this passage Tolkien explains that
God allowed "the fall so that he could manifest His own sovereignty
over Satan all the more, of Christ's incarnation, the spread of His light
from one person to another, and the final consummation at Christ's
return."[80]

It is at the end of the Third Age that Tolkien's readers see most
clearly the role of grace in salvation. As Tolkien told Father Murray,
the entire story of *The Lord of the Rings* reflects God's grace, but
while God is always present, he is never named. For example, when
Frodo asks Gandalf how the Ring came into his possession, Gandalf
answers: "Behind that there was something else at work, beyond any
design of the Ring-maker. I can put it no plainer than by saying that
Bilbo was meant to find the Ring, and not by its maker. In which
case you also were meant to have it. And that may be an encouraging thought."[81] In *Unfinished Tales*, Gandalf declares that what one
calls chance is really one's will accepting Ilúvatar's direction.[82] When
Elrond calls the council to order, deciding what to do with the Ring,
he says: "Called, I say, though I have not called you to me, strangers
from distant lands. You have come and are here met, in this very nick
of time, by chance as it may seem. Yet it is not so. Believe rather that
it is so ordered that we, who sit here, and none others, must now find
counsel for the peril of the world."[83] But beyond these hints, God
remains off stage in *The Lord of the Rings*. He is, rather, contained
within the very fiber of the story.[84]

  While there are many manifestations of grace in *The Lord of
the Rings*, the most important and the most telling example revolves
around the relationship between Gollum and Frodo. At the beginning
of the first part of the *Lord of the Rings*, Frodo and Gandalf debate

the merits of killing the corrupted hobbit, Gollum. Frodo states without hesitation, "He deserves death." Gandalf, one of the wise, replies, "Deserves it! I daresay he does. Many that live deserve death. And some that die deserve life. Can you give it to them? Then do not be too eager to deal out death in judgement. For even the very wise cannot see all ends."[85]

As Frodo, the suffering servant, carries his burden, the evil Ring, to its destruction in Mount Doom in Mordor, he slowly learns how it had corrupted and reshaped Gollum. He feels pity and mercy for the poor creature. He also realizes how blessed Bilbo was to be rid of the Ring and survive unscathed, never becoming a Gollum. Amazingly, rather than making him evil or bitter, or filling him with lies, the Ring is finally unable to corrupt Frodo, and he even learns mercy in spite of its painful presence.

In fact, Frodo's acts of mercy and pity almost redeem the seemingly irredeemable Gollum. In a passage that Tolkien believed to be one of the most moving in *The Lord of the Rings*, Gollum nearly repents of his past crimes.

> Gollum looked at them. A strange expression passed over his lean hungry face. The gleam faded from his eyes, and they went dim and grey, old and tired. A spasm of pain seemed to twist him, and he turned away, peering back up towards the pass, shaking his head, as if engaged in some interior debate. Then he came back, and slowly putting out a trembling hand, very cautiously he touched Frodo's knee—but almost the touch was a caress. For a fleeting moment could one of the sleepers have seen him, they would have thought that they beheld an old weary hobbit, shrunken by the years that had carried him far beyond his time, beyond friends and kin, and the fields and streams of youth, an old starved pitiable thing.[86]

But at this point Sam awakens. Distrusting the motives of Gollum, he harshly reprimands him, and Gollum slinks back into his abyss, ready now, finally, to betray the two hobbits to Shelob.[87]

It is precisely because Frodo learns to understand the wisdom of mercy that the Ring is destroyed in the end. As Frodo fails on top of Mount Doom, overcome with the desire to wield the Ring and declare himself Lord of Middle-earth, grace intrudes in the form of the corrupted hobbit Gollum. The foul creature bites off the finger of Frodo, gleefully dances along the precipice, and falls to his death, destroying the Ring once and for all.

Though Frodo failed in the end, overcome as he was by desire and greed, he succeeded at a much greater task: living out the advice of Gandalf and performing Christ-like acts of mercy to Gollum.[88] Had he not done that, his failure would have been infinitely greater, as no Gollum would have been on Mount Doom to finish the task of destroying the Ring. Instead, Frodo might have declared himself Lord of Middle-earth, succumbing to the temptation first presented in the Garden of Eden—"ye too shall be as gods." Sauron would have then overpowered Frodo, who would have been too small to wield the Ring effectively. Ilúvatar thus demonstrates his sovereignty and his love through the unlikely character of Gollum. One should not, as Gandalf warns, violate God's laws, no matter how little sense those laws, at times, make to us, but should instead trust in his plan.

For Tolkien, Frodo's greatest failure came after he claimed the Ring as his own. Losing hope on the Stairs of Cirith Ungol, Frodo despaired, "All is lost. I tarried on the way. All is lost. Even if my errand is performed, no one will ever know. There will be no one I can tell. It will be in vain."[89] After the Ring is destroyed, Frodo is stunned that he remains alive. To be a true hero, he thought, he would have had to have sacrificed himself, thus seeking his own glory. He failed to realize that God's task for him was over; he was to live. The "Divine economy [is] limited to what is sufficient for the accomplishment of the task appointed to one instrument in a pattern of circumstances and other instruments," wrote Tolkien.[90] To claim more, would be to claim the sole right of Jesus Christ, as the savior of mankind. "In its highest exercise," Tolkien explained, mercy "belongs to God."[91] Certainly not to men—or hobbits.

While no single character or place within *The Lord of the Rings* directly parallels the places, events, and people of the Christian story—to do so would have made the myth a formal allegory—the myth is, as Tolkien explained "consonant with Christian thought and belief."[92] Throughout the story, one finds strong Christian symbolism, especially symbolism of a Catholic flavor having to do with prayer, the Eucharist, and the Virgin Mary. The legendarium should "be accepted—well, shall we say baldly," Tolkien concluded, "by a mind that believes in the Blessed Trinity."[93]

One of the most important Christian symbols in the mythology comes in the form of invocations, petitions, and prayers to higher powers. In one telling scene, the Gondorian brother of Boromir, Faramir, "turned and faced West in a moment of silence" prior to dinner. Frodo questions him about this, and Faramir lamely answers that it is the custom to recognize the lost home of Númenor and the lands beyond.[94] Faramir goes through the motions but misunderstands the essence of his actions. His is a piety without substance.

In the same way, Frodo and Sam almost unwillingly, or at the very least unconsciously, invoke the name of Elbereth numerous times. Frodo invokes her when the Ringwraiths attack at Weathertop as well as when they pursue him to the ford outside of Rivendell.[95] While Aragorn commends Frodo for stabbing his blade into the Ringwraith, he states, "More deadly to him was the name of Elbereth."[96] As Sam thrusts Sting into Shelob, full of anger and spite, he too calls on Elbereth, just as a Roman Catholic or Eastern Orthodox believer would invoke the name of a saint.[97] "O Elbereth Gilthoniel, gazing afar to thee I cry, here beneath death-horror. Look towards me."[98] The prayer gives him the strength necessary to defeat the evil creature, the spawn of Ungoliant.[99]

Tolkien, however, noted that neither Frodo nor Sam deliberately called for the intercession of higher powers. Frodo finds himself calling on Elbereth unconsciously. Sam finds himself speaking in a language unknown to him. Thus, grace moved Frodo and Sam to call on grace; the servants of Ilúvatar aided other servants of Ilúvatar. As Tolkien stressed, only Ilúvatar is sovereign,[100] but in the pre-incarnational time in which Tolkien's tale takes place one could reach Ilúvatar only by speaking to and through the Valar, Ilúvatar's delegates in Arda.[101] "The Fall of Man is in the past and off stage; the Redemption of Man in the far future," Tolkien wrote. "We are in a time when the One God, Eru, is known to exist by the wise, but is not approachable save by or through the Valar."[102] Tolkien also argued that since the events of *The Lord of the Rings* occur in a pre-Christian world, a natural monotheistic theology exists. "All this is 'mythical', and not any kind of new religion or vision," he cautioned.[103]

That myth, however, is deeply rooted in Christian theology. In one of the most dramatic moments of *The Fellowship of the Ring*, Gandalf faces an ancient enemy, a Balrog. As he confronts the incarnate demon, Gandalf names his source of power. "You cannot pass," he cries. "I am a servant of the Secret Fire, wielder of the flame of Anor. You cannot pass."[104] Indeed, the Balrog cannot pass, and Gandalf falls to his death, sacrificing himself and becoming entangled with and destroying his evil counterpart. As Tolkien admitted to Clyde Kilby, the "Secret Fire," Gandalf's master, is the Holy Spirit.[105]

When the potential producer of a movie version of *The Lord of the Rings* showed Tolkien the script, Tolkien was aghast. In addition to too many oversimplifications and wrongheaded ideas that ran contrary to the spirit of the tale, Tolkien discovered that the scriptwriter had changed the "lembas," the food given by Galadriel to the Fellowship to sustain the members for their journey, to a "food concentrate." No chemical analysis, Tolkien wrote, could uncover the *lembas'* properties. Instead, it "has a much larger significance, of what one might hesitatingly call a 'religious' kind."[106] Properly translated, *lembas* means "way-bread" or "life-bread."[107] Thus, as Frodo struggles up Mount Doom to destroy the Ring, the *lembas* sustains him.

> The *lembas* has a virtue without which they would long ago have lain down to die. It did not satisfy desire, and at times Sam's mind was

filled with the memories of food, and the longing for simple bread and meats. And yet this waybread of the Elves had a potency that increased as travellers relied on it alone and did not mingle it with other foods. It fed the will, and it gave strength to endure, and to master sinew and limb beyond the measure of mortal kind.[108]

The *lembas* plays a vital role throughout the entirety of *The Lord of the Rings*. Not only does it sustain Frodo and Sam as they complete their mission, but it also protects and feeds the wills of Merry and Pippin as captives of the Orcs, and of Aragorn, Legolas, and Gimli as they search for the demonic enemies who have captured the two hobbits.[109] Conversely, evil refuses to partake of it, and when some Orcs find the *lembas* on Frodo's person, they attempt to destroy it.[110]

Lembas also appears several times in *The Silmarillion* and the *History of Middle-earth*. The first man to receive it, Túrin Turambar, received it from a Maia, Melian, mother of Lúthien. In no way, Tolkien wrote, could Melian have paid Túrin a greater honor. It served Túrin and his company well, as it quickly healed all wounds and illnesses during their mission. Rarely, though, did the Elves share it with men.[111] The men of Númenor also made a form of *lembas*, but it never equaled the quality or enchantment of the Elven *lembas*. Tellingly, Isildur carried the man-made substitute en route to his death on the Gladden Fields.[112]

As Charles Columbe has written, the stories surrounding the *lembas* reflect numerous medieval legends regarding the Blessed Sacrament.[113] Indeed, the Elven *lembas* arguably serves as Tolkien's most explicit symbol of Christianity in *The Lord of the Rings*; it is a representation, though pre-Christian, of the Eucharist. For Tolkien, nothing represented a greater gift from God than the actual Body and Blood of Christ. "I put before you the one great thing to love on earth: the Blessed Sacrament," Tolkien wrote to his son Michael. "There you will find romance, glory, honour, fidelity, and the true way of all your loves upon earth."[114] Like all devout pre–Vatican II Catholics, Tolkien always attended confession before receiving the

Sacrament.[115] Indeed, the sacraments for Tolkien served as the best and perhaps only effective means of preventing Satan from taking over the world. Tolkien encouraged his children to receive it daily, as it "must be continuous and grow by exercise."[116] Even the screaming children of others failed to distract or taint Tolkien's reception of the Blessed Sacrament.[117] The Sacrament wielded so much power that only the most corrupt soul would lose faith after taking it, he believed. To deny this was to "call Our Lord a fraud to His face."[118]

Tolkien once experienced a holy vision while praying before the Blessed Sacrament. "I perceived or thought of the Light of God and in it suspended one small mote (or millions of motes to only one of which was my small mind directed), glittering white because of the individual ray from the Light which both held." Tolkien also witnessed his guardian angel in the vision, not as a go-between but as the personalization of "God's very attention."[119]

Second only in importance to the Blessed Sacrament for Tolkien was the Theotokos, Mary the mother of God. As Tolkien noted, Mary provided him with a model of "beauty in majesty and simplicity."[120] Tolkien did not believe he was alone in such a belief. God presented the world with Mary as worthy of devotion to "refin[e] so much our gross manly natures and emotions, and also of warming and colouring our hard, bitter, religion."[121] The very idea that she served as a human tabernacle for the Second Covenant, the Christ, meant that she must be impeccably and awesomely beautiful, Tolkien argued.[122] Anything, therefore, of beauty that Tolkien created, he claimed, came from his own limited notions of Mary.[123] Mary, as the only "unfallen human," also demonstrates what death was to have been like prior to the fall of Adam and Eve. The "'assumption' was the natural end of each human life, though as far as we know it has been the end of the only 'unfallen' member of Mankind."[124]

Losing his own mother may have acted to increase Tolkien's devotion to Mary. He spoke of Mary often, and even debated the doctrine of the Immaculate Conception with Warnie Lewis on occasion.[125] Several Marian figures appear in Tolkien's legendarium. None are actual representations of Mary, but they share many common traits with her. The most obvious Marian figure is Galadriel. The Elven queen of Lorien, a timeless realm she created and sustained with the ring Nenya, Galadriel spent much of the Second and Third Ages resisting the power of Sauron. She also created the White Council, which was dedicated to overthrowing the darkness.[126] Even though she must repent for her crimes against the Valar in the First Age, Tolkien wrote, "it is true that I owe much of this character to Christian and Catholic teaching and imagination about Mary."[127] In a letter to Kilby, Tolkien all but affirmed that Galadriel must serve as the most important Marian figure, as "[t]here is something missing from any form of 'Christian thought' that could make such an omission. A failure (I think) to accept full *all* the consequences of the Incarnation-story as it is told to us in scripture."[128]

Elbereth serves as another Marian figure in the legendarium. The angelic wife of Manwë and maker of light and stars, she serves, like Mary in Roman Catholic theology, as the "Queen of Heaven." As noted earlier, the Elves invoke her in prayer and revere her more than any other of the Valar. In turn, she listens to their prayers.[129] She also answers the prayers of hobbits, including Sam's pleas for aid during battle with Shelob. Together with Manwë, it is Elbereth who sends Gandalf to aid in Middle-earth against Sauron.[130] Prior to the Last Battle, the final triumph of Ilúvatar over Morgoth and evil, Elbereth forms the constellation of Menelmacar as a sign of the battle's approach.[131] In short, her features are reminiscent of the description of Mary given in chapter 12 of the "Apocalypse of St. John": "A great and wondrous sign appeared in heaven: a woman clothed with the sun, with the moon under her feet and crown of twelves stars on her head."[132]

In 1969, a young girl asked Tolkien to explain "the purpose of life." Naturally, Tolkien provided a theological answer. First, we should study the created order, the universe. While the universe is not God, we honor the creator by studying his creation. Second, and more important, we find the real and final answer in the *Gloria in Excelsis*: "We praise you, we call you holy, we worship you, we proclaim your glory, we thank you for the greatness of your splendour."[133]

As a true subcreator, Tolkien desired to glorify God's work. Not only did he see *The Lord of the Rings* as his way of glorifying and praising God, but he also hoped it would help redeem the world.[134] Indeed, Tolkien viewed its potential influence with great hope. "I feel as if an ever darkening sky over our present world had been suddenly pierced, the clouds rolled back, and an almost forgotten sunlight had poured down again," he wrote in 1971.[135]

Nonetheless, as did Frodo in his journey to Mount Doom, Tolkien knew he was merely an instrument for God's will, not a hero in and of himself. All good that he did, he knew, came ultimately from God's grace, unmerited on Tolkien's part. As he once told Lewis, apologizing for his unkind comments regarding Lewis's book on sixteenth-century literature, "The only just literary critic is Christ, who admires more than does any man the gifts He Himself has bestowed."[136]

Chapter 4

Heroism

As philosopher Eric Voegelin has argued, great thinkers have often provided their communities with an *anamnesis*, or the recovery of past encounters with transcendence. Aristotle, Cicero, and St. Augustine, for example, all served their contemporaries in this way.

Much as St. Augustine had, Tolkien confronted a world and culture that seemed to many on the verge of collapse. And, as with St. Augustine, Tolkien hoped that his myth would serve as an *anamnesis*, a return to right reason. Both Augustine and Tolkien viewed this world and its history as irredeemable through sheer human will or reason. In Tolkien's mythology, as he stated in writings published posthumously, all of earth has been corrupted by Morgoth.[1] In the end, though, evil will fail to corrupt the good, which to Tolkien meant those saved and sanctified through Christ. Paraphrasing and baptizing the words of Cicero, St. Augustine wrote: "For the good man is neither uplifted with the good things of time, nor broken by its ills; but the wicked man, because he is corrupted by this world's happiness, feels himself punished by its unhappiness."[2] Aragorn speaks in a similar fashion when encountering the Riders of Rohan in *The Two Towers*. When one of the riders asks Aragorn how to discern right from wrong in complicated times, Aragorn responds: "As he ever has judged," for "[g]ood and ill have not changed since yesteryear; nor are they one thing among Elves and Dwarves and another among Men. It is a man's part to discern them, as much in the Golden Wood as in his own house."[3] To discern good and evil, and to suffer the ills of this world, serves to make one better, more sanctified, and more able to serve as a fire that "causes gold to glow brightly."[4]

For neither Tolkien nor St. Augustine does this fact mean that in despair one should simply abandon this world to the enemy and his allies or isolate oneself from society. To the contrary, one of the most prevalent and important themes in all of Tolkien's work—whether academic or fictional—is the importance of heroism, not as an act of will, but as a result of grace. Through his mystery, majesty, and grace, God allows evil to happen so that the good may do good. "Evil labours with vast power and perpetual success," Tolkien wrote. Ultimately, though, evil works "in vain: preparing always only the soil for unexpected good to sprout in."[5] St. Augustine contended that the world ultimately destroyed the wicked, as they could not suffer reverses in the world they revered with too much pride.[6]

Tolkien believed that as a part of one's preparation for heaven, or one's sanctification, one should perform acts of Christian heroism. For Tolkien, that meant doing God's will and being a part of Christ's army. As the great medieval theologian Hugh of St. Victor described it:

> For the Incarnate Word is our King, who came into this world to war with the devil; and all the saints who were before His coming are soldiers as it were, going before their King, and those who have come after and will come, even to the end of the world, are soldiers following their King. And the King himself is in the midst of His army and proceeds protected and surrounded on all sides by His columns. And although in a multitude as vast as this the kind of arms different in the sacraments and the observance of the peoples preceding and following, yet all are really serving the one king and following the one banner; all are pursuing the one enemy and are being crowned by the one victory.[7]

Christ's army is "the church" traversing time and space, the continuance of Christ incarnate. James Patrick claims that Tolkien's Fellowship of the Ring is the mythological equivalent of the church, "moving across the dark landscape, enduring every privation, frightened but full of courage, fulfilling the providence of God."[8] The church's many parts, the unique gifts and the bearers of those gifts, collectively form the body of Christ.[9]

While God may not be directly visible at all times, he is always and intimately involved in the formation and guidance of his Church and his creation. As we saw in the previous chapter, Tolkien firmly believed that God intervenes directly and indirectly in the real world, as well as in Tolkien's subcreated world. *The Silmarillion*, for example, provides a mythical account of God's creation and intervention in the affairs of men. Ilúvatar works through his agents, specifically the loyal Valar and Maiar.[10] Ilúvatar, though, distributes his gifts of grace to all his servants—Valar, Maiar, Elves, men, Dwarves, and hobbits. And he distributes them in surprising ways, ways known only to him, which makes life endlessly complex and fascinating. The "great policies of world history," Tolkien wrote, "are often turned not by the Lords and the Governors, even gods, but by the seemingly unknown and weak—owing to the secret life in creation, and the part unknowable to all wisdom but One, that resides in the intrusions of the Children of God into the Drama."[11] Thus, within Morgoth's ring—that is, Arda itself—Ilúvatar depends on his army to do his will. He aids them directly at times, relying on the "Flame Imperishable," Tolkien's mythological equivalent of the Holy Spirit, to spark creativity and the moral imagination in his creation.[12] But ultimately, whether through his gifts of grace or direct intervention, all good activities come from Ilúvatar alone.

All this Tolkien thought clear enough, which is why he was frustrated by readers who failed to find God in his mythology. The "religious element is absorbed into the story and the symbolism," Tolkien explained to a Jesuit friend.[13] One may find God in the plot itself. Indeed, the elements of true Christian heroism are severally represented in the four major characters of *The Lord of the Rings*: Gandalf, the prophet; Aragorn, the king; Frodo, the priest; and Sam, the common man and servant.[14] An Australian academic, Barry Gordon, was the first critic to demonstrate the presence of the Christian offices of priest, prophet, and king in Tolkien's work. Tolkien forwarded Gordon's article, "Kingship, Priesthood and Prophecy in *The Lord of the Rings*" to Clyde Kilby. Tolkien admitted in the letter to Kilby that the Gordon thesis was true, but that such a scheme had been unconscious on Tolkien's part.[15] In his own notes expounding on the Gordon thesis, Kilby wrote: "M-e.[Middle-earth] is saved through the priestly self-sacrifice of the hobbit Frodo, thru wisdom and guidance of Gandalf and mastery of Aragorn, heir of kings. Also forces beyond these. As each agent responds to his 'calling' he grows in power and grace. Each becomes increasingly 'Christian.'"[16] In other words, Tolkien's myth echoes Christian teaching in that once one accepts one's specific calling or vocation and employs one's gifts for the good of the Body of Christ, the journey of sanctification begins.

At first glance, Frodo seems the hero in *The Lord of the Rings*. Fulfilling the role of priest, he carries the Ring—the cross of Christ, the sins of the world—into the heart of hell (Mordor). Frodo does this out of profound love for his friends and for life itself.[17] And, perhaps equally important, he understands and accepts that this is his duty alone. Ilúvatar chose him, though Frodo does not know that name.

Frodo survives the journey, but the experience of carrying the Ring, and ultimately succumbing to its temptation, transforms him profoundly. He knows the experience of mortal sin firsthand, and he repents by embracing mercy. In the "Scouring of the Shire," Tolkien shows Frodo asking his fellow hobbits not to kill, even for defensive purposes. He even allows Saruman to escape, unpunished, only to have Grima Wormtongue betray and fall on the defrocked wizard, killing him. Frodo seems to have so embraced mercy that he has become a thoroughgoing pacifist.[18]

In accepting and carrying the burden of the Ring, Frodo has poured his spiritual as well as his physical being into the task, taxing both to the breaking point. Though he served in politics briefly as the mayor of Michael Delving and wrote the history of the "War of the Ring," he remains restless and, ultimately, without his pre-quest physical constitution. Mentally, he seems to have slipped as well. In Tolkien's poem,

"The Sea Bell," Frodo appears to be slowly descending into madness. "For a year and a day there must I stay: beetles were tapping in the rotten trees, spiders were weaving, in the mould heaving puffballs loomed about my knees," says Frodo. "Never again, as in sad lane, in blind alley and in long street ragged I walk. To myself I talk; for still they speak not, men that I meet."[19] To heal, Frodo crosses the sea to Tol Eressëa with Gandalf and many of the leaders of the Third Age. Frodo's final journey, Tolkien explained, was a purgatorial one, but one of healing, not suffering.

Yet, although he appears to be the hero of *The Lord of the Rings*, Frodo lacks the depth and nuanced personality possessed by several of the other characters in the legendarium. "Frodo is not so interesting, because he has to be highminded, and has (as it were) a vocation," Tolkien explained. He "will naturally become too ennobled and rarefied by the achievement of the Quest."[20] Though Frodo develops a deep appreciation of pity and mercy, he remains throughout the story "a fixed point." Other characters around him change, such as Sam, but Frodo continues in the role of "suffering servant," heading toward Mordor to fulfill his specific purpose. And though he grows weary, he remains faithful to his task to almost the very end. Only in the last moments of his quest does he falter, as the burden of the Ring—representing the weight of sin and temptation—becomes too great for him. Even at the Cracks of Doom, he has merely played out God's role for him. Carrying the cross changes him permanently, and he fails to reenter normal existence with any real degree of success. Until he departs for the Grey Havens, he remains somewhat alienated from the hobbitic life, which now seems too quaint.[21] The purpose of his quest was for others to live normal, productive, and happy lives. When he leaves for Tol Eressëa, he departs the world he preserved for them but cannot now enjoy himself.

It is the hobbit in Frodo's shadow, Samwise, who proves to be the true hero of *The Lord of the Rings*.[22] The unsuspecting reader expects little from Sam. At the beginning of *The Fellowship of the Ring*, he appears merely the ignoramus and the fool. The reader first encounters him in a pointless and frustrating argument with Ted

Sandyman. In a Bywater bar, Sam speaks openly about rumors of Trolls and walking trees and of darknesses spreading outside the Shire and possibly even penetrating the Shire itself. Others in the bar, all provincials who have never traveled outside the boundaries of the Shire, led by the cynical Ted Sandyman, poke fun at Sam's ideas. Sam, tellingly, refuses to back down, but his evidence does seem shaky.[23] Even his first name, Samwise, does not portend great things, meaning merely "half wise."

Yet Sam has one great virtue, and it proves the virtue that sanctifies his character: loyalty. Sam's is the loyalty, for Tolkien, that characterized the common man in the trenches of World War I. "My 'Sam Gamgee,'" Tolkien wrote, "is indeed a reflexion of the English soldier, or the privates and batmen I knew in the 1914 war, and recognized as so far superior to myself."[24] During the quest, Sam's loyalty is also biblical. Indeed, Sam plays the character of St. John the Evangelist to Frodo's Jesus.[25] Like St. John, Sam remains faithful to Frodo throughout his journey. And like St. John, who stood at the foot of the cross, Sam stands with Frodo at the Cracks of Doom. Sam also recalls another famous Christian figure, Sir Gawain. In his famous commentary on the meaning of Sir Gawain's heroism, Tolkien wrote: "His motive is a humble one: the protection of Arthur, his elder kinsmen, of his king, of the head of the Round Table, from indignity and peril, and the risking instead of himself, the least of the knights (as he declares), and the one whose loss could most easily be endured. He is involved therefore in the business, as far as it was possible to make the fairy-story go, as a matter of duty and humility and self-sacrifice."[26]

Finally, Sam is reminiscent of Wiglaf in *Beowulf*. Wiglaf, of course, is also a St. John figure, never abandoning Beowulf, even when ten of his eleven companions do so. For Tolkien, Wiglaf was a truer hero than his master. Beowulf, for example, often falls because of his own pride. And Tolkien believed that the "heroic" acts of men like Beowulf were usually motivated by a desire for personal glory rather than a sense of duty, especially duty to God. That's why the subordinate, especially the immediate subordinate, proved so important a figure to Tolkien—he followed orders out of love and duty, not for personal gain. Of such common men, Tolkien wrote approvingly, "personal pride was . . . in [them] at its lowest, and love and loyalty at their highest."[27] The most profound heroism, then, stems from "obedience and love not of pride or wilfulness."[28] Like St. John, Wiglaf, and Sir Gawain, Sam demonstrates his love for and obedience to Frodo throughout the story. Their relationship is pure. Sam especially proves this when he fears that Shelob has killed Frodo. Wielding Sting, an Elven blade, and the sacramental Phial of Galadriel, Sam prays to Elbereth as he confronts the grotesque spider. "As if his indomitable spirit had set its potency in motion, the glass blazed suddenly a white torch in hand," Tolkien wrote. "It flamed like a star that leaping from the firmament sears the dark air with intolerable light."[29]

Sam is the ultimate personification, representative, and defender of the Shire. As Tolkien put it, Sam, not Frodo, is the new Bilbo.[30] Tolkien thought that "the simple 'rustic' love of Sam and Rosie (nowhere elaborated) is absolutely essential to the study of his (the chief hero's) character, and to the theme of the relation of the ordinary life (breathing, eating, working, begetting) and quests, sacrifice, causes, and the 'longing for Elves,' and sheer beauty."[31] In the end, the quest to Mount Doom is as much about Sam as it is Frodo the priest, Gandalf the prophet, or Aragorn the king. Rooted to the Shire's soil like an Anglo-Saxon warrior-farmer in the early Middle Ages, Sam understands the true necessity of the quest. After his first encounter with the Elves while still within the Shire, Sam says, "I seem to see ahead, in a kind of way. I know we are going to take a very long road, into darkness; but I know I can't turn back. It isn't to see Elves now, nor dragons, nor mountains, that I want—I don't rightly know what I want: but I have something to do before the end, and it lies ahead, not in the Shire."[32] As fellow Inkling Charles Williams explained, Sam's character lies at the root of the story, for he represents "freedom, peace, [and] ordinary life."[33] Undoubtedly, Sam would rather stay at home and garden and farm than walk into the heart of Hell itself. But God has a different task for him, and Sam accepts his duty, as all good men do. He follows Frodo with pure loyalty and without question. Still, throughout the story he keeps his mind focused on the Shire. The destruction of the Ring represents the victory of "Christ's army," allowing persons (men, Elves, or hobbits) like Sam to lead the peaceful lives they were meant to lead, and to thus freely enjoy the gifts that God gave them and intended them to use.

In an unpublished chapter of *The Lord of the Rings*, Tolkien told the story of Sam as it takes place several years into the Fourth Age. As noted above, Tolkien considered it essential to understand the nature of Sam, as well as to understand the beauty of ordinary life.[34] However, he feared that this final chapter might be too trite, and so did not include it.[35] There are two extant versions of the omitted chapter, which are similar. Each takes place just a week before the seventeenth anniversary of the destruction of the Ring. Sam, the reader happily discovers, is the mayor of the Shire. Aragorn—"Elfstone King of Gondor and Lord of the Westlands"—and his wife Arwen desire to meet with Sam and his family. As he had promised, the restored king has forbidden men from either living in or traversing the Shire. Therefore, he also may not enter the realm of hobbits, but can only meet Mayor Sam on the border, where he intends to present the unsuspecting Sam with a great honor, the "Star of the Dúnedain."[36] In the invitation, Aragorn touchingly translates Sam's name in Elvish not properly as "Half-wise," but instead as "Plain-wise" and "Full-wise," reflecting Sam's significant growth during and after the quest to destroy the Ring. As Aragorn's letter reveals, Sam has grown from the silly hobbit arguing with Ted Sandyman in the pub to a wise and virtuous statesman. His children treat him with immense love and respect, respecting his authority as father. When Sam speaks, Tolkien wrote, his children respond to him "as hobbit-children of other times had watched the wizard Gandalf."[37] Indeed, the adult Samwise carries the authority of an incarnate angel.

Tolkien reveals much about the ultimate fate of the other heroes of The War of the Ring in the epilogue. The reader discovers, for example, that Shadowfax departed with Gandalf for the West. He also learns that numerous Orcs and Elves, including Celeborn, still reside in Middle-earth and most likely will for a long time to come.

The Orcs, of course, present a problem, but Aragorn and his military forces are slowly isolating them, attenuating their power. To do so, though, Aragorn's men must dig deep into the "dark places" of Middle-earth, such as Moria. Finally, the reader learns that Gimli and the Dwarves have helped rebuild Gondor to its former glory, and the Dwarves and Elves have healed their deep wound and have developed a strong friendship.

As Tolkien explained in his letters, the final epilogue reveals life as it should be, as it was before the Dark Lord rose, as Frodo and the eight of the Fellowship would have wanted it. Clearly, Sam loves his wife and his children. In fact, God has blessed him and Rosie with many offspring, and it seems likely that more are on the way. "Regular ragtag and bobtail," Sam says of his children, "old Saruman would have called it."[38] Evil sees children merely as obstacles. Sam wisely knows they are essential for the good life. Sam also notes that while Frodo received proper acclaim for his deeds, he himself has "had lots of treasures."[39] At the end of the epilogue, Tolkien writes of a conversation between Sam and his wife Rosie. Discussing the events of seventeen years earlier, when Gollum fell with the Ring into the Cracks of Doom, ending the reign of the Dark Lord, Sam notes that he was unsure if he would ever make it back to the Shire, "[t]o the most beloved place in all the world . . . [t]o my Rose and my garden." "They went in, and Sam shut the door," Tolkien wrote. "But even as he did so, he heard suddenly, deep and unstilled, the sigh and murmur of the Sea upon the shores of Middle-earth."[40] Eternity beckons Sam. He too will one day depart from the Grey Havens to the Blessed Realm and experience, like Frodo, a purgatorial rest. But until then, Sam will enjoy his family and his garden.

Though Gandalf appears in all of Tolkien's major works—*The Silmarillion, The Hobbit, The Lord of the Rings,* and *Unfinished Tales*—his origin remained a mystery to Tolkien throughout his life.[41] Gandalf first appeared, albeit briefly, in *The Silmarillion* as Olórin. He was the wisest of the second order of angels, the Maiar. Full of "pity and patience," which he learned from one of the Valar, Olórin moved invisibly among the Elves in the First Age, offering them "fair visions or the promptings of wisdom."[42]

In the year 1000 of the Third Age of Arda, the Valar sent Olórin with four other Maiar in incarnate form to Middle-earth to rouse its inhabitants "from despair and put away the imaginations of darkness."[43] It was only through Ilúvatar's direct permission, though, that a Maiar could enter the natural world.[44] In incarnate form, Gandalf arrived in Middle-earth as the least of his order, the Istari, or "the Wise." Four arrived before him: Saruman, Radagast, and the two unknown blue wizards. Each, save Gandalf, fails in his mission to stop the workings of the Enemy. Saruman, the greatest of the order, studied too long "the arts of the Enemy" and became an ally of evil.[45] Radagast grew too enamored with creation, coming to love the birds, trees, animals, and land so much that he forgot his mission and creator. The two unnamed wizards most likely were also corrupted by Sauron, Tolkien reasoned, possibly founding Eastern mystery cults.[46] Gandalf, though, became to Manwë what Sauron was to Morgoth, his greatest servant and lieutenant.[47]

Gandalf succeeded where the others failed because he understood the temptations that incarnation would bring: pleasures of the flesh and the lust for power. The asceticism St. Paul recommends to Timothy—"We brought nothing into the world; for that matter we can take nothing with us when we leave, but if we have food and covering we may rest content"—is taken to heart by Gandalf.[48] Indeed, when Gandalf returns from death, reborn as the White rather than the Grey, he announces: "Naked I was sent back—for a brief time, until my task is done. And naked I lay upon the mountain-top."[49] Here he echoes Job: "Naked I came from the womb, naked shall I return whence I came."[50] Thus does Gandalf do all he can to attenuate the desires of the flesh.

Gandalf serves directly the Secret Fire. When he arrives in Middle-earth, Gandalf is recognized by the Elven guardian of the Grey Havens, Cirdan. Though Gandalf has been created as the least among the Istari, Cirdan believes him to be the greatest of the order. To further Gandalf's mission to inspire the inhabitants of Middle-earth to fight the enemy, Cirdan gives Gandalf one of the three Elven rings, Narya. This is the "ring of fire," and with it, Gandalf can "rekindle hearts to the valour of old in a world that grows chill."[51] Narya helps Gandalf oppose "the fire that devours and wastes with the fire that kindles."[52] It also symbolizes Gandalf's service to the "Flame Imperishable," or the Holy Spirit. At the Bridge in Khazad-dûm immediately before his fight and fall with the Balrog, a demon of fire, Gandalf declares: "I am a servant of the Secret Fire, wielder of the Flame of Anor. You cannot pass."[53] Saruman too fears Gandalf, seeing within his rival "the great power and strange 'good fortune' that went with" him.[54] Ilúvatar, the Flame Imperishable, and Manwë, Saruman suspects, have their fingers of protection on Gandalf.

Whether as the Gray or the White, though, Gandalf carries immense spiritual burdens, the weight of which is betrayed by his tired body. He rarely shows his true self or nature to ordinary beings, as shown in his relationship with the hobbits. As Aragorn explains to Frodo: "Gandalf is greater than you Shire-folk know—as a rule you can only see his jokes and toys."[55] Even to a High Elf such as Galadriel, Gandalf never reveals his full purpose. "Needless were none of the deeds of Gandalf in life," Galadriel assures the remaining fellowship after the wizard's death in Khazad-dûm. "Those that followed him knew not his mind and cannot report his full purpose."[56] Prior to his death in Khazad-Dûm, Gandalf is also unsure of his abilities, but he never flounders in his mission. "There are many powers in the world, for good or for evil. Some are greater than I am," he admitted to Frodo. "Against some I have not yet been measured. But my time is coming."[57]

Upon his return as the White, Gandalf is filled with confidence. Merry notes that Gandalf is more intense, "both kinder and more alarming, merrier and more solemn."[58] His spirit had presumably consulted with Manwë or Ilúvatar while his incarnate form was dead, obtaining new strength and new instructions. "I have passed through fire and deep water," Gandalf says. "I have forgotten much that I thought I knew, and learned again much that I had forgotten."[59]

"Indeed my friends, none of you have any weapon that could hurt me," he tells the startled Aragorn, Legolas, and Gimli upon his return from death.[60] As Gandalf the White, his mission is to protect Middle-earth and inspire Ilúvatar's forces to defeat Sauron.[61] With Sauron defeated at the end of the Third Age, Gandalf's mission concludes, and he must depart. "The Third Age was my age. I was the Enemy of Sauron; and my work is finished. I shall go soon. The burden must lie now upon you and your kindred."[62] His job accomplished, Gandalf's immense and direct holy power can no longer be permitted to linger in Middle-earth. There is a danger that he will distort the inhabitants' free will in choosing the good because of his virtue and charisma as an incarnate Maiar.[63] The world of myth allows for such beings to walk the earth. The world of history rarely abides such intrusions.

In addition to his own moral imagination, Tolkien drew on a number of sources to create the character of Gandalf. The name Gandalf comes from Snorri Sturluson's thirteenth-century *Poetic Edda*. It is one of many names listed in one of the most famous pre-Christian northern stories, the Voluspa, or the "Seeress's Prophecy," most of which Tolkien used for the names of the company of Dwarves in *The Hobbit*. The story involves Odin, the Scandinavian mythological "All-Father," consulting with a seeress in an attempt to discover the nature of men and the world. (The Voluspa, is, perhaps, the best extant synopsis of northern pre-Christian religion.)[64]

Tolkien once referred to Gandalf as an "Odinic wanderer."[65] When Odin appears in the Icelandic thirteenth-century *Saga of the Volsungs*, he appears as a wandering, old man, dressed in grey.

> It is now told that when people were sitting by the fires in the evening a man came into the hall. He was not known to the men by sight. He was dressing in this way: he wore a mottled cape that was hooded; he was barefoot and had linen breeches tied around his legs. As he walked up to barnstock he held a sword in his hand while over his head was a low-hanging hood. He was very tall and gray with age, and he had only one eye. He brandished the sword and thrust it into the trunk so that it sank up to the hilt. Words of welcome failed everyone.[66]

Throughout northern mythology, Odin serves as one who inspires certain heroes. Like Gandalf, Odin not only gives them courage, but he also gives them powerful, supernatural gifts as aids in their exploits. And like Gandalf, Odin has a supernaturally endowed horse.[67]

Tolkien also drew on numerous Christian sources for the character of Gandalf. One important source was the New Testament's "The Acts of the Apostles," in which God sends an angel to let Peter out of prison.[68] The other Christian source and inspiration that Tolkien never made explicit seems to be St. Boniface (Wilfred) of Mainz/Crediton. According to the cultural historian Christopher Dawson, it was the Anglo-Saxon missionary St. Boniface who first realized the significance of the Anglo-Saxons and their isolated and protected home in the British Isles. The British Isles served as the intellectual base of Boniface's larger plan to create medieval Christendom out the ruins of Rome and to protect it from the continuous threat of the invading and pagan barbaric tribes. As Charles Martel and his sons protected France from Islamic invasion from its new base in Iberia, classical and Christian learning remained safe and protected on the northwest edge of Europe in the British Isles. Like Tolkien's hobbits who lead a normal, happy lifestyle unaware, prior to the War of the Ring, of the troubles of the larger world, the Anglo-Saxon Christian monasteries of the medieval period, especially in Northumbria, protected all that was good from the classical and early Christian worlds in virtual isolation.[69]

> The work of St. Boniface did more than any other factor to lay the foundations of medieval Christendom. His mission to Germany was not an isolated spiritual adventure like the achievements of his Celtic predecessors; it was part of a far-sighted programme of construction and reform planned with all the method and statesmanship of the Roman tradition. It involved a triple alliance between the Anglo-Saxon missionaries, the Papacy, and the family of Charles Martel, the de facto rulers of the Frankish kingdom, out of which the Carolingian Empire and the Carolingian culture ultimately emerged.[70]

In *The Making of Europe*, Dawson takes this view even further. St. Boniface "had a deeper influence on the history of Europe than any other Englishman who has ever lived,"[71] he asserts.

St. Boniface seems as likely a source as Odin for the character of Gandalf. Tolkien enjoyed mixing the pagan with the Christian, and like the spirited and intrepid St. Boniface, Gandalf creates a triple alliance between different peoples, in this case hobbits, Elves, and the men of Númenórean descent. And like Gandalf, Boniface refused to operate from any one base of power, but chose the life of a wandering pilgrim instead.

Other parallels between early-medieval Europe and the Third Age of Middle-earth exist. The hobbits, as noted previously, are analogous to the best of Anglo-Saxon common society. The Elves of Rivendell and Lothlorien resemble the Benedictines of the early and high middle ages. Like their Benedictine counterparts, the Elves preserve tradition and create art. They also act as citizens of the Blessed Realm, knowing that they are immortal, as did the monks, who knew that they lived half on Earth and half as citizens of God's heavenly kingdom. Finally, the Elves sing in timelessness (time has little meaning in their realm) and in the style of Gregorian chant— the "pure language" of St. Gregory, a Benedictine.[72]

The northern men of Númenórean descent seem to resemble the Christianized northern Germanic tribes, like the Anglo-Saxons, mixed with a Romanized nobility. As after the fall of the Roman Empire, the Franks especially attempted to protect the frontiers, in the Third Age of Middle-earth, the northern men of Númenórean descent, led by Aragorn, serve as Rangers who protect the borders of the Shire and other realms of good. And as with Rome after the destruction of the empire, the two Númenórean kingdoms are in dire straits. Arnor, the northern kingdom, is long gone, its remnants such as Weather Top (Amon Sûl) and the Barrow-downs in ruin. Gondor, the southern kingdom, has decayed considerably, and its ultimate destruction seems imminent. Denethor and Boromir, descendants of Númenor, even strike an uncanny resemblance to Charles Martel and his sons, who cared more for the trappings and prestige of the Roman empire than the Christianity that could animate it effectively.

As we saw in chapter 2, Tolkien ultimately wanted his myth to end in something "like the re-establishment of an effective Holy Roman Empire with its seat in Rome."[73] Gandalf, like St. Boniface, inspired all of Middle-earth to stop the invasion from the south and southeast. The Orcs, indeed, are the great armies of evil on the borders, attempting to penetrate the heart of northwestern Middle-earth, just as the Muslims attempted in the seventh and eighth centuries to penetrate western Europe. Gandalf, Tolkien wrote, "was thinking only of the defence of the West against the Shadow."[74] Finally, while Tolkien's conception is mythological, his special knowledge of, and interest in, the early- and high-medieval periods must have informed his worldview and his view of myth. Certainly, as a Roman Catholic, it is easy to see how he would have idealized the medieval period as the high-water mark of Christendom.

Whether Tolkien intended him as a St. Boniface figure or not, Gandalf proves indispensable in the fight against Sauron. Indeed, it is only the moral imagination of Gandalf, and his fortitude, that leads to Sauron's defeat. Like a true prophet, Gandalf, the servant of the Flame Imperishable, inspires men to use their gifts for the greater good of society, to live up to the best of the past, and to transmit this tradition to future generations.

Toward the end of The War of the Ring, Legolas reflects on how dangerous Aragorn might have been as a dark king. "In that hour I looked on Aragorn and thought how great and terrible a Lord he might have become in the strength of his will, had he taken the Ring to himself. Not for naught does Mordor fear him."[75] From his shadowy and mysterious introduction as Strider in the pub at Bree, Aragorn emerges as the most powerful man in all of Middle-earth. Sauron fears him—and rightfully so. Even when he is just Strider, Aragorn is a formidable figure. He leads the men of Númenórean descent in the North of Middle-earth in their roles as rangers, men dedicated to watching the borders and frontiers, guarding against penetration of the Shire by the forces of the Dark Lord. "Lonely men are we," Aragorn admitted to Boromir at the Council of Elrond. "Rangers of the wild, hunters—but hunters ever of the servants of the Enemy; for they are found in many places, not in Mordor only."[76] Loneliness was not the only burden of a Ranger. Most residents of the North distrusted them, misunderstanding their need for secrecy as an art of evil. "'Strider' I am to one fat man who lives within a day's march of forces that would freeze his heart, or lay his little town in ruin," Aragorn states, "if he were not guarded ceaselessly."[77] Aragorn's ancestors and relatives have accepted the role of ranger for generations, awaiting the proper time for the emergence of the king. According to prophecy, he will rule over a recreated Arnor and Gondor.

From his meeting with the hobbits in Bree, to his search for Pippin and Merry after they have been kidnapped by Orcs, and to his challenge of Sauron in the Palantír, Aragorn proves his ability to lead. Additionally, he exhibits a stunning fortitude and bravery. Though Aragorn provides a glimpse of his abilities in the struggle with Sauron over the Palantír, it is not until he serves as a healer that he reveals himself fully as the prophesied king. Old Middle-earth lore had stated: "The hands of the king are the hands of a healer."[78] Aragorn heals Faramir and Eowyn, both of whom have been wounded by the deepest darkness of the Enemy. Word of his deeds spreads quickly through Gondor, giving hope to the besieged city. The king has returned, and his strength and love flow throughout his kingdom. His closest friends feel it most intensely. Gimli notes that only "the will of Aragorn" gave him strength to endure trials, while Legolas says that "all those who come to know him come to love him after their own fashion." Indeed, even the dead follow Aragorn.[79]

Gandalf, the prophet, and Aragorn, the divinely appointed king, formulate and execute the last plan of the War of the Ring: to attack the very gates of Mordor. "To waver is to fall," Aragorn tells his followers.[80] This last act is both brilliant and desperate. The attack at the gates will distract Sauron, thus attenuating his vigilance while the

Ring Bearer and Sam make their way up Mount Doom. In essence, the king and the prophet do what is demanded of them by Providence. They willingly place themselves and their forces in a position that may prove their undoing and their death. As true servants of Ilúvatar, they are willing to sacrifice themselves for the opportunity to serve the greater good.

Aragorn resembles the best of the high-medieval kings; historically, he is similar to Pepin and Charlemagne, but in spirit he is more akin to a non-Frankish king—specifically, a Christian Anglo-Saxon or a virtuous pagan Scandinavian king, like Beowulf. Jane Chance, in her detailed and learned study of Tolkien, argues that in the legendarium Denethor is a bad barbarian king, Théoden a good barbarian king, and Aragorn a good Christian king.[81] Yet it should not surprise the reader that Aragorn embodies both pagan and Christian elements. Indeed, the notion of medieval kingship itself represented a synthesis of the barbarian virtues with the classical and Christian virtues. Typically, in the Middle Ages, the king represented entire tribes and ethnic groups. But the king was beholden to God as well as to his subjects. Kingship could be revoked if the king refused to act like Christ. But when a king did act as Christ would, it was clear to his people that he had been chosen by God. He ruled by divine right, as kingship and true power could only be conferred by God.[82] Tolkien made it quite clear in his letters that the king was Ilúvatar's representative on Earth.[83] If Manwë was Ilúvatar's regent of the whole earth, Aragorn was Ilúvatar's regent of Middle-earth, the steward of men, hobbits, Dwarves, and Elves.

Aragorn's coronation is medieval in form. The people have consented, and Frodo, the priest, carries the crown to Gandalf, the prophet. As with the prophets Samuel and Nathan and the kings Saul and David, the prophet Gandalf places it upon the king's head. Gandalf, Aragorn explains, "has been the mover of all that has been accomplished, and this is his victory."[84] As St. Boniface crowned Pepin king in 752 and successfully united Christendom against outside forces, especially Islam, Gandalf's crowning of Aragorn unites all of Middle-earth against the forces of evil, Sauron's remnants.

After crowning Aragorn, Gandalf identifies Aragorn with the Valar of Arda: "Now come the days of the King, and may they be blessed while the thrones of the Valar endure!"[85] When Aragorn stands, all recognize him as a man reborn as king, chosen by Ilúvatar.[86]

As king, Aragorn acts as would a virtuous medieval monarch. Many of the nations and peoples who had sided with Sauron are forgiven and are free to leave the court without punishment. Aragorn liberates Sauron's slaves, redistributing the arable lands to them as recompense for their enslavement. He rewards his allies in the war with just words and gifts. As one character notes, Aragorn acted with "mercy and justice"—the most laudatory words that could be applied to a medieval king.[87] Most importantly, Aragorn unites all of Middle-earth, reestablishes the kingdoms of Arnor and Gondor, and roots out the remaining strongholds of evil. In a mythological sense, Christendom has been united, and its enemies isolated and dealt with. Through his marriage to Arwen, Aragorn becomes king of the Elves as well.[88]

Understanding his great burden, Aragorn rules not arbitrarily, but through the most Christian and medieval of institutions, the Council, known in Tolkien's mythology as the "Great Council of Gondor." With it, Aragorn "governed the realm with the frame of ancient law, of which he was administrator (and interpreter) but not the maker."[89] Demonstrating further that Aragorn is the true king, the descendant sapling of the oldest of trees of Valinor blooms and blossoms again in Middle-earth.[90]

Interestingly enough, like the Virgin Mary in Catholic theology, Aragorn dies of his own free will.[91] It is not, however, suicide; he simply decides when to end his earthly journey and begin his eternal journey with God. As Tolkien described it in 1958, a man "would or should *die* voluntarily by surrender with trust *before being compelled.*"[92] Such a death only glorifies God and acknowledges even more his sovereignty. When Arwen, Aragorn's wife and queen, regrets Ilúvatar's decision to allow Aragorn to end his life voluntarily, Aragorn comforts her: "In sorrow we must go, but not in despair. Behold! We are not bound for ever to the circles of the world, and beyond them is more than memory."[93] As Tolkien explained in his letters, "Death is not an Enemy."[94]

To understand Aragorn fully, one must also understand his "second," Faramir. In 1944, Tolkien expressed surprise at Faramir's appearance in his stories: "I am sure I did not invent him, I did not even want him, though I like him, but there he came walking into the woods of Ithilien."[95] C. S. Lewis and Charles Williams both liked Faramir immediately,[96] and Tolkien considered him to be the closest character to himself in *The Lord of the Rings*.[97] Tolkien and Faramir shared the recurring "Great Wave Dream," in which a monstrous wave destroys a civilization. It was a dream that Tolkien seems to have had throughout his life.[98]

Faramir first appears in *The Two Towers* as a beacon of hope for Frodo and Sam. The son of Denethor and brother of Boromir, Faramir is of Númenórean descent; Tolkien even titled the chapter in which Faramir appears, "A Window on the West," implying that Faramir offers a glimpse of the best of Númenor. Faramir refuses to lie or to deceive in any way, even in his dealings with the enemy. He is honorable to a fault. He is highly intelligent, and he kills even the enemy reluctantly.[99]

Unlike his brother and father, however, Faramir does not resent his family's position as one of stewardship rather than royalty. Faramir is a man of integrity and great courage, not a seeker of power. In his initial meeting with Frodo and Sam, Faramir recounts the views held by his brother and father. "How many hundreds of years needs it to make a steward a king, if the king returns not," Boromir asked his father. After hearing his father's answer, Boromir responded in frustration: "In Gondor ten thousand years would not suffice."[100] Unlike his brother, but like Sam, Faramir does what is right, not what is profitable, expedient, or politic. His father, Denethor, distrusted his second son, Tolkien explained in his letters, because he himself "was tainted with mere politics."[101] Sauron and Mordor had, in his mind, become just another rival power to his polity, not to the world, to humanity, or to God. Faramir knows his place in creation, and he desires nothing more than to play out Ilúvatar's role for him.

Though a man, Faramir best resembles the Elves, who allowed their sanctuaries of sublime beauty to be sacrificed for the greater and common good with the destruction of the One Ring.

Faramir embodies grace at a number of levels. First, Tolkien had not planned on his appearance. God had created him and inspired Tolkien to include him in the story—or so the Oxford don believed. Second, it was the healing of Faramir, along with Eowyn and Merry, that revealed the true nature and kingship of Aragorn. Third, and perhaps most important, Faramir offers one of the very few obvious allusions to religion in *The Lord of the Rings*. Just before his dinner with Frodo, "Faramir and all his men turned and faced west in a moment of silence."[102] Though Faramir is unsure of the meaning of the act, he follows the pious forms that have come to him through tradition.

Each of these figures in The Lord of the Rings—Frodo, Sam, Gandalf, Aragorn, and Faramir—represent different heroic acts: Gandalf is the prophet, Aragorn is the "Christian" king, Frodo is the sacrificial priest, Sam is the common man, and Faramir is the man who knows and respects his place in God's creation. Tolkien filled his legendarium with many heroes, and each deserves a chapter of his own: Túrin Turambar, Luthien, Beren, Eärendil, and Tom Bombadil, to name a few. But Frodo, Sam, Gandalf, Aragorn, and Faramir best represent the sanctified heroes Tolkien had in mind for a Christian-centered mythology. Each separately and combined fulfills not only St. Augustine's post-Roman vision of heroism—a synthesis of Stoic realism and Christian hope—but particularly St. Paul's notion that each individual was a member of the larger and eternal Body of Christ.

These heroes, Tolkien wrote in his letters, knowingly fought for good against evil. "The story is cast in terms of a good side, and a bad side, beauty against ruthless ugliness, tyranny against kingship, moderated freedom with consent against compulsion that has long lost any object save mere power."[103] In 1971, just two years before his death, Tolkien praised the role of human will in survival:

"I've always been impressed that we're here surviving because of the indomitable courage of quite small people against impossible odds: jungles, volcanoes, wild beasts . . . they struggle on, almost blindly in a way."[104] Still, as each of Tolkien's heroes reveal, true heroism comes from grace, not human will. In 1968, Russell Kirk commented that Sauron's "scheme would destroy man as the son of God; it would abolish the moral freedom which distinguishes men from brutes. Only the sacrifice of heroes can save us from such degradation; and Tolkien appeals to the gallantry which still is latent in the youth of the twentieth century."[105]

Tolkien also knew that though there were times of renewal in which men accepted God's grace and used their gifts wisely, thus fulfilling the needs of the Church, there were evil times that needed to be renewed and redeemed. In such times, as Tolkien aptly put it, "men slept."[106]

Chapter 5

The Nature of Evil

In 1942, C. S. Lewis published a book of theological fiction about
two demons—one a new trainee and the other an expert tempter—
who write letters to one another regarding their attempts to prevent
a young man from becoming a Christian. In thanks for their then
thirteen-year-old friendship, Lewis dedicated *The Screwtape Letters*
to Tolkien and inscribed in the copy he gave his friend, "In token
payment of a great debt."[1] Lewis's dedication angered Tolkien, for
the book had deeply disturbed him.[2] How could Lewis have delved
so deeply into the arts of the Enemy, Tolkien must have wondered?
In no uncertain terms, Tolkien disapproved of such ventures—even
when undertaken by good Christians like Lewis. The devil was too
powerful for a human to trifle with or to write too much about.
After the publication of *The Screwtape Letters*, another Oxford
don only compounded Tolkien's unease when he referred to two of
Lewis's fictional demons, asking him, "Say, are you Wormwood or
Slubgob?"[3]

Throughout his life, Tolkien believed strongly in the immediacy
of evil. Evil manifested itself in two possible ways, he thought. The
first, the predominant way during pre-history or in myth, was as a
physical or spiritual entity.

> [T]his story *[The Lord of the Rings]* exhibits 'myth' passing into
> History of the Dominion of Men; for of the course the Shadow
> will arise again in a sense (as is clearly foretold by Gandalf), but
> never again (unless it be before the great End) will an evil daemon
> be incarnate as a physical enemy; he will direct Men and all the

complications of half-evils, and defective goods, and the twilights of doubts as to sides, such situations as he most loves.[4]

Melkor and Sauron represent the two most explicit manifestations of evil in Tolkien's mythology, though numerous others abound throughout the legendarium: Balrogs, dragons, werewolves, Orcs, goblins, half-Orcs, Ringwraiths, wights, hounds of hell, vampires, wargs, wolves, and trolls, to name just a few. The second way evil becomes manifest is indirectly: for example, through the lies, pride, and mistrust bred and spread by the likes of Melkor and his chief servant Sauron. While neither Melkor nor Sauron have the power to change the nature of an entire race or species, they can corrupt individuals with the foul lies and deceptions they leave in their wake. Like Satan, his mythological equivalent, Morgoth is "a liar and the father of lies."[5]

Tolkien believed that a virtuous person should understand that evil exists, but should acknowledge or act on little more than that. When trying to explain why Saruman had renounced the vows of the Istari in their fight against Sauron, Elrond explained: "It is perilous to study too deeply the arts of the Enemy, for good or for ill."[6] Earlier, Gandalf had explained to Frodo that as Saruman's knowledge grew, so did his pride.[7] Even to mimic evil could lead to the irrevocable alteration of the virtuous person's understanding of the world. Thus, Tolkien thought C. S. Lewis's *Screwtape Letters* a hazardous experiment.[8] Lewis had gotten too far into the mind of "The Enemy," as Tolkien commonly referred to evil, much to the danger of Lewis and possibly all of the Inklings. Furthermore, Lewis was acting too much like Charles Williams, who Tolkien had called a "witch doctor."[9]

Tolkien's failure to explore or explain evil in much depth has led many critics to chide him for being too simplistic and childlike. Horror writer Fritz Leiber, for example, complained that Tolkien "does not explore and even seems uninterested in exploring the mentality and consciousness and inner life of his chief villains." His villains are merely "sneaks, bullies and resentful cowards."[10] Perhaps Tolkien's chief critic in this area is fantasy writer Michael Moorcock, who accuses Tolkien of having created a "not so evil" evil character in Sauron. Tolkien's "courageous characters take on the aspect of retired colonels at last driven to write a letter to *The Times* and we are not sure—because Tolkien cannot really bring himself to get close to his proles and their satanic leaders—if Sauron and Co. are quite as evil as we're told." (After all, Moorcock bitterly notes, "anyone who hates hobbits can't be all bad.")[11] Tolkien will only "take you to the edge of the Abyss and point out the excellent tea-garden at the bottom, showing you the steps carved into the cliff and reminding you to be a bit careful because the hand-rails are a trifle shaky."[12]

Yet Tolkien would most likely not be too bothered by the criticism of Leiber or Moorcock. Evil, for Tolkien, was not about being scared by monsters. Rather, evil is very real and perilous, whether in fairy tales, in the trenches of World War I, or in the Soviet gulags. The monsters of fiction and nightmares are merely manifestations of the true, original evil—the perversion and mocking of God's creation. In its essence, evil is and always will be merely derivative and perverse. Therefore, as Hannah Arendt famously explained, evil is, finally, banal. Even Sauron is nothing but a poor substitute for Morgoth. "The operations of Sauron naturally and inevitably resembled or repeated those of his master," Tolkien explained.[13]

There is, in fact, something brilliant in Tolkien's refusal to discuss evil in depth. By placing evil in the background of *The Lord of the Rings*, Tolkien has created an evil that is outright ominous, for it seems to be everywhere, pervading the entire landscape of Middle-earth, surrounding the Fellowship of the Ring on all sides. Even the birds and the mountains seem corrupted, watching and informing on every movement of the Fellowship, forcing them, for example, to take the road through Moria and to face the Balrog.

Throughout *The Lord of the Rings* and the entire legendarium, then, evil appears in both its direct and indirect forms. It is all the more terrifying because we approach the story from the hobbits', that is, the common man's, perspective. Our imaginations, rather than

Tolkien's, allow us to contemplate the worst when considering the vaguely described but omnipresent evil encroaching upon the heart of Middle-earth. Fantasy writer Ursula Le Guin noted this in 1977, arguing that Tolkien's depiction (or lack thereof) of evil is Platonic. Those "who do wrong are not complete figures, but complements; Saruman is Gandalf's dark-self, Boromir Aragorn's; Wormtongue is, almost literally, the weakness of King Theoden," she writes. "Gollum is Frodo's shadow."[14] It is in the goodness of the heroes who are fighting for Middle-earth that one understands the evil that good opposes. And as philosopher Peter Kreeft rightly contends, it is in making the good interesting that the Inklings may have made their greatest contribution.[15]

"Like Lewis, Tolkien was an Old Western Man who was staggered at the present direction of civilization," wrote Clyde Kilby.[16] History was, Tolkien believed, one "long defeat," with victory only at its end, and even then attained only by and through God.[17] Tolkien admitted that the various crises of the twentieth century crept into his mythology and helped shape it.[18] But the evil of Tolkien's world did not parallel any one specific evil in the primary world. *The Lord of the Rings* is not an allegory about the development of the hydrogen bomb or the rise of Stalin or Hitler. Russell Kirk described Tolkien's method well:

> Although political significance may be read into some of the more influential fantasies of our century, it is notable how successfully our fabulists have sheered away from ideology in an age of political religions. Some critics may identify the evil power in Tolkien's *Lord of the Rings* with Nazi or Communist dominations; yet Tolkien himself did not intend to be bound by yesterday's or today's ideological encounters. His three volumes are a picture of the perpetual struggle between good and evil; his concern is the corrupting intoxication of power.[19]

As Tolkien put it, a "small knowledge of history depresses one with the sense of the everlasting weight of human iniquity."[20] The twentieth century may have been notable for the volume of bloodshed and horror it had witnessed, but evil had always been, and always would be, present in the world. "[T]he presence (even if only on the borders) of the terrible is, I believe, what gives this imagined world its verisimilitude," Tolkien wrote in 1937. "A safe fairy-land is untrue to all worlds."[21]

In a poem written to celebrate the conversion of his friend C. S. Lewis to Christianity, Tolkien wrote: "Evil it will not see, for evil lies/not in God's picture but in crooked eyes/not in the source but in malicious choice/and not in sound but in the tuneless voice."[22] God makes nothing evil; rather, all that he makes is good. As Elrond stated at his Council: "[N]othing is evil in the beginning."[23] Even Morgoth, the devil figure of Tolkien's mythology, was created out of pure goodness and unadulterated love. Indeed, Ilúvatar gave him more gifts than any other entity. But Morgoth craved more. Rather than singing Ilúvatar's song at the creation of Arda, he desired to create on his own and become a god himself. His pride proved his undoing, and he became the Diabolus. After his rebellion, Morgoth thrived on destruction and enslavement.[24] "To corrupt or destroy whatsoever arose new and fair was ever the chief desire of Morgoth," Tolkien explained.[25] "[H]is dominion was torment."[26] Tolkien's other strictly diabolical figure, Ungoliant, is one of the most frightening creatures to appear in the mythology. She feeds on life and light, absorbing all as she passes by any living creature. She is, in essence, a monstrous and demonic black hole.[27]

The attempts of Evil to create, in Tolkien's world, result in the perverted mockery of Ilúvatar's creation.[28] The Orcs are the most obvious example.[29] Translated from Anglo-Saxon, "Orc" means "demon." The Orcs are, as Tolkien originally conceived them, Elves corrupted by Morgoth and Sauron.[30] "They are servants of the Dark Power, and later of Sauron, neither of whom could, or would, produce living things," Tolkien noted, and, therefore, "they must be 'corruptions.'"[31] *The Silmarillion* records that the Elves taken prisoner by Melkor were "by slow arts of cruelty . . . corrupted and enslaved; and thus did Melkor breed the hideous race of the Orcs in envy and mockery of the Elves."[32] Tolkien proposed that had Morgoth truly "created" the Orcs from nothing, they would act "more like puppets filled (only at a distance) with their maker's mind and will, or ant-like operating under direction of a queen-centre."[33] Even as corruptions of what was once good, Orcs despise the individuality characteristic of God's creatures. This is reflected in their cult of mechanization, hatred of the light, and contempt for beauty. As Tolkien wrote in *The Hobbit*:

> Now goblins are cruel, wicked, and bad-hearted. They make no beautiful things, but they make many clever ones. They can tunnel and mine as well as any but the most skilled dwarves, when they take the trouble, though they are usually untidy and dirty. Hammers, axes, swords, daggers, pickaxes, tongs, and also instruments of torture, they make very well, or get other people to make to their design, prisoners and slaves that have to work till they die for want of air and light. It is not unlikely that they invented some of the machines that have since troubled the world, especially the ingenious devices for killing large numbers at once, for wheels and engines and explosions always delighted them.[34]

Tolkien cautioned against thinking of the Orcs in too fantastic terms. One should not judge them too harshly, he thought, for they "are fundamentally a race of 'rational incarnate' creatures, though horribly corrupted, if no more so than many Men to be met today."[35] Orcs, like all sentient creatures except the devil, are ultimately redeemable.[36] But they have fallen far; the Eucharistic *lembas* terrifies them, and they most eagerly eat man-flesh when Saruman feeds it to them.[37]

Strangely, the creation of the Dwarves parallels Morgoth's torture and the ultimate perversion of Elves into Orcs. But unlike Morgoth, the Vala Aulë made the Dwarves out of joy, hoping to share with them all of Ilúvatar's creation. Loving creation too much, Aulë desired to serve as their mentor in earthly crafts and skills. Ilúvatar reprimanded Aulë, and noted that the creation of the seven Dwarves was beyond the authority he had delegated to him. Immediately,

Aulë realized his error. When Ilúvatar informs him that the Dwarves can only act as puppets, as Aulë is too limited to ever give them free will, Aulë is ashamed and distraught. Like Abraham with Isaac, Aulë attempts to kill the Dwarves in obedience, but Ilúvatar prevents their destruction, as he has given each of the Dwarves independent consciousness and free will. Their race, however, must wait until the Elves and the men emerge in Time before they may also enter Time. Until then, they must dwell in the earth, estranged from the Elves and all creatures who live above ground.[38]

One can find the theme of "the fall" throughout Tolkien's mythology. It served as one of the most important concerns of his stories. Almost without exception, pride goeth before the fall, and the desire to be something more than God, or what God intended, can corrupt even the best being. Sometimes it is angelic pride, as in the cases of Morgoth and Sauron; sometimes it is individual pride, as with Isildur, who failed to destroy the One Ring when he had the chance to do so, shortly after the success of the Last Alliance; sometimes it is the pride of an entire race, as with men, though *the* Fall occurs offstage in Tolkien's mythology.[39] In the conversation between Finrod and Andreth, Andreth refuses to tell Finrod the reason why men fell. Andreth explains that men do not speak of it with outsiders, and those men who do speak of it do not agree on what the specifics were. They only know that they greatly angered Ilúvatar at some point in the distant past.[40] One extant story claims that men traded their independence for greater knowledge. Soon, though, they came to possess neither knowledge nor independence, and they began to pray to Morgoth. Unlike Ilúvatar, though, Morgoth only answered their prayers if men performed deeds and works for him.[41] Therefore, men now lament over the fall, even if its specifics remain unknown:

> Thereafter we were grievously afflicted, by weariness, and hunger, and sickness; and the Earth and all things in it were turned against

us. Fire and Water rebelled against us. The birds and the beasts
shunned us, or if they were strong they assailed us. Plants gave us
poison; and we feared the shadows under trees.[42]

The elf Finrod contends that man's fall could not have been the
sole result of Morgoth's actions. Morgoth, Finrod states, has neither
the power to create nor the power to utterly destroy or wholly corrupt. "Melkor could seduce individual minds and wills," he says to
Andreth, "but he could not make this heritable, or alter (contrary to
the will and design of Eru) the relation of a whole people to Time and
Arda."[43] Only the Creator, the Prime Mover, could change the relationship with the Creator, and only because of some ill-chosen action
on the part of his creatures. Morgoth's role was simply to exploit the
unrest that men already felt, not to create that unrest or ill will toward
Ilúvatar. Specifically, he exploited the fear men had of mortality, of
death. Originally, Ilúvatar gave men short lives as a gift. Indeed, Ilúvatar did not intend for men to fear death. Instead, the restlessness
he placed in man was intended to prompt them to accept and desire
eternal life with him. But because of the disorder Morgoth's actions
introduced prior to the birth of man, men misunderstood Ilúvatar's
intentions and feared death.[44]

Tolkien's most explicit rendering of a fall—and in some ways
most fascinating, if highly undeveloped—is that of Númenor in the
Second Age, or, as Tolkien labeled it, the Akallabêth. As a reward
to men—the Edain—who had fought against Morgoth at the end
of the First Age rather than succumbing to his perverted will, Ilúvatar blessed them with a realm of their own, Andor. In it, the Edain,
now calling themselves the Númenóreans, lived long lives, created
beautiful works of art, and became the greatest mariners the world
had ever seen. The waters, controlled by the Vala Ulmo, protected
them from harm, and the rest of the Valar watched over them in a
variety of ways.[45] Two restrictions, though, were placed upon them.
First, the Númenóreans were still mortal. Unlike the Elves, it was in
their nature to be mortal, and the Valar had neither the authority
nor the desire to grant them anything beyond that. Second, to pre-

vent the Edain from misunderstanding the gift of mortality and from suffering jealousy, as had happened to the earliest men, they were forbidden from sailing to the Blessed Realm and witnessing the lives of the immortals. The Númenóreans knew the second rule as "the Ban." Meneltarma, also known as the Pillar of Heaven, was built by the Númenóreans as a temple to praise Ilúvatar. Within it, only the King, who also served as priest, could speak.[46] The first king, Elros, son of Eärendil and brother of Elrond, ruled wisely for over four centuries.[47]

As the Númenóreans attained increasingly greater skills, craftsmanship, and wisdom, they expanded their explorations to the East, finding and exploring the shores of Middle-earth. There they found backwards peoples—those men in Middle-earth who had either remained neutral or sided with Morgoth in the last great war and now lived in a deep age of darkness. Pitying those they found, the Númenóreans served as missionaries, teaching the ignorant men the agricultural arts and the well-ordered life. The men of Middle-earth believed the Númenóreans divine and, with selfish pride, the Númenóreans began to agree. They were certainly superior to the men they encountered outside of Númenor. In their arrogance, they began to wonder why the Valar had imposed mortality and the Ban upon them.[48]

The more the Númenóreans dwelt upon their suspicions, the greater became their pride. They came to resent the Valar and to fear death, seeing it not as a gift but as a curse. Over the centuries, they attempted to prolong their mortal lives as long as possible, and they built "tombs in which the thought of death was enshrined in the darkness."[49] Their missionary work in Middle-earth became nothing but colonization. In imperialist manner, they exploited Middle-earth's natural resources and labor, mined for silver and gold, and demanded tribute from those they "helped."[50] Discussing one famous Númenórean sea captain, Aldarion, Tolkien wrote: "[H]e dreamed of the glory of Númenor and the power of its kings, and he sought for footholds whence they could step to wider dominion."[51] At the same time, Sauron slowly began to reassume physical form. Rather than stop the growing evil of Sauron, the men of Númenor "hardened their hearts," full of anger and spite against the Valar.[52] To demonstrate their anger, the kings of Númenor began to take the blasphemous title "Lord of the West," which had been reserved for Manwë alone. Becoming ever more prideful, they forbade the use of the Elvish tongues.[53]

When the Númenóreans finally did confront Sauron and his rising power in Middle-earth, they did so out of vanity and concern for their own power rather than out of mercy for the peoples of Middle-earth. They could not share the known world with an equal or superior power, and they decided to destroy Sauron and his forces. Their combined naval and land forces so overwhelmed Sauron that Morgoth's lieutenant deceivingly humbled himself before the Númenórean king. He begged for forgiveness and offered his services as a prophet and man of great knowledge. Deceived by this flattery, the king accepted Sauron as an advisor.

Just as the earliest men had been tempted with knowledge, so too were the Númenóreans. Taken into the confidence of the Númenóreans, Sauron soon provided a Gnostic interpretation and reading of what was left of traditional Númenórean theology. Ilúvatar was the false god, the "God of Darkness," said the dark prophet and priest Sauron. Melkor was the true god, the "Giver of Freedom" to men.[54] "The wretched soul has strayed into a labyrinth of torment and wanders without a way out," ancient Gnostic writings teach, "It seeks to escape from the bitter chaos, but knows not how to get out."[55] In Tolkien's mythology, Sauron presents himself as the Gnostic savior, urging the Númenóreans away from the labyrinth of Ilúvatar's time and space and toward the "true god" Melkor.

Sauron, wrote Tolkien, "had gone the way of all tyrants: beginning well, at least on the level that while desiring to order all things according to his own wisdom he still at first considered the (economic) well-being of other inhabitants of the Earth. But he went further than human tyrants in pride and the lust for domination, being in origin an immortal (angelic) spirit."[56] Sauron slowly took advantage of Númenórean weaknesses and the disorder in their souls. He tore apart their prideful culture from the inside with his Gnostic inversions. A small minority, known as Elf-friends or "The Faithful," remained true to Ilúvatar, but they were persecuted and driven underground. Sauron cut down the White Tree, the symbol of the allegiance between the Valar and the Númenóreans, and built his own temple. His first sacrifice was the White Tree, offered to the false and fallen god Melkor. The sacrifices soon included the burning of men, those who were Elf-friends. Worshiping the Darkness, the Númenóreans became even more powerful and wealthy, and, tellingly, more industrial and technologically astute. They even enslaved the men of Middle-earth.[57]

With their pride at its height, Middle-earth subdued, and Sauron as their head priest and prophet, the Númenóreans decided to invade the Blessed Realm. Why not? Were they not the greatest beings in all of Arda? Why should the Valar and the Elves enjoy immortality when their superiors suffered? Sauron declared himself a god, offering a human holocaust in the heart of Meneltarma, the true Temple to Ilúvatar, and Númenóreans accepted his deification.[58]

Incensed by the blasphemy of Sauron and the Númenóreans, Ilúvatar intervened in the world directly, bypassing even the Valar, his regents. He remade the shape of the earth into a sphere (it had been flat). He then opened a "great chasm in the sea between Númenor and the Deathless Lands," into which the Númenórean fleet disappeared.[59] Finally, Ilúvatar completely destroyed The Land of Gift. "Then suddenly fire burst from Meneltarma, and there came a mighty wind and a tumult of the earth, and the sky reeled, and the hills slid, and Númenor went down into the sea, with all its children and its wives and its maidens and its ladies proud."[60] Like Noah and his few followers, only the Elf-friends were spared Ilúvatar's wrath. They had departed the island just prior to the Númenóreans' attempted invasion of the Blessed Realm. In nine ships, they had taken with them all that they could, including a sapling of the white tree named Nimloth, history books, and the seven Palantíri.[61] They became the founders of Gondor and Arnor, returning the remnants of Númenórean society to a well-ordered culture and society.

Not only did this remnant, through Ilúvatar's Grace, succeed, but Evil fled; during Ilúvatar's destruction of Númenor, Sauron lost his pleasing incarnate form. He traveled to Middle-earth as a black wind and took shape again in Barad-dûr as the Lidless Eye.[62] A revived Númenórean culture thrived for hundreds of years in Middle-earth, preserving right reason and peace in the realms of Gondor and Arnor, though the men there still remained fallen and easily susceptible to the sin of pride.

Tolkien died before he could fill out much of the history of the Second Age. The primary accounts of it are given in "The Lost Road," "A Description of the Island of Númenor," "The Mariner's Wife," and "The Line of Elros." Perhaps because there is relatively little description of it, the Second Age appears unduly fascinating, as one's imagination must of necessity complete what has been given. But Tolkien's tale of the Second Age also fascinates because, more than any other of Tolkien's "ages," it has a ring of familiarity that prompts the reader to long to delve into it. Even in its "raw" form one sees within it several important themes. First, the story of Númenor represents Tolkien's incorporation of the Atlantis myth into his own legendarium.[63] Tolkien believed that Atlantis, or a version of it, was "fundamental to 'mythical history'" whether it contained a basis in reality or not.[64] Lewis must have agreed with Tolkien, as he referred to Tolkien's version of Númenor several times in his famous *Space Trilogy* and also alludes to it in *The Chronicles of Narnia*. Second, the Númenórean myth incorporates Tolkien's own rather disturbing and vivid "Wave Dream," which he shared with one of his sons as well as his character Faramir.[65] Third, Tolkien's Númenórean myth demonstrates the follies of pride and retells the story of the fall of man. Indeed, Tolkien's version touches us so deeply because as humans created in God's image we long for Eden. Fourth, the Númenórean story reveals the arrogance and dangers of imperialism, exploitation, and industrialization. It is, in essence, another Tolkienian comment on the character of modernity. An Elf-friend aptly described the changes Sauron brought to Númenor, as the divinely inspired desire for beauty became the diabolical lust for power.

At first he revealed only secrets of craft, and taught the making of many things powerful and wonderful; and they seemed good. Our ships go now without the wind, and many are made of metal that sheareth hidden rocks, and they sink not in calm or storm; but they are no longer fair to look upon. Our towers grow ever stronger and climb ever higher, but beauty they leave behind upon earth. We who have no foes are embattled with impregnable fortresses—and mostly on the West. Our arms are multiplied as if for an agelong war, and men are ceasing to give love or care to the making of things for use or delight. But our shields are impenetrable, our swords cannot be withstood, our darts are like thunder and pass over leagues unerring.[66]

Or, as a Númenórean woman wisely described the ultimate result of Sauron's reign: "We cannot dwell in the time that is to come, lest we lose our now for a phantom of our own design."[67] Tolkien clearly implied these comments as descriptions of modernity.

Finally, on a narrative level, the Númenórean myth connects the First and Third Ages. It allows us to see the source of the animosity between men and Elves, between those of Númenórean descent and the indigenous men of Middle-earth, and the animosity among the exiled Númenóreans. Within their blood runs both faith and blasphemy. One also discovers how Sauron became the Lidless Eye. And the importance of the return of king Aragorn is explained: with him, "the worship of God would be renewed."[68]

In Tolkien's legendarium, a character's invocation of magic is often a sign of the presence of evil. Magic plays a central role in all fantastic literature. "A 'fairy-story' is one which touches on or uses Faërie, whatever its own main purpose may be: satire, adventure, morality, fantasy," Tolkien explained. "Faërie itself may perhaps most nearly be translated by Magic."[69] Most authors, though, employ magic in a very different manner than did Tolkien. More often than not, fantasy writers use magic to represent raw power, either drawn from the character himself or from the character's companion spiritual force.

As a Roman Catholic, Tolkien believed that magic in the sense of power was evil.

To Tolkien, the story of Simon the Magician in the Acts of the Apostles would have provided ample proof of magic's reality. Simon practiced magic throughout Samaria, and many, including Simon, believed his gift came from the Christian God. When Simon witnessed Peter and John receive power from the Holy Spirit, he desired to possess and wield it. Approaching them with confidence, Simon offered to pay them for the knowledge and gift of their holy power. Horrified and angry at his insolence, Peter rebuked him: "Your silver perish with you, because you thought you could obtain the gift of God with money."[70] The point is clear: one obtains such a gift as that wielded by St. Peter by faith alone, and only through God's sovereign decision to give it freely to his creature. Such power may not be bought or bartered for. St. Paul had a similar encounter with a magician, Elymas, also recorded in Acts. Through God, St. Paul temporarily blinded Elymas, thus demonstrating the superiority of the miracle to magic.[71]

Just as two types of supernatural power are described in the New Testament, Tolkien believed that what is usually labeled as "magic" exists in two forms: "*magia* and *goeteia*."[72] While not strict about the definitions, Tolkien generally used the former, *magia*, to mean "enchantment," and the latter, *goeteia*, to mean power derived from a demonic source and intended to dominate others and deprive its victim of their free will. Galadriel speaks of this division when she, Frodo, and Sam stand before her enchanted mirror. "For this is what your folk would call magic, I believe," Galadriel states to Sam, "though I do not understand clearly what they mean; and they seem also to use the same word for the deceits of the Enemy."[73] Galadriel's "elvish craft" was a form of *magia*, or enchantment. Enchantment is the process and result of a non-prideful subcreation, a glorification of God's world and a furthering of his desires for his creation. "Uncorrupted it does not seek delusion, nor bewitchment and domination," Tolkien explained in "On Fairy-Stories," but instead "seeks shared enrichment, [as] partners in making and delight, not slaves."[74]

In contrast, the person who invokes *goeteia* feels disdain for God's world as it is and hopes to overpower it and manipulate it into an alien image. This form of magic, Tolkien wrote, "produces, or pretends to produce, an alteration in the Primary World. It does not matter by whom it is said to be practised, fay or mortal, it remains distinct from the other two; it is not an art but a technique; its desire is *power* in this world, domination of things and wills" (emphasis in original).[75] One uses *goeteia*, Tolkien wrote in a letter, to "terrify and subjugate."[76] It is the "perversion of . . . art to power."[77] Sauron was so corrupted by the time of the War of the Rings, that he could only understand power and, therefore, this form of magic. Art eluded him, as his moral imagination no longer existed. He had habituated himself to sin, a disordered state of body, mind, and soul.[78] The idea of free peoples anywhere—full of joy, using the land and the gifts God gave them, such as the hobbits in the Shire—infuriates Sauron.[79]

Tolkien viewed machines, industrialization, and modern science as variants of *goeteia*, as all three sought to control others and to reorder the world in the finite image of man rather than in the infinite and ultimately incomprehensible image of God. In a letter written in 1950, Tolkien wrote that *The Lord of the Rings* is about three intimately related things: the "Fall, Mortality, and the Machine." Perversion and the Fall occur when

> the sub-creator wishes to be the Lord and God of his private creation. He will rebel against the laws of the Creator—especially against mortality. Both of these (alone or together) will lead to the desire for Power, for making the will more quickly effective,—and so to the Machine (or Magic).[80]

Elven enchantment, in contrast, is about "Art not Power, sub-creation not domination and tyrannous re-forming of Creation." "The Enemy in successive forms is always 'naturally' concerned with sheer Domination, and so [is] the Lord of magic and machines."[81] Tolkien's dichotomous classification of magic echoes Romano Guardini's dichotomous classification of technology. Technology, according to

Guardini, could work with nature or could seek to dominate it. With the first type of technology, "the aim is to penetrate, to move within, to live with," Guardini argued. "The other, however, unpacks, tears apart, arranges in compartments, takes over and rules."[82] The latter, dominating kind of technology soon takes on a life of its own, and man becomes subsumed by it. "It is destructive because it is not under human control," Guardini concluded. "It is surging ahead of unleashed forces that have not yet been mastered, raw material that has not yet been put together, given a living and spiritual form, and related to humanity."[83]

Similarly, in his studies on modern Gnosticism, Eric Voegelin claimed that the postmedieval scientific revolution had produced "'the greatest power orgy in the history of mankind' caused by 'a gigantic outburst of magic imagination after the breakdown of the intellectual and spiritual form of medieval high civilization.'"[84] In Tolkien's mythology, one sees this clearly in the corruption of Saruman. He becomes more and more reliant upon machinery and his servant Orcs. In turn, he becomes more confident in his own power. As Merry explains after witnessing the Ents decimate the machinery of Saruman: "I think he has not much grit, not much plain courage alone in a tight place without a lot of slaves and machines and things."[85] Although believing himself a master of the machine, Saruman had become a slave to it, and was nearly impotent without it.

In Tolkien's mythology, the ultimate symbol of magic and the machine is the One Ring of Power, Sauron's Ring, forged in Mount Doom, and into which Sauron poured much of his spirit and will. He made it to dominate the other rings of power: the three of the Elves, the seven of the Dwarves, and the nine of the men. Indeed, the sole purpose of the One Ring is to re-order the world in Sauron's image, to mock, to corrupt, and to pervert Ilúvatar's creation. Of the nineteen lesser ring-bearers, only the Elven ring-bearers had understood Sauron's machinations and prevented his control over them with the One Ring. Still, all of the works they produced and preserved with the three rings were subject, ultimately, to the One Ring. If he obtained it, he would turn their subcreations to dust. And even the Elves were not free from pride, though their motives remained good. As Tolkien wrote, immortality brought sadness to the Elves, and their art became "antiquarian, and their efforts all really a kind of embalming."[86]

At one level the One Ring represents the machine, as both aid the desire to control others. At a more fundamental level the Ring represents sin itself, specifically the first sin, as recorded in Genesis: "ye too shall be as Gods." Like Plato's Ring of Gyges, it renders one invisible, and it gives "power according to [one's] stature."[87] To Gollum, it is his "precious." It consumes him. One who wears it becomes slowly habituated to sin rather than to goodness, decorum, and virtue. The more one uses it, the more one "fades: [one] becomes in the end invisible permanently, and walks in the twilight under the eye of the dark power that rules the Ring," Gandalf explains, and "sooner or later the dark power will devour him."[88] The Ring as sin reshapes Gollum. Formerly a hobbit, he is now a disfigured shell of his former self, "stretched" beyond what nature or Ilúvatar had intended.[89] Bilbo, too, becomes stretched. Though 111 years old at the beginning of *The Lord of the Rings*, he appears to be about fifty. The Ring has "preserved" him, much like it had preserved the much older Gollum. At the beginning of *The Lord of the Rings*, the Ring is slowly and subtly beginning to possess him. When Bilbo refuses to leave it to Frodo, Gandalf reprimands him: "It has got far too much hold on you. Let it go! And then you can go yourself, and be free."[90] Gandalf refuses to touch it, knowing the temptation to use it for good would be too strong within him. "Yet the way of the Ring to my heart is by pity, pity for weakness and the desire of strength to do good," Gandalf explains to Frodo.[91] Other characters become tempted by it throughout the story: Galadriel, Boromir, and Denethor, to name just a few. The former resists, the latter two fail, and it proves their ultimate undoing. Even Frodo fails to resist it completely, almost declaring himself Lord of the Ring.

If power tempts even the good, it ultimately consumes the evil. Sauron's lust for power proved his ultimate demise. It blinded him and thus left him unable to fathom the motives of the side of good.[92] The

Ring, he assumed, would be used as a weapon against him in the War of the Rings. When looking at his own enemies, Sauron understood Saruman's corruption and greed perfectly well, since both Sauron and Saruman were corrupted Maiar. They would follow the same path, and Sauron anticipated Saruman's moves perfectly, which allowed him to dominate Saruman while all the while hastening his corruption. But Sauron mistakenly thought that the Istari were "emissaries from the Valar, seeking to establish their lost power again and 'colonize' Middle-earth, as a mere effort of defeated imperialists (without knowledge or sanction of Eru)."[93] Gandalf baffled Sauron. He too was a Maia, though one of slightly less power and intelligence than Sauron or Saruman, and slightly more power and intelligence than Radagast. That Gandalf would choose to have the Ring destroyed rather than wield it himself as a new dominating power eluded Sauron. Only in his final moments, when Frodo declares himself the new lord in the Crack of Mount Doom, does Sauron realize his error. Hence, Frodo and Sam journey into Mordor unseen and unexpected, as the Dark Lord would never think to look for them there.

All secondary evils—whether corrupt trees, spiders, Orcs, or Balrogs, to name a few mischievous and clever evils within Tolkien's mythology—seem to be controlled, or at the very least, heavily influenced, by the wills of either Morgoth, Sauron, or Saruman (himself, of course, unwittingly controlled by Sauron). This reverses, or, at the very least, puts a new spin on, Aristotle's metaphysical notions of love, order, and the Prime Mover's motivations and actions. Aristotle argued that the Prime Mover threw forth his love and called it back to himself. Tolkien presented the diabolical Morgoth as the mirror image of Divine Love, a grotesque evil calling all evil back to him in his strongholds in the North (*The Silmarillion*). Sauron and his secondary evils behave in a similar fashion and have a similar relationship in *The Lord of the Rings*. "Mordor draws all wicked things," Gandalf told Frodo, "and the Dark Power was bending all its will to gather them there."[94]

In the late 1950s or early 1960s, Tolkien began a sequel (a "thriller") to *The Lord of the Rings* titled "The New Shadow."[95] Tolkien abandoned "The New Shadow" fairly quickly, finding the work extraordinarily depressing. But a fragment of the story remains extant, and it revolves around a mysterious meeting at which secrets will be revealed.

"The New Shadow" takes place roughly a century after Aragorn's death. The men of Middle-earth have again become bored with goodness and beauty. Inevitably, restlessness has set in, disordering both the rulers and the younger generation. The new kings have been concerned only with power, and the young men have created violent gangs in imitation of the Orcs.[96] The thesis of the story is stated wisely by the main character Borlas: "Deep indeed run the roots of Evil . . . and the black sap is strong in them. That tree will never be slain. Let men hew it as often as they may, it will thrust up shoots again as soon as they turn aside. Not even at the Feast of the Felling should the axe be hung up on the wall."[97] As Gandalf warns prior to the defeat of Sauron in the War of the Ring: "Other evils there are that may come; for Sauron is himself but a servant or emissary. Yet it is not our part to master all the tides of the world, but to do what is in us for the succour of those years wherein we are set, uprooting the evil in the fields that we know, so that those who live after may have clean earth to till. What weather they shall have is not ours to rule."[98] Apparently, Tolkien did not feel it was in him to write another story bearing out the truth of Borlas and Gandalf's assertions.

Tolkien's reluctance is understandable. Leiber and Moorcock are right: Tolkien is far more concerned with understanding the intricacies of the Good than he is with delving into the dark complexities of evil. As Tolkien makes clear throughout his legendarium, it is Good that can rightly claim the true possession and ownership of imagination. And he firmly believed that although evil will continue to manifest itself, the Good is ultimately more powerful, and will in time emerge the victor.

Chapter 6

Middle-earth and Modernity

Since the publication of *The Lord of the Rings* in the mid-1950s, Tolkien's Middle-earth stories have often been dismissed as escapist. Tolkien, the critics argue, lived in a dream world. Andrew Rissik, writing for the *London Guardian*, has voiced the standard view of Tolkien's detractors: "After the annihilating traumas of the last century, it's merely perverse to ascribe greatness to this airy but strangely simplified mock-Teutonic never-never land, where races and species intermingle at will and great battles are fought but there is never any remotely convincing treatment of those fundamental human concerns through which all societies ultimately define themselves—religion, philosophy, politics and the conduct of sexual relationships."[1] Journalist Roz Kaveney has argued in a similar vein, noting that advocates of Tolkien's work often use his books as bludgeons in a "broadside attack on modernism and even on realism."[2] And feminist critic Germaine Greer has contended that Tolkien's works dismiss the "great struggles of the twentieth century," such as "politics, war, the black movement, and [the] sexual revolution."[3]

Tolkien, it is true, did not embrace the twentieth century. But neither did he run from it. Rather, he forced his readers to confront their world from a different perspective, a perspective informed by the power of myth, symbol, and examples of true heroism. The modern and industrialized world seemed to have little use, he knew, for the older way of seeing and knowing represented by his mythology. Nor did it have much use for the decentralized mode of social and political organization in which he believed. Rather, tyranny characterized Tolkien's century, and Tolkien passionately hated tyranny, whether it came from the Left or Right of the political spectrum. And as to the "escapist" charge? As Tolkien once told C. S. Lewis, those who most hate escapism are jailers.[4]

———————

Man is nothing, Tolkien believed, if not a subcreator made in the image of the true creator. God places each uniquely created individual in a certain time, in a certain place, with certain gifts, for a certain reason. For Tolkien, modernity was committed to the denial of God as the author of man and the world. And once man denies God, he denies his true self. When Harvey Breit of the *New York Times Book Review* asked Tolkien in 1955 what made him tick, Tolkien responded: "I don't tick. I am not a machine. (If I did tick, I should have no views on it, and you had better ask the winder.)"[5] Tolkien was not just being flippant or curmudgeonly. The question, which reflected modernity's tendency to mechanize man, deeply bothered him. Tolkien, on the whole, despised mechanization, arguing that it reflected modernity's attack on nature, its attempt to dominate and subjugate all aspects of the given world. "There is a tragedy and despair of all machinery laid bare," he wrote, and human fallenness "makes our . . . devices not only fail of their desire but turn to new and horrible evil." He referred to technology in general as "Mordor-gadgets," and to fighter planes during World War II as "Nazgul-birds."[6] When Tolkien learned of the American dropping of the atomic bomb on Hiroshima, he responded with horror. "The utter folly of these lunatic physicists to consent to do such work for war-purposes: calmly plotting the destruction of the world!"[7] Allies of Mordor, he later noted mockingly, had created the atomic bomb, "to use the Ring for their own (of course most excellent) purposes."[8]

Though Tolkien especially disliked the machines of war, he frequently complained about the machines that were increasingly coming to be associated with everyday life in the twentieth century. He had once owned a car, but in his later life he refused to own one after he saw what the planners did to change the city of Oxford to accommodate automobiles.[9] Once, when Clyde Kilby was visiting Tolkien, a motorcycle passed by. "That is an Orc," Tolkien proclaimed.[10] When his fellow Inkling George Sayer brought out a tape recorder in 1952 and asked Tolkien to read some of his then-unpublished *Lord of the Rings*, Tolkien seemed both amused and frightened. Sayer had himself carefully considered whether to show Tolkien the recording device, knowing of his extreme dislike of machines. "He might curse it and curse me with it," Sayer feared.[11] "He had never seen one before," Sayer later wrote, "and said whimsically that he ought to cast out any devil that might be in it by recording a prayer, the Lord's Prayer in Gothic."[12] When the owners of the first hydrofoil attempted to honor Tolkien by christening it *Shadowfax*, Tolkien labeled the plan "monstrous."[13] Shadowfax, the majestic horse rode by Gandalf, was a gift of the angelic Valar, not a man-made abomination. Tolkien's disdain for machines reveals itself throughout the Middle-earth works. Along with the Orcs, Sauron and the corrupted Saruman design and employ machines frequently, a fact that for Tolkien adequately served to symbolize their corruption.

For Tolkien, the tree stood in opposition to the machine, and as such served to represent the premodern era. To him, trees appeared beautiful and wise. He "had loved trees since childhood and pointed out the trees he had himself planted," Kilby wrote of his first visit to Tolkien's home in Oxford. "One easily understands Michael Tolkien's remark that from his father he 'inherited an almost obsessive love of trees' and considered the massive felling of trees 'the wanton murder of living beings for very shoddy ends.'"[14]

Tolkien found the abuse of trees unacceptable. "I am (obviously) much in love with plants and above all trees, and always have been," Tolkien wrote to his publisher, Houghton Mifflin, "and I find human maltreatment of them as hard to bear as some find ill-treatment of animals."[15] Discussing the inspiration for his wonderful short story about purgatory, "Leaf by Niggle," Tolkien wrote:

> There was a great tree—a huge poplar with vast limbs—visible through
> my window even as I lay in bed. I loved it, and was anxious about it. It
> had been savagely mutilated some years before, but had gallantly grown
> new limbs—though of course not with the unblemished grace of its for-
> mer natural self; and now a foolish neighbour was agitating to have it
> felled. Every tree has its enemy, few have an advocate. (Too often the hate
> is irrational, a fear of anything large and alive, and not easily tamed or
> destroyed, though it may clothe itself in pseudo-rational terms).[16]

Tolkien always took the side of trees in their disputes with humans.
He lamented that "[t]he savage sound of the electric saw is never silent
wherever trees are still found growing."[17]

Tolkien employed trees, as both symbols and characters, throughout his Middle-earth works. In *The Silmarillion*, the Two Trees of
Valinor, Telperion and Laurelin, first give light to the earth. Two of
the angelic Valar created them, and Fëanor, the greatest of the Elven
craftsmen, created the Silmarils, which captured the light of the two
trees. Repulsed by their beauty, Morgoth and his ally, Ungoliant,
attacked the trees and mortally wounded them.

> Then the Unlight of Ungoliant rose up even to the roots of the
> Trees, and Melkor sprang upon the mound; and with his black
> spear he smote each Tree to its core, wounded them deep, and their
> sap poured forth as it were their blood, and was spilled upon the
> ground. But Ungoliant sucked it up, and going then from Tree to
> Tree she set her black beak to their wounds, till they were drained;
> and the pain of Death that was in her went into their tissues and
> withered them, root, branch, and leaf; and they died.[18]

In Platonic fashion, the Valar created the Sun and the Moon, only
poor reflections of the true light of the trees. In the end of all things,
Ilúvatar (God the Father) may allow the return of Telperion and Laurelin, though the end cannot be clearly foretold by mortals. And when
the white tree grows again in Gondor at the end of the Third Age, the
residents of Middle-earth recognize this as a further sign that Aragorn
is the true king.

One of Tolkien's more revealing creations is Treebeard, the ultimate personification of Tolkien's anti-modernism. Treebeard, a giant, sentient tree-like creature first introduced in *The Lord of the Rings*, despises Orcs, axes, and machines. With his deep, woodwind-like voice, Treebeard speaks deliberately, letting his newfound friends, the hobbits Merry and Pippin, know that "real names tell you the story of the things they belong to in my language, in the Old Entish."[19] He and his kind, the Ents, serve as shepherds for all trees as well as historians and chroniclers of events in Middle-earth. Treebeard convinces the other Ents to attack Saruman, the traitorous wizard at Isengard. "He is plotting to become a Power," Treebeard says. "He has a mind of metal and wheels; and he does not care for growing things, except as far as they serve him for the moment." With that, Treebeard and his army of Ents march on the unsuspecting Saruman and his fortress. There they find Saruman's "treasuries, store-houses, armouries, smithies, and great furnaces. Iron wheels revolved there endlessly, and hammers thudded. At night plumes of vapour steamed from the vents, lit from beneath with red light, or blue, or venomous green."[20] The attack was a furious one, especially for the deliberate, long-lived Ents: "An angry Ent is terrifying," Merry explains, having witnessed the destruction of Isengard. "Their fingers, and their toes, just freeze on to rock; and they tear it up like bread-crust. It was like watching the work of great tree-roots in a hundred years, all packed into a few moments."[21]

The mechanization of man and nature revealed its full diabolical potential in the statist crimes committed during the twentieth century, a century Tolkien loathed.[22] Considering the death and brutality littering its landscape, it is hard to admire much in the century just passed. From the beginning of recorded history to 1900, governments murdered an estimated 133 million of their own citizens. Between 1901 and 1987, governments killed nearly 170 million of their own citizens. Stalin slaughtered 41 million, Mao 35 million, and Hitler 21 million. Another 38.5 million died in state-sponsored wars during the same period.[23] When some demographer gets around to making the final count for the century, including those killed in Africa, the former Yugoslavia, and China since 1987, the figure may push beyond 200 million.

Overwhelmed by the bloodshed of his era, Tolkien confronted in his works this deadly mix of war, industrialism, and nationalism. In one of the most haunting passages in *The Lord of the Rings*, Tolkien wrote:

> Dreadful as the Dead Marshes had been, and the arid moors of the Noman-land, more loathsome far was the country that the crawling day now slowly unveiled to his [Frodo's] shrinking eyes. Even to the Mere of Dead Faces, some haggard phantom of green spring would come; but here neither spring nor summer would ever come again. Here nothing lived, not even the leprous growths that feed on rottenness. The gasping pools were choked with ash and crawling muds, sickly white and grey, as if the mountains had vomited the filth of their entrails upon the lands about. High mounds of crushed and powdered rock, great cones of earth fire-blasted and poison-stained, stood like an obscene graveyard in endless rows, slowly revealed in the reluctant light.[24]

C. S. Lewis observed that only someone who had witnessed the trenches of war firsthand could have written this passage.[25] For Lewis, Tolkien's ability to transform reality into "symbol" precipitated his ability to describe war, and the results of war, so effectively and with such penetrating realism.[26] This is not to suggest that *The Lord of the Rings* serves as a simple allegory for the events of the twentieth century, a common charge of Tolkien's critics. In the preface to *The Fellowship of the Ring*, Tolkien wrote:

> The real war does not resemble the legendary war in its process or its conclusion. If it had inspired or directed the development of the legend, then certainly the Ring would have been seized and used against Sauron; he would have not been annihilated but enslaved, and Barad-dûr would not have been destroyed but occupied. Saruman, failing to get possession of the Ring, would in the confusion

and treacheries of the time have found in Mordor the missing links in his own researches into Ring-lore, and before long he would have made a Great Ring of his own with which to challenge the self-styled Ruler of Middle-earth. In that conflict both sides would have held hobbits in hatred and contempt: they would not long have survived even as slaves.[27]

Though Tolkien especially loathed Adolf Hitler, the Germans of the Third Reich fascinated him. The Germans, he wrote in a letter to his son Michael, were "enemies whose virtues (and they are virtues) of obedience and patriotism are greater than ours in the mass." Because they were led by Hitler, however, they lived "under the curse of God." The one thing holding the German people together was Hitler's perversion of Northern European myth. Tolkien especially disliked the term "Nordic," viewing it as an adulteration of the true and rooted goodness of Germanic myths. "I have in this War a burning private grudge . . . against that ruddy little ignoramus Adolf Hitler," Tolkien continued to Michael, for "[r]uining, perverting, misapplying, and making for ever accursed that noble northern spirit, a supreme contribution to Europe, which I have ever loved, and tried to present in its true light. Nowhere, incidently, was it nobler than in England, nor more early sanctified and Christianized."[28] Unlike many of the prominent Englishmen of his day, Tolkien desired a soft peace with the German people after the war, laying the blame for the war at the feet of Hitler and his immediate subordinates.[29] "The destruction of Germany, be it 100 times merited," Tolkien wrote his son Christopher in January 1945 as Soviet tanks raced toward Berlin, "is one of the most appalling world-catastrophes."[30]

Some of Tolkien's critics—and even some of his friends—have claimed that Tolkien's Middle-earth works can be read as arguing for a benign, moderated type of middle-class fascism. Fred Inglis, for one, believes that Tolkien desired an English "steady vegetable pressure" variety of fascism. "Tolkien is no Fascist," writes Inglis, but "his great myth may be said, as Wagner's was, to prefigure the genuine ideals and nobilities of which Fascism is the dark negation.

Instead of the raucous bawling of Il Duce, the pentameter; instead of tanks and the goose step, horses and cloaks and lances; instead of Nuremberg, Frodo's farewell."[31] The Italian Fascists have even appropriated Tolkien and his works as their own. Though they have only recently adopted Bilbo Baggins as their symbol, their affiliation with Tolkien started in 1970, when a right-wing publisher first introduced a version of *The Lord of the Rings* to the Italian public. Echoing Inglis, journalist Nick Farrell assures his readers that Tolkien was no fascist. "Yet his world view was similar in many ways to that of fascists," Farrell writes. "He exalted order, hierarchy, the countryside and the mythical past [and] he despised industrialization and modernisation."[32]

But the readings of Inglis and Farrell are too simplistic. Like Lewis, Tolkien was strongly opposed to tyranny of any form. Lewis wrote penetratingly of communism and fascism, recognizing them both as manifestations of modernity's turn away from God and its embrace of the first sin, "ye too shall be gods." Like Tolkien, he recognized that both ideologies contained the trappings of goodness but had corrupted essences. "Fascism and Communism, like all other evils, are potent because of the good they contain or imitate," Lewis wrote. "And of course their occasion is the failure of those who left humanity starved of that particular good. This does not for me alter the conviction that they are very bad indeed. One of the things we must guard against is the penetration of both into Christianity."[33] Tolkien wrote that the saints living in the modern world were those "who have for all their imperfections never finally bowed head and will to the world or the evil spirit (in modern but not universal terms: mechanism, 'scientific' materialism, Socialism in either of its factions now at war)."[34]

As with many Roman Catholics of the 1930s and 1940s, Tolkien believed that communism represented a more dangerous form of tyranny than did fascism. If he hated fascism, he *really* hated communism. Many of the so-called fascists, he believed, such as Franco in Spain, actually protected the Roman Catholic Church, whereas the communists had always assaulted any form of theism, substituting their own ideology for Christian beliefs as rapidly and as violently as possible.[35] Tolkien was especially taken with the bullfighting ally of Franco, poet and Roman Catholic convert Roy Campbell. Meeting with Tolkien and Lewis in October 1944, Campbell reported the atrocities against Roman Catholics being committed by the communists and socialists in Spain. By the end of the evening, Tolkien concluded that Campbell was a modern-day Trotter (the earlier name for the character who would become Aragorn), ranging the world and struggling against the powers that be to defend God's glory. Lewis, though shaken by the conversation, remained less convinced of the purity of Campbell's motives.[36]

Tolkien also feared communism because of its potential to do evil after the end of the war. "[W]hat of the red Chrysanthemum in the East?," Tolkien asked. "[W]hen [World War II] is over, will ordinary people have any freedom left (or right) or will they have to fight for it, or will they be too tired to resist?"[37] Tolkien feared the loss of any part of the West to the Soviets, which he viewed as a truly foreign and eastern power, totally alien to the West. He labeled the Teheran conference of November 1943, at which the "Big Three" compromised their principles and sought to define the contours of the postwar world, a "ballyhoo." Tolkien sickened at the thought of "that old bloodthirsty murderer Josef Stalin inviting all nations to join a happy family of folks devoted to the abolition of tyranny and intolerance."[38] The worst scenario Tolkien could imagine was a world divided by the brutal, totalitarian Soviets and the commercially aggressive Americans. The world, Tolkien predicted, would become one homogeneous, cosmopolitan entity, with England a mere suburb. "May the curse of Babel strike all their tongues till they can only say 'baa baa,'" Tolkien wrote to Christopher. "I think I shall have to refuse to speak anything but Old Mercian."[39] Here, Tolkien echoed Christopher Dawson, a close friend of Inkling R. E. Havard. Only a year earlier, Dawson had written: "The time is approaching when the cities become one city—a Babylon which sets its mark on the mind of every man and woman and imposes the same pattern of behaviour on every human activity."[40]

Catholics had a special dislike of communism because of two important events in the late nineteenth and early twentieth centuries. First, in 1884 Pope Leo XIII had a vision in which he saw devils roaming the twentieth-century earth, laying much of it waste. Consequently, he composed the "Prayer to St. Michael," which asks God to unleash St. Michael the Archangel to fight with the demons and the devil, and instituted this as the concluding prayer at all masses.[41] Not surprisingly, then, many devout twentieth-century Catholics, Tolkien among them, viewed communism as a satanic irruption into the world. It is no coincidence that Tolkien gave Manwë a prominent role in the affairs of Middle-earth, since Manwë represents St. Michael.

Second, in 1917 in Fatima, Portugal, the Virgin Mary appeared to three children, giving them several secret prophecies regarding the course of the twentieth century. One of these was that communism would become the greatest worldly enemy of the Church in the twentieth century. The Bolshevik Revolution in late 1917, only months after the appearance at Fatima, gave credence to Mary's warnings. The Church quickly approved the apparition, and it no doubt was another important factor in the development of Tolkien's belief that communism was man's primary enemy. Throughout the century, devout Roman Catholics offered the prayer of the rosary for the fall of communism and the conversion of the Russians to Christianity. This remains one of the great untold stories of twentieth-century Catholic piety.

Interestingly, during the 1980s Tolkien's works served as handbooks for peaceful, Christian, anticommunist underground movements in Eastern Europe and Russia.[42] One former Czech dissident, Michal Semin, writes:

> Mordor was understood to be the "evil empire" of the Soviet Union. It was also placed in [the] east. The rings, of course, represent the seduction of the devil to take everything into merely human hands with no reference to [the] transcendent[al] end of man. They follow the path of the original "non serviam." Then the special role of the [hobbits], creatures of no special or magic powers, very simple

and to a certain degree worldly. This served to remind us that even ordinary Czech citizens may stand against the evil of totalitarianism without tanks and artillery. The whole book is also anti-utopian. It helped us to understand that . . . no paradise on earth should be expected.[43]

Not surprisingly, the Soviet Union forbade books by Tolkien, understanding that Moscow and Mordor were similar in essence if not in form. They also feared that Tolkien's Orcs might represent the proletariat. Nevertheless, prior to 1991, poorly translated, photocopied works circulated throughout the Russian underground.[44]

Evil does not always come in the form of war or totalitarian terror. Tolkien saw in the impersonal, machine-driven capitalism of the twentieth century, and especially its handmaiden, the democratic bureaucracies of the Western world, a form of soft tyranny almost as oppressive as fascism and communism. As much as Lewis in *The Abolition of Man* and *That Hideous Strength*, Tolkien feared the democratic conditioners and the "men without chests" who planned for the sake of planning, draining life of its vast richness and wonders. Bureaucrats especially targeted languages, Tolkien's speciality, and to the author, the spice of real life. "In modern England the usage has become disastrously confused by the maleficent interference of the Government with the usual object of governments: uniformity."[45]

When Merlin reappears after fifteen centuries of sleeping in Lewis's *That Hideous Strength*, he asks where they might find allies to combat the evil that threatens what remains of Christendom. Ransom responds:

> The poison was brewed in these West lands but it has spat itself everywhere by now. However far you went you would find the machines, the crowded cities, the empty thrones, the false writings, the barren books: men maddened with false promises and soured with true miseries, worshiping the iron works of their own hands, cut off from Earth their mother and from the Father in Heaven.

You might go East so far that East became West and you returned
to Britain across the great ocean, but even so you would not have
come out anywhere into the light. The shadow of one dark wing is
over all.[46]

Democracy, a newly fashionable word in England during the war,
was nothing but a sham, according to Tolkien. In ancient Greece,
democracy served as a fancy name for mob rule. Any Greek city-
state worth remembering, Tolkien wrote, is worth remembering precisely because of its centralized ability to mobilize and attack another
power.[47] Furthermore, Tolkien argued, democracy naturally ends in
slavery. "I am not a 'democrat' only because 'humility' and equality
are spiritual principles corrupted by the attempt to mechanize and
formalize them, with the result that we get not universal smallness
and humility, but universal greatness and pride, till some Orc gets
hold of a ring of power—and then we get and are getting slavery,"
Tolkien lamented, echoing a number of democracy's critics, from
Plato in the *Republic* to Tocqueville in *Democracy in America*.[48]

Tolkien never referred to himself as a member of one or another of
England's political parties, though he seems to have favored the Conservatives far more than Labor.[49] Discussing in 1965 the influence of
his surrogate parent, Father Morgan, however, Tolkien stated that the
priest's teachings "pierced even the 'liberal' darkness out of which I
came."[50] At other times, he revealed his own politics rather forcefully.
"My political opinions lean more and more to Anarchy (philosophi-
cally understood, meaning abolition of control not whiskered men
with bombs)—or to 'unconstitutional' Monarchy," Tolkien wrote to
his son Christopher. "I would arrest anybody who uses the word State
(in any sense other than the inanimate realm of England and its inhabitants, a thing that has neither power, rights nor mind); and after a
chance of recantation, execute them if they remained obstinate!"[51]

Hating machines and socialism of any shade—communist, fascist, or democratic—Tolkien's true affection fastened on rural and

agrarian society. Tolkien "once remarked to me that the feeling about home must have been quite different in the days when a family had fed on the produce of the same few miles of country for six generations, and that perhaps this was why they saw nymphs in the fountains and dryads in the wood—they were not mistaken for there was in a sense a real (not metaphorical) connexion between them and the countryside," Lewis wrote to a close friend. "What had been earth and air & later corn, and later still bread, really was in them." Instead, Tolkien concluded, according to Lewis, "We are synthetic men, uprooted. The strength of the hills is not ours."[52] In his diary in 1933, Tolkien recorded:

> I pass over the pangs to me of passing through Hall Green—become a huge tram-ridden meaningless suburb, where I actually lost my way—and eventually down what is left of beloved lands of childhood, and past the very gate of our cottage, now in the midst of a sea of new red-brick. The old mill still stands, and Mrs. Hunt's still sticks out into the road as it turns uphill; but the cross beyond the now fenced-in pool, where the bluebell land ran down into the mill lane, is now a dangerous crossing alive with motors and red lights. The White Ogre's house (which the children were excited to see) is become a petrol station, and most of Short Avenue and the elms between it and the crossing have gone. How I envy those whose precious early scenery has not been exposed to such violent and peculiarly hideous change.[53]

Whenever he came upon a countryside damaged by the forces of industrialization, Tolkien's mood would change dramatically, and he would speak of Orcs and their ravages.[54] "The dread Orcs, who look like the Chinese army, the Nazis, and our highways and streets, are what humanity looks like when deference has been replaced by power and civilization by efficiency," Guy Davenport wrote perceptively in his obituary of Tolkien.[55]

According to Joseph Pearce and Colin Wilson, both Tolkien scholars, Hilaire Belloc's and G. K. Chesterton's agrarian and distributist ideas strongly influenced Tolkien.[56] Like Jeffersonian agrarians, distributists argued that private property should be as evenly divided as possible and spread out among many rather than concentrated among the few. They viewed themselves as a middle way between state-centralized socialism and free-wheeling capitalism, which, they believed, tended toward concentration and monopoly. "That our free modern society in which the means of production are owned by a few being necessarily in unstable equilibrium," Belloc wrote in his 1912 book, *The Servile State*, "it is tending to reach a condition of stable equilibrium by the establishment of compulsory labor legally enforceable upon those who do not own the means of production for the advantage of those who do."[57]

Furthermore, if they do not own land individuals tend to become urbanized sophisticates, Belloc and Chesterton argued, thus destroying the continuity between generations that depends on rootedness in community. Finally, without land the individual's economic autonomy is drastically diminished. Simply put, the distributists desired a middle-class nation of independent and autonomous yeoman farmers and shopkeepers, a nation that promoted rather than retarded the discovery and development of the gifts God had given each individual uniquely. Belloc, Chesterton, and their allies were by no means the first to argue for such a vision. Classical republican political philosophers from Cicero to James Harrington and Thomas Jefferson have all claimed that decentralized, agrarian homesteads best promote a virtuous citizenry.[58]

In one of their most important arguments, the distributists claimed that with the loss of land, independence, and faith, uprooted modern men and women would turn to new symbols and new myths in which to root themselves. "There is a new religion which is not exactly the worship of the State, but the worship of the collective body (formerly called England, now quite commonly called the Empire), of which the individual is a member," Belloc wrote.[59] The Empire, Belloc warned, was becoming for secularized Englishmen a sacrosanct, self-justifying entity. Tolkien concurred, and in defiance of the trend he proclaimed during World War II, "I love England (not Great Britain and certainly not the British Commonwealth (grr!))."

The distributists and others, like Tolkien, who distrusted the modern, centralized secular state saw their views echoed in the Roman Catholic Church's social teaching. Pope Leo's 1879 encyclical, *Aeterni Patris* ("On the Restoration of Christian Philosophy"), and his 1891 encyclical, *Rerum Novarum* ("On the Condition of Labor"), provided especially powerful blueprints for the development of a truly Catholic social philosophy.[60]

The Shire serves as Tolkien's conception of the ideal agrarian republic. The Shire is a pre-modern society, and the hobbits who live there often seem innocent and childlike because they are: they live in a pre-cynical age. As farmers, shopkeepers, and craftsmen, hobbits live the good life. They eat, they drink, they smoke, they argue, they gossip, they collect too many gifts ("mathom"), they garden, and they love. "Hobbits are unobtrusive but very ancient people, more numerous formerly than they are today; for they love peace and quiet and good tilled earth: a well-ordered and well-farmed countryside was their favourite haunt," Tolkien wrote in the prologue to *The Fellowship of the Ring*. "They do not and did not understand or like machines more complicated than a forge-bellows, a water-mill, or a hand-loom, though they were skilful [sic] with tools."[61]

Tolkien confessed that the Shire was modeled on the pre-industrial England of his youth. "'The Shire' is based on rural England and not any other country in the world," Tolkien wrote to his publisher. "The toponymy of the Shire, to take the first list, is a 'parody' of that of rural England, in much the same sense as are its inhabitants: they go together and are meant to."[62] Politically, the Shire is, as C. S. Lewis described it, "almost anarchical."[63] Tolkien referred to it as "half republic half aristocracy," meaning essentially an isolationist Jeffersonian society ruled by natural elites.[64] In such a society, a good deal of one's reputation comes from family and kinship. Bilbo Baggins, for instance, is part Took, one of the most audacious of families in the Shire. Prior to the quest related in *The Hobbit*, Gandalf is taken with Bilbo almost exclusively for this reason.[65] In the

Shire, the head of a family group usually serves as a "chieftain."[66] No one hobbit or group of hobbits decreed new laws. Instead, the hobbits voluntarily obeyed the laws of a king who had been absent for one thousand years. These laws were known as "The Rules" because they were "both ancient and just."[67] In emergencies, which were few and far between, the head of the Took family served as president of the Shire-moot (a type of parliament) and as the leader of the local militia.[68] Twelve shirriffs policed the Shire, wearing a feather in their caps for identification. Their main job was to capture stray animals. A group of men also patrolled the borders of the Shire "to see that Outsiders of any kind, great or small, did not make themselves a nuisance."[69]

Families in the Shire, however, usually protected themselves. One of the more powerful and independent-minded hobbit families, the Brandybucks, lived on the edge of the Shire as a sort of hobbit colony called "Buckland." The head of the family, the "Master of the Hall," wielded considerable power over his own kin group. To protect themselves, the Brandybucks over generations built a twenty-mile-long hedge, known as the "High Hay."[70] When three Ringwraiths appeared in Buckland, searching for Frodo and the Ring, traditions long kept but usually unneeded proved effective. Signaling danger, "horns rang out. It rent the night like fire on a hilltop. AWAKE! FEAR! FIRE! FOES! AWAKE!" The Brandybucks grabbed arms and came to the rescue, driving away the evil, at least for the time being.[71]

In one of the most politically interesting chapters of *The Lord of the Rings*, "The Scouring of the Shire," Frodo, Sam, Merry, and Pippin return to find the Shire turned into a fascist industrial state run by "The Chief." The Chief has set up smoke-belching factories, built ugly houses to replace hobbit holes, and has torn up rows of trees, gardens, and homes, displacing a number of hobbits. The Chief has established new rules, mostly laws taxing and regulating the use and consumption of foodstuffs and various materials. Like a puritan dictator, the Chief has also outlawed beer. The hobbits have become enslaved, working under the watchful eyes of gangs of men. Perhaps most disturbing, several hobbits are collaborating with the fascist bullies. "'This is worse than Mordor!' said Sam. 'Much worse in a way. It comes home to you, as they say; because it is home, and you remember it before it was all ruined.'"

The hobbits, of course, are victorious against the Chief and his men. Under the leadership of Sam, Merry, and Pippin, the hobbits respond by issuing the traditional alarm of danger. Very quickly, and with only limited bloodshed, thanks to the influence of the now-pacifist Frodo, the hobbits take back the government of the Shire, driving out the men and their leader, Sharkey.

The harder part, as with any war, comes with the clean-up. Working as a cohesive and harmonious community, the hobbits release the political prisoners, many of whom had been nearly starved to death, tear down every one of the factories, and rebuild the gardens of the Shire. Sam replants trees throughout the Shire, using one grain of the mysterious gift of Galadriel with every seedling. The following spring, the Shire returns to normal, blessed by Sam's efforts and Galadriel's gift. Indeed, the Shire had never experienced such a spring or summer. The year 1420 witnessed in the Shire

> an air of richness and growth, and a gleam of a beauty beyond that of mortal summers that flicker and pass upon this Middle-earth. All the children born or begotten in that year, and there were many, were fair to see and strong, and most of them had a rich golden hair that had before been rare among hobbits. The fruit was so plentiful that young hobbits very nearly bathed in strawberries and cream; and later they sat on the lawns under the plum-trees and ate, until they had made piles of stones like small pyramids or the heaped skulls of a conqueror, and then they moved on. And no one was ill, and everyone was pleased, except those who had to mow the grass.[72]

Tolkien was not a strict republican in the classical sense, even though the Shire suggests such a reading. Like many Catholics of his day and age, Tolkien retained a fondness for monarchy throughout his life.[73] However indirect or imagined, the Shire was ruled by a monarch for nearly a thousand years prior to the crowning of Aragorn. That the king did not exist does not matter. The members of the Shire acted as though he did. Tolkien's story therefore faithfully reflects the image of the "good king" that remained powerful in the Roman Catholic imagination of his era. "After the calamities of the Reformation, English Civil War, Glorious, French, Industrial, and Russian Revolutions, etc.," Charles Coulombe explains, "the king became . . . the exiled leader of the faithful, whose return alone would bring a return to the old ways, and an end to change and unrest."[74] Aragorn represents the ideal king: noble, chivalrous, powerful, and healing.

"My opinion of current affairs is not as depressed as some people's," Tolkien told an interviewer in 1966. "I should say I'm a bit frightened that the Greeks hadn't got something in the saying that those whom the gods wish to destroy they first drive mad. Our modern world is like the tower of Babel—wild noise and confusion. But I think that a little history cures you. Living at the end of the sixteenth century would have been just as bad, but then there weren't so many people around." Today, machines have destroyed "certain things that were good, were beautiful, were more nourishing to the human person."[75] But we cannot choose our time or place, only what we do with the time that is given to us. "I look East, West, North, South, and I do not see Sauron," Tolkien told a Dutch audience. "But I see that Saruman has many descendants. We Hobbits have against them no magic weapons. Yet, my gentle hobbits, I give you this toast: To the Hobbits. May they outlast the Sarumans and see spring again in the trees."[76] Tolkien wrote to Lewis, in defiance,

> *I will not walk with your progressive apes,*
> *erect and sapient. Before them gapes*
> *the dark abyss to which their progress tends—*
> *if by God's mercy progress ever ends,*
> *and does not ceaselessly revolve the same*
> *unfruitful course with changing of a name.*[77]

The Nature of Grace Proclaimed

In the summer of 2000, a Unitarian church in Bloomington, Indiana, held a citywide forum to discuss an eco-terrorist attack that had
recently been perpetrated by a group calling itself the Environmental
Liberation Front (E.L.F.). E.L.F. had burned down a house that was
being built in an area alleged to be environmentally sensitive. Just as
the forum proceedings were about to begin, a lawyer representing an
environmentalist group known as Elf Lore issued a subpoena claiming
a misuse of the term and word "E.L.F." Said a member of Elf Lore,
while pointing at the spokesperson for E.L.F., "you all are not Elves of
any kind, but Orcs!"[1]

Elf Lore, which sees itself as attempting to live out the hobbits'
message of communalism and harmony with nature, is just one
example of the Tolkien-inspired environmental groups that flour-
ished primarily in the 1960s and early 1970s. Indeed, Tolkien's association with the youth rebellion of that era is one reason why, with
a few notable exceptions, several generations of academics have
viewed Tolkien's mythology as little more than a psychedelic "sword
and sorcery" story. Harold Bloom, for one, has contended that *The
Lord of the Rings* is "inflated, over-written, tendentious, and mor-
alistic in the extreme. Is it not a giant Period Piece?"[2] Simply stated,
writes Bloom, Tolkien "met a need in the early days of the Coun-
ter-Culture."[3] Specifically, the need for escape. "Didn't we bury all
that stuff along with patchouli oil and LSD?" one Scottish commentator has asked. "The wise will recall that Tolkien fanaticism
has long been a barometer of idiocy and poor personal hygiene."[4]

Indeed, Tolkien's critical reputation is not helped when books like *The Tolkien Reader*, reissued by Ballantine in spring 2002, appear with psychedelic covers. On that book the conservative Roman Catholic Oxford don appears to have just dropped acid.

It is interesting to speculate as to what Tolkien would have made of all this. Doubtless he would not necessarily have recognized modern environmentalists as his allies. Unlike some radical greens, he did not believe that for nature to be conserved and respected humanity had to be devalued. Rather, he thought that the natural world was a gift from God and that man was obligated to act as its steward. In his unfinished story of the Fourth Age, "The New Shadow," Tolkien addressed the question directly.

> You spoke of the judgement of trees in these matters. But trees are not judges. The children of the One are the masters. My judgement as one of them you know already. The evils of the world were not at first in the great Theme, but entered with the discords of Melkor. Men did not come with these discords; they entered afterwards as a new thing direct from Eru, the One, and therefore they are called His children, and all that was in the Theme they have, for their own good, the right to use—and rightly, without pride or wantonness, but reverence.[5]

"In truth, nature begins to relate to us only when we begin to indwell it, when culture begins in it," Romano Guardini wrote in the mid-1920s. "Culture then develops and, bit by bit, nature is refashioned. We create our own world, shaped by thoughts and controlled not merely by natural urges but by ends that we set to serve ourselves as intellectual and spiritual beings, an environment that is related to us and brought into being by us."[6] In Tolkien's mythology, Rivendell best represents living with nature, the Shire represents the agrarian use of nature, and Orthanc and Mordor represent the exploitation, domination, and, consequently, the destruction of nature.

Tolkien also dealt with the worship of nature with his character of Radagast, one of the Istari, who becomes so enamored with nature and creation that he ultimately forsakes its author. He even unwittingly aids Saruman in the capture and imprisonment of Gandalf at the beginning of the War of the Ring. Known as Gandalf's cousin, Radagast the Brown lives on the southern edge of Mirkwood and is "a worthy wizard, a master of shapes and changes of hue; and he has much lore of herbs and beasts, and birds are especially his friends," says Gandalf.[7] If Gandalf embodies elements of St. Boniface and Odin, Radagast embodies elements of St. Francis of Assisi and the Czech mythological figure, Radegast, often imagined as a bird tamer.[8] Like St. Francis, Radagast is described in *The Silmarillion* as "the friend of all beasts and birds" and in *Unfinished Tales* as dressed in "earthen brown," like a Franciscan.[9] Too enamored with nature and forgetting his mission to aid Middle-earth in the fight against Sauron, however, he gives aid to the enemy by lending him birds as messengers and, ultimately, as spies.[10] "Radagast the Bird-tamer! Radagast the Simple! Radagast the Fool!," Saruman sneers mockingly—but truthfully.[11] One wonders if Tolkien intended a comment on the thought of St. Francis as well.

Environmentalists are not the only ones who have laid claim to Tolkien's legacy. Perhaps more preponderant are the legions of fantasy writers, fantasy readers, occult card players (such as *Magic: The Gathering*), and *Dungeons and Dragons* players. While fantasy as a medium has existed for thousands of years, the commercialization and categorization of fantasy as a distinct genre began in the 1960s with the immense popularity of Tolkien. At times it seems nearly impossible not to read "At last, a worthy successor to Tolkien," on the back of a fantasy book.[12] Though Tolkien did not invent fantasy, "he elevated it and redefined it, to such an extent that it will never be the same again," as acclaimed fantasy author George R. R. Martin has argued.[13] Tolkien "has had many imitators, and imitators of imitators, and imitators of imitators of imitators, until some heroic-quest fantasies resemble nothing so much as blurry sixth-generation photocopies of his great work," complains professional historian and novelist Harry Turtledove.[14] Many fantasy stories are at best simple good versus evil stories, while a goodly number are but bizarre explorations and glorifications of faux medievalism and the occult. As Jane Yolen writes, fantasy often has "degenerated into a kind of mythic silliness—elves in fur loinclothes, pastel unicorns, coy talking swords, and a paint-by-number medieval setting with the requisite number of dirty inns, evil wizards, and gentle hairy-footed beings of various sexual persuasions."[15] Ursula Le Guin, one of the greatest living fantasy writers, contends that "[c]ommodified fantasy takes no risks: it invents nothing, but imitates and trivializes. It proceeds by depriving the old stories of their intellectual and ethical complexities, turning their action into violence, their actors to dolls, and their truth-telling to sentimental platitude."[16] Tolkien would find little in common with the contemporary fantasy genre. For Tolkien, faerie and myth had a significance far beyond anything most contemporary fantasy writers and fans imagine.

Nonetheless, Tolkien's fantasy appeal is largely responsible for the unpredictable spread of his popularity. For example, Tolkien's popularity in Russia has soared since the fall of communism.[17] Some Tolkien fan clubs there simply meet to discuss Tolkien and the meaning of his mythology. Others, however, take it much further, dressing in faux-medieval garb and gathering in places like Gorky Park to, as one female fan explained, "act out scenes from fantasies, not just Tolkien but writers like the Strugatsky brothers and Ursula Le Guin. People hitchhike from all over the country. Sometimes as many as 500 turn up. We divide into camps and fight with swords."[18] "They took me up the hill to Eglador, or the Forgotten Land," writes one reporter, "where dozens of teenagers gathered around a small campfire. All kinds of young people were there—punks, hippies, fans of heavy metal—but their petty differences were unimportant compared with their common love of Tolkien. They seemed to be the intellectual cream of Russian youth."[19] Why are the Russians so taken with Tolkien? They may see in his world an escape from social anarchy: "Young people who remember the old system are instinctively trying to rediscover it. Soviet communist propaganda has gone, but they find many of the same rules in Tolkien's medieval mystical world. Tolkien characters live by the principle of the public good being superior to the private needs. The same principles were drummed by the communists into little boys and girls."[20] In the former Soviet Republic of Kazakhstan, Tolkien followers, known there, as in Russia, as the Tolkienisti, have been arrested for carrying such "concealed weapons" as rubber axes and wooden swords, which they use for mock battle.[21] Kazakhstan's pro-Islamic government has arrested such Tolkien devotees for "being Satanists and conducting dark rituals."[22]

Then there are the fanatics. Three decades after the great writer's death, Tolkien cultists still harass the Tolkien children mercilessly. "The Tolkien family is under perpetual abuse of one kind or another," Father John Tolkien revealed in 2001. "It goes on all the time." Tolkien's son Christopher "doesn't live in England any more and when he comes to England he doesn't use his own name. Christopher lives in France and has had some trouble recently with people trying to get at him. He keeps wild boars in his garden, which is a little bit dangerous but they are useful when people become a nuisance."[23]

But in the end Tolkien's popularity goes well beyond the environmentalists, the fantasy devotees, and the freaks. Approximately 150,000,000 copies of *The Lord of the Rings* have sold throughout the world.[24] His American publisher, Houghton Mifflin, regards Tolkien as its "great and treasured crown jewel."[25] Given the phenomenal success of Peter Jackson's film adaptation of *The Lord of the Rings*, there is no indication that it is a jewel that will lose its luster anytime soon.

When New Line Cinema's first installment of *The Lord of the Rings* trilogy appeared in summer 2002, the true Tolkien fan had every right to be apprehensive of director Peter Jackson's project. It seemed unlikely that anyone who could direct *Heavenly Creatures*—a chilling movie about two teenagers who murder one of their mothers by crushing her skull with a brick—could ever properly capture Tolkien's vision. It seemed a reasonable fear that Jackson would, at worst, pervert Tolkien's mythology for immoral ends, and that at best he would produce an action movie devoid of Tolkien's deeper meaning. And yet, from the opening chords of the epic-style soundtrack and Galadriel's narration—"History became legend, legend became myth"—Jackson's version of Middle-earth justly captivated audiences worldwide. From the Elvish and Númenórean armies of the Last Alliance to the breaking of the Fellowship, Jackson faithfully captured the spirit and essence of Tolkien's vision in *The Fellowship of the Ring*.[26] At times, indeed, the viewer desires to jump into the landscapes portrayed in the film, especially the pastoral Shire and the ethereal Rivendell. Some of Jackson's additions are similarly brilliant: Boromir teaching Pippin and Merry to sword fight; Sam using pots and pans to fight Orcs; the Orcs scurrying down pillars like insects in Moria.

But most importantly, Jackson's film version includes even more explicit religious symbolism than does Tolkien's book. When Arwen first appears—one of the Jackson changes many fans had particularly dreaded prior to seeing the movie—she does so as a female St. Raphael from the deuterocanonical Book of Tobias. She partially heals Frodo's Morgul wound with a prayer: "By grace given to me, I give freely of myself to you." Here, Jackson adopts T. A. Shippey's interpretation of the Elves as semi-fallen angels. In his learned *Road to Middle-Earth*, Shippey claims that Tolkien's Elves represent the "neutral angels" of the early medieval poem, "The Legend of St. Michael," in which a number of angels declared neutrality in the war between St. Michael and Satan. Some lean toward God's side, others toward the devil's.[27]

In another of Jackson's additions, the future king Aragorn twice makes a rudimentary sign of the cross: when Galadriel first appears and when Boromir dies heroically. And, in possibly the most powerful moment in the movie, Gandalf faces the ancient demon Balrog at the Bridge of Khazad-dûûm, declaring his service to the Secret Fire. Jackson could have easily left this out, as it is rather confusing to almost any viewer who has not read the books. But much to his credit, Jackson keeps in this line, the most important religious statement in the book, and one of the only direct references to Ilúvatar in the entire trilogy.

In terms of cinematography, Jackson borrowed heavily from 1990s epics such as "Last of the Mohicans" and "Braveheart." Filled with action, few moments of respite exist in the film. For three hours, one sits on the edge of one's seat, as Frodo and the rest of the Fellowship make their way through Middle-earth, besieged on all sides by increasingly powerful evils from Mordor and Isengard. As I noted in an earlier chapter, one Tolkien critic has contended—rightly, I think—that the Fellowship represents the Church struggling through time and space against its many enemies. Jackson depicts that image beautifully. Whatever happens with the rest of the trilogy, the first installment is a faithful adaptation and representation of Tolkien's sacramental vision.

———————————

Regardless of what the entertainment industry, environmentalists, fantasy enthusiasts, Italian Fascists, or any other element of the modern and postmodern world does to, or with, Tolkien and his legacy, Tolkien's own vision, in which he was always confident, remained consistent throughout his adult life. That vision, which attempted to use myth to return the Western world to faith and right reason, in its essence parallels the sentiments of numerous twentieth-century scholars and artists collectively known as Christian humanists. We saw in the introduction that the Christian humanist asks two fundamental questions: 1) what is the role of man within God's creation? and 2) how does man order himself within God's creation?

Perhaps the primary burden of the work of the Christian humanists was to show that man is not the creator of his own world, but is a creature who inevitably lives under the natural and divine law. He is obligated, therefore, to assume an attitude of humility and piety before the world—and before its transcendent source and governor. Indeed, to apotheosize man and his works is to succumb to the words of the first temptation: "ye too shall be as gods." In the view of Tolkien and the rest of the Christian humanists, these are the words on which all ideology—whether communism, fascism, or any of the variants of either—is based. To the Christian humanist, ide-

ology, one of the chief characteristics of modernity, can be defined
as "a political formula that promises mankind an earthly paradise."
But, as Russell Kirk points out, "in cruel fact what ideology has created is a series of terrestrial hells."[28] Instead of trying to force real,
living, historically rooted human beings to fit the abstract imagin-
ings of ideologies, man must live within and order himself according
to the natural law, something Cicero understood:

> True law is right reason in agreement with nature; it is of universal
> application, unchanging and everlasting; it summons to duty by its
> commands, and averts from wrongdoing by its prohibitions. And it
> does not lay its commands or prohibitions upon good men in vain,
> though neither have any effect on the wicked. It is a sin to try to
> alter this law, nor is it allowable to attempt to repeal any part of
> it, and it is impossible to abolish entirely. We cannot be freed from
> its obligation by senate or people, and we need not look outside
> ourselves for an expounder or interpreter of it. And there will not
> be different laws at Rome and at Athens, or different laws now and
> in the future, but one eternal and unchangeable law will be valid
> for all nations and all times, and there will be one master and ruler,
> that is, God, over us all, for he is the author of this law, its promul-
> gator, and its enforcing judge.[29]

St. Paul affirms the universal visibility of the natural law in his letter to
the Romans, when he writes: "Ever since the creation of the world his
invisible nature, namely, his eternal power and deity, has been clearly
perceived in the things that have been made."[30]

In addition, for the Christian humanist the Incarnation proves
the intrinsic worth of each human person, despite the fallenness that
each human person has inherited because of Adam's sin. Thus, persons are never to be used as means to a "higher" ends. Rather, each
life possesses a unique dignity. As Pope John Paul II has explained,
"the concept of [the] person as the unique and unrepeatable center of freedom and responsibility, whose inalienable dignity must be
recognized . . . , has proved to be the cornerstone of any genuinely
human civilization."[31] Of course, the devaluation of personal dig-

nity is one of the hallmarks of the ideologue. It is no surprise, then, that the ideologically motivated dictators of the twentieth century perpetrated by far the greatest slaughter any century of human history has ever seen. T. S. Eliot stated it bluntly: "If you will not have God (and He is a jealous God) you should pay your respects to Hitler or Stalin."[32]

Another characteristic of Christian humanism is its belief that, as a creature of God, each person has a responsibility to strive for excellence and creativity. As St. Paul wrote in his Letter to the Philippians: "Finally, brethren, whatever is true, whatever is honorable, whatever is just, whatever is pure, whatever is lovely, whatever is gracious, if there is any excellence, if there is anything worthy of praise, think about these things."[33] By using one's gifts for the Body of Christ, one glorifies creation and praises God for the gifts he has lent. Sanctifying one's work makes it *opus Dei*, the work of and for God. For Tolkien, especially, one of the greatest gifts of God to each human person was the power of imagination; wielded properly and accompanied by grace, it would readily outwit evil.

To find the context of Christian humanism—its sources of inspiration as well as its animation—one must look to two profound nineteenth-century papal encyclicals, both issued by Pope Leo: the 1879 encyclical *Aeterni Patris* ("On the Restoration of Christian Philosophy"), and the 1891 encyclical *Rerum Novarum* ("Condition of Labor"). The former re-examined philosophy in light of progressivist and humanist thought, while the latter reaffirmed the church's position on industry, labor unions, socialism, and capitalism. Each became a call to arms for twentieth-century Roman Catholic scholars, and each was also influential on a number of Anglo-Catholic, Orthodox, and Protestant writers.

Such scholars and writers include: Jacques Maritain (French), Romano Guardini (Italian/German), Eric Voegelin (Austrian/American), Etienne Gilson (French), Aleksandr Solzhenitsyn (Russian), Russell Kirk (American), C. S. Lewis (Northern Irish), E. I. Watkin (English), and T. S. Eliot (American/English), to name just a few. In some areas, these men radically disagreed. C. S. Lewis, for example, thought little of Jacques Maritain and, initially, T. S. Eliot. But in the main, these thinkers are far more similar than they are different.

For the English Christian humanists, the most important intellectual influences, in chronological order, were John Henry Newman, G. K. Chesterton, and Christopher Dawson. Each of these thinkers played a vital role in advancing Christian humanism during his own era. For Tolkien, the most important of the English Christian humanists was the historian Dawson, probably the most important English Roman Catholic scholar of the first half of the twentieth century.[34] "When the future historian describes the Catholic Renaissance of the twentieth century, it is my guess that he will pay particular attention to the emergence, during the great wars and at the darkest moment before the dawn, of the great 'doctors' who were the prophets of the new age," writes one commentator. "He will point to men like Etienne Gilson and Jacques Maritain and Edward Watkin and, certainly, to Christopher Dawson." And also Tolkien. In terms of influence, sheer numbers alone dictate his inclusion. He reached far more people with his Middle-earth mythology than did any of the other Christian humanist thinkers, including Lewis. Outside of the scriptural authors, he may be the most widely read Christian author of our time.

What will Tolkien's legacy be? Will his mythology have its desired effect on its millions of readers? If a person has been profoundly moved by Tolkien's legendarium what is he, finally, to do? The answer for Tolkien was as simple as it is infuriatingly difficult. We, as human persons, are to sanctify our own gifts by putting them to the service of the betterment of our selves, our community, our society, the Church, and, ultimately, the world. In Gandalf's words: "All we have to decide is what to do with the time that is given us."[35]

Tolkien had no one overarching plan for society. Indeed, he loathed the thought of delivering on high some plan to remake the world, and hence he would have loathed the idea of his mythology serving as a blueprint for some new system, ideology, or religion. If Tolkien wanted to renew Christendom, it was not in a superficial structural or even political sense in which he sought such a renewal, but rather in the sense that he wished there to be instilled in society an ethic that embraced the purpose God has for each of his creations and his Church. This ethic was not esoteric, but was instead encoded in the natural and divine law. The Middle-earth mythology was to serve as a wake-up call to this law, a law once better recognized, Tolkien believed, than in the modern era. Hence, his legendarium was also a call to defend all that was best in the long history of Western civilization.

The lessons of Tolkien's mythology, finally, are simple, straightforward, old-fashioned, and hence, unfashionable. For one, Tolkien wanted to teach his readers that God's grace, like faerie, is everywhere. But we must be open to it, willing to accept it as a freely given gift, and realize, as Frodo did not when he desired martyrdom at the Cracks of Mount Doom, that we are given just enough to achieve our given task, and no more. Tolkien's myth calls us to embrace the sanctity of each human person and our obligation to act as faithful stewards of creation. We are also called, like Beowulf or Aragorn, to fight for the protection of the good and the oppressed, even to the point of self-sacrifice. And we must not shy from doing the right thing, regardless of what those around us may think as a result. As Tolkien once wrote to his wife: "I do so dearly believe that no half-heartedness and no worldly fear must turn us aside from following the light unflinchingly."[36] And finally, we must expect dark ages, as man is fallen and easily succumbs to sin. "The evil of Sauron," Gandalf laments, "cannot be wholly cured."[37] The gulags, holocaust camps, and killing fields of the twentieth century refute utopian optimism.

And yet, Tolkien believed just as firmly that there is always hope. Even deep in Mordor, "Sam saw a white star twinkle for a while. The beauty of it smote his heart, as he looked up out of the forsaken land, and hope returned to him that in the end the Shadow was only a small and passing thing: there was light and high beauty forever beyond its reach."[38] That hope, and especially the grace imparted by the Incarnation, reminds us that we must sanctify the world and "redeem the time." When asked about the meaning of life, Tolkien wrote that

> the chief purpose of life, for any one of us, is to increase according to our capacity our knowledge of God by all the means we have, and to be moved by it to praise and thanks. To do as we say in the Gloria in Excelsis . . . . We praise you, we call you holy, we worship you, we proclaim your glory, we thank you for the greatness of your splendour. And in moments of exaltation we may call on all created things to join in our chorus, speaking on their behalf . . . all mountains and hills, all orchards and forests, all things that creep and birds on the wing.[39]

Tolkien the subcreator fulfilled his purpose as best he could. His vocation was to redeem the time through a Christ-inspired and God-centered mythology, to counter the dryness and devastation of the modern world with enchantment, to provide a glimpse of the True Joy, and to speak for all things: Valar, Maiar, incarnate angels, Elves, Dwarves, ents, hobbits . . . even modern men and women. His achievement helps one believe, indeed, that there is always hope.

Notes

Introduction

1. Tolkien spelled Fairy in a variety of ways throughout his life: fairy, faerie, and fäerie were the most common ways.

2. J. R. R. Tolkien, *Smith of Wootton Major and Farmer Giles of Ham* (Garden City, N.Y.: Nelson Doubleday, 1976), 13.

3. Ibid., 17.

4. Ibid.

5. Ibid., 18.

6. Chesterton, *The Everlasting Man*, 112.

7. J. R. R. Tolkien, "Sir Gawain and the Green Knight," 73.

8. Chesterton, *The Everlasting Man*, 108.

9. Humphrey Carpenter, ed., *The Letters of J. R. R. Tolkien* (Boston: Houghton Mifflin, 1981), 144.

10. J. R. R. Tolkien, "Mythopoeia," in *Tree and Leaf, including the Poem Mythopoeia* (Boston: Houghton Mifflin, 1988), 99.

11. Carpenter, ed., *Letters*, 147.

12. Chesterton, *The Everlasting Man*, 104–5.

13. Russell Kirk, *Prospects for Conservatives* (Washington, D.C.: Regnery, 1989), 18. On Tolkien's significant influence on Kirk, see James E. Person Jr., *Russell Kirk: A Critical Biography of a Conservative Mind* (Lanham, Md.: Madison Books, 1999), 18.

14. Chesterton, *The Everlasting Man*, 105.

15. G. K. Chesterton, *Orthodoxy* (Colorado Springs: Shaw, 1994), 47.

16. Donald Lutz, ed., in the preface to *Colonial Origins of the American Constitution* (Indianapolis, Ind.: Liberty Fund, 1998), xv.

17. Chesterton, *The Everlasting Man*, 109.

18. Romano Guardini, *Letters from Lake Como: Explorations in Technology and the Human Race* (Grand Rapids, Mich.: Eerdman's, 1994), 20.

19. Tolkien, *Smith of Wootton Major*, 26.

20. Mark Hollis, "New Grass," *Laughing Stock* (Polydor/EMI, 1991).

21. Quoted in Kirk, *Prospects*, 196. For Tolkien and Burke, see Roger Lancelyn Green and Walter Hooper, *C. S. Lewis: A Biography*, rev. ed. (New York: Harcourt Brace, 1994), 158–59.

22. See, for example, Christopher Dawson, *Christianity and the New Age* (1931; Manchester, N.H.: Sophia Institute Press, 1985).

23. For an excellent overview of Christian Humanism in the late twentieth century, see George Weigel, "John Paul II and the Crisis of Humanism, *First Things* 98 (December 1999): 31–36; and Gleaves Whitney, "Sowing Seeds in the Wasteland: The Perennial Task of Christian Humanists," an ISI/Trinity Christian College Evening Lecture (Palos Heights, Ill.), 13 October 1997, paper in possession of the author.

Chapter 1

1. Charlotte and Denis Plimmer, "The Man Who Understands Hobbits [interview with Tolkien]," *London Daily Telegraph Magazine*, 22 March 1968, 31. For a good description of Tolkien's study, see Michael Coren, *J. R. R. Tolkien: The Man Who Created* The Lord of the Rings (Toronto: Stoddart, 2001).

2. David Crumm, "The Spirit of Fantasy: 'Lord of the Rings' Fervor Might Lead Readers to Other Authors of Fairy Tale and Faith," *Detroit Free Press*, 14 May 2001.

3. Michael Tolkien, "J. R. R. Tolkien—The Wizard Father," *London Sunday Telegraph*, 9 September 1973.

4. Humphrey Carpenter, *Tolkien: A Biography* (Boston: Houghton Mifflin, 1977), 264.

5. Carpenter, *Tolkien*, 264–66.

6. John Garth, "Tolkien Fantasy Was Born in the Trenches of the Somme," *London Evening Standard*, 13 December 2001, 22.

7. Bill Cater, "We Talked of Love, Death, and Fairy Tales," *London Daily Telegraph*, 29 November 2001, 23.

8. Carpenter, *Tolkien*, 265.

9. Carpenter, ed., *Letters*, 9–10.

10. Tolkien, "On Fairy Stories," in *The Monsters and the Critics*, ed. Christopher Tolkien (Boston: Houghton Mifflin, 1983), 135; "Tolkien Talking," *London Sunday Times*, 27 November 1966, 9.

11. Keith Brace, "In the Footsteps of the Hobbits [interview with Tolkien]," *Birmingham Post*, 25 March 1968.

12. When a copy editor once attempted to change a word of Tolkien's during the 1950s, Tolkien responded with anger, "Why, I wrote the O.E.D.!" See Herbert Mitgang, "Behind the Best Sellers: J. R. R. Tolkien," *New York Times*, 2 October 1977, 48.

13. Tolkien, "English and Welsh," in Christopher Tolkien, ed., *The Monsters and the Critics and Other Essays* (Boston: Houghton Mifflin, 1984), 162.

14. Carpenter, *Tolkien*, 265–66; and C. S. Lewis, "Professor J. R. R. Tolkien: Creator of Hobbits and Inventor of a New Mythology," *London Times*, 3 September 1973.

15. Guy Davenport, "Hobbits in Kentucky," *New York Times*, 23 February 1979, A27.

16. Ruth Harshaw, "When Carnival of Books Went to Europe," *ALA Bulletin*, February 1957, MU JRRT COLLECTION, Series 5, Box 1, Folder 2.

17. J. R. R. Tolkien, Oxford, to Mr. Archer, Milwaukee, Wisconsin, 5 August 1957, MU JRRT COLLECTION, Tolkien Acquisition File, 1957–59.

18. William Ready, *The Tolkien Relation: A Personal Inquiry* (Chicago: Regnery, 1968), 23.

19. Lewis quoted in George Sayer, "Recollections of J. R. R. Tolkien," in Joseph Pearce, ed., *Tolkien: A Celebration* (London: Fount, 1999), 2.

20. W. H. Auden, "Making and Judging Poetry," *Atlantic Monthly*, January 1957, 46.

21. Quoted in Ready, *The Tolkien Relation*, 23.

22. Anonymous student, quoted in "J. R. R. Tolkien," *New York Times*, 3 September 1973, 18.

23. Antony Curtis, "Remembering Tolkien and Lewis," *British Book News*, June 1977, 429.

24. Quoted in William Cater, "More and More People Are Getting the J. R. R. Tolkien Habit," *Los Angeles Times*, 9 April 1972, 14; and Philip Norman, "The Prevalence of Hobbits," *New York Times*, 15 January 1967.

25. Cater, "More and More People Are Getting the J. R. R. Tolkien Habit," 14.

26. Robert Burchfield, "My Hero," *Independent Magazine*, 4 March 1989.

27. See, for example, Sayer, "Recollections," 3; and Priscilla Tolkien, "Memories of J. R. R. Tolkien in His Centenary Year," *The Brown Book* (December 1992): 12.

28. John Lawlor, *C. S. Lewis: Memories and Reflections* (Dallas, Tex.: Spence, 1998), 31–32; and Walter Hooper, "Tolkien and C. S. Lewis: An Interview with Walter Hooper," in Pearce, ed., *Tolkien: A Celebration*, 191.

29. J. R. R. Tolkien to George Sayer, quoted in "Letters Reveal Tolkien as a Grouchy Hobbit," *London Independent*, 2 November 2001, 11.

30. Michael Tolkien, "J. R. R. Tolkien," *London Sunday Telegraph*, 9 September 1973.

31. Priscilla Tolkien, "Memories," 13; and Shirley Love, "Talk with Priscilla Tolkien, on The Father Christmas Letters," December 1976, in MU, JRRT COLLECTION, Series 5, Box 1, Folder 32.

32. Carpenter, *Tolkien*, 130.

33. Lawlor, *C. S. Lewis*, 32.

34. Excerpt from a letter about JRRT, from Norman S. Power, Ladywood, Birmingham, England, author of THE FIRLAND SAGA," WCWC, Kilby Files, 3–8, "Tolkien the Man" from TOLKIEN AND THE SILMARILLION.

35. Carpenter, *Tolkien*, 130.

36. Humphrey Carpenter, "The Lord of the Rings: J. R. R. Tolkien, Our Brief Encounter," *London Sunday Times*, 25 November 2001 (special section on Tolkien).

37. Lewis, "Professor J. R. R. Tolkien." Samuel Johnson supposedly hated to sleep at night, preferring to work as late, or as early as the case might be, as possible.

38. Walter Hooper, ed., *All My Road before Me: The Diary of C. S. Lewis, 1922–1927* (San Diego, Calif.: Harcourt Brace, 1991), 393.

39. Ibid., 440.

40. Walter Hooper, ed., *The Letters of C. S. Lewis to Arthur Greeves, 1914–1963* (1979; New York: Collier Books, 1986), 317.

41. J. R. R. Tolkien, *The Lays of Beleriand* (Boston: Houghton Mifflin, 1985), 150–51.

42. Hooper, "Tolkien and C. S. Lewis: An Interview with Walter Hooper," 192.

43. See, for example, W. H. Lewis, *Brothers and Friends: The Diaries of Warren Hamilton Lewis* (San Francisco: Harper and Row, 1982), 127.

44. Lawlor, *C. S. Lewis*, 29.

45. John Wain, *Sprightly Running: Part of an Autobiography* (New York: St. Martin's Press, 1962), 138–39.

46. Curtis, "Remembering Tolkien and Lewis," 429.

47. Wain, *Sprightly Running*, 138–39.

48. Quoted in John Bayley, "A Passionate Pilgrim," *Times Literary Supplement*, 12 July 1974.

49. Hooper, ed., *The Letters of C. S. Lewis to Arthur Greeves*, 421.

50. Ibid.

51. Ibid., 425. See also Tolkien, "Mythopoeia," 97–101; and C. S. Lewis, *Surprised by Joy: The Shape of My Early Life* (New York: Harcourt Brace, 1955), 209.

52. J. R. R. Tolkien, Oxford, to William Luther White, 11 September 1967, in William Luther White, *The Image of Man in C. S. Lewis* (Nashville, Tenn.: Abingdon Press, 1969), 221–22; and George Sayer, *Jack: C. S. Lewis and His Times* (San Francisco: Harper and Row, 1986), 149.

53. Sayer, *Jack*, 150–51.

54. For a comprehensive list and mini-bio of each member, see Humphrey Carpenter, *The Inklings: C. S. Lewis, J. R. R. Tolkien, Charles Williams and Their Friends* (Boston: Houghton Mifflin, 1979), 255–59. On Hardie, see "Colin Hardie," *London Times*, 20 October 1998.

55. W. H. Lewis, ed., *Letters of C. S. Lewis* (San Diego: Harcourt Brace, 1993), 481.

56. Douglass Gresham, *Lenten Lands* (New York: Macmillan, 1988), 43, 51.

57. Sayer, "Recollections," 14.

58. Lawlor, *C. S. Lewis*, 38.

59. W. H. Lewis, ed., *Letters of C. S. Lewis*, 292.

60. Sayer, *Jack*, 151–52; and Shirley Sugerman, ed., "A Conversation with Owen Barfield," in *Evolution of Consciousness: Studies in Polarity* (Middletown, Conn.: Wesleyan University Press, 1975), 9.

61. James Dundas-Grant, "From an 'Outsider,'" in James T. Como, ed., *C. S. Lewis at the Breakfast Table and Other Reminiscences* (New York: Collier, 1979), 231.

62. Wain, *Sprightly Running*, 184.

63. C. S. Lewis, preface to *Essays Presented to Charles Williams* (1947; Grand Rapids, Mich.: Eerdman's, 1974), v.

64. W. H. Lewis, ed., *Letters of C. S. Lewis*, 363.

65. Nathan C. Starr, "Good Cheer and Sustenance," in Como, ed., *C. S. Lewis*, 122–23; Robert E. Havard, "Philia: Jack at Ease," in Como, ed., *C. S.*

Lewis, 217; and James Dundas-Grant, "From an 'Outsider,'" in Como, ed., *C. S. Lewis*, 231.

66. Tolkien to White, 11 September 1967, in White, *The Image of Man in C. S. Lewis*, 222.

67. W. H. Lewis, *C. S. Lewis: A Biography*. Unpublished ms. in WCWC.

68. Dyson, quoted in A. N. Wilson, *C. S. Lewis: A Biography* (New York: W.W. Norton, 1990), 217; and W. H. Lewis, *Brothers and Friends*, 200.

69. Dyson quoted in Davenport, "Hobbits in Kentucky," A27. See also Havard, "Philia: Jack at Ease," 217.

70. C. S. Lewis to Charles Moorman, 15 May 1959, quoted in Lin Carter, *Tolkien: A Look behind The Lord of the Rings* (New York: Ballantine, 1969), 18; Sayer, "Recollections," 10; CSL to Father Gardiner, 5 October 1962, in W. H. Lewis, *C. S. Lewis: A Biography* (unpublished), 460, in WCWC; W. H. Lewis, ed., *Letters of C. S. Lewis*, 376; Clyde Kilby, unpublished parts of chapter "Woodland Prisoner," 11, in WCWC, Kilby Files, 3–8, "Tolkien the Man" from TOLKIEN AND THE SILMARILLION; and Edmund Fuller, "A Superb Addition to Tolkien's Mythological Realm," *Wall Street Journal*, 19 September 1977.

71. Plimmer, "The Man Who Understands Hobbits," 32.

72. W. H. Lewis, *Brothers and Friends*, 268.

73. See, for example, ibid., 189, 212, 218. In what can only be regarded as brilliant writing, Humphrey Carpenter recreated what he thought a typical Inklings meeting must have been like. See Carpenter, *The Inklings*, 127–52. Tolkien recreated an Inklings discussion as well. See Tolkien, "The Notion Club Papers, parts 1 and 2," in *Sauron Defeated: The End of the Third Age*, ed. Christopher Tolkien, *History of Middle-earth*, vol. 9 (Boston: Houghton Mifflin, 1992), 145–327.

74. W. H. Lewis, ed., *Letters of C. S. Lewis*, 337.

75. Wain, *Sprightly Running*, 181. See also Havard, "Philia: Jack at Ease," 226.

76. Wain, *Sprightly Running*, 181.

77. C. S. Lewis, The Kilns, to Warnie Lewis, 17 March 1940, WCWC, CSL Letters to Warnie Lewis, Letter Index 172.

78. Wain, *Sprightly Running*, 181–85.

79. Carpenter, ed., *Letters*, 349.

80. Ibid., 33, 113, 151, 224, 303, 361, 378.

81. Ibid., 341.

82. Ibid., 265.

83. Tolkien quoted in Green and Hooper, *C. S. Lewis: A Biography*, 241. See also Sayer, "Recollections," 14.

84. A. N. Wilson, *C. S. Lewis*, 273.

85. Ibid., 294.

86. Brian Barbour, "Lewis and Cambridge," *Modern Philology* 96 (May 1999): 439–84.

87. Carpenter, *Tolkien*, 237.

88. Hooper, "Tolkien and C. S. Lewis: An Interview with Walter Hooper," 190.

89. Gresham, *Lenten Lands*, 152.

90. Michael A. Foster, "Dr. Clyde S. Kilby Recalls the Inklings" [interview], 6 October 1980, JRRT Series 5, Box 1, Folder 23, p. 4, Tolkien Papers, Marquette University Archives.

91. Carpenter, ed., *Letters*, 341.

92. "Tolkien [obituary]," New York Times, 3 September 1973, 18.

93. Carpenter, ed., *Letters*, 366.

94. Quoted in Joseph Pearce, *Tolkien: Man and Myth* (San Francisco: Ignatius Press, 1999), 70.

95. Hooper, ed., *The Letters of C. S. Lewis to Arthur Greeves*, 449.

96. "Tolkien [obituary]," *New York Times*, 18.

97. Carpenter, ed., *Letters*, 25–27

98. Christopher Tolkien explains this in J. R. R. Tolkien, *The Lays of Beleriand*, 366.

99. Carpenter, ed. *Letters*, 34

100. Quoted in Lynn Williams, "Tolkien Is Still Fantastic, 100 Years after His Birth," St. Louis Post-Dispatch, 12 January 1992, 1C.

101. W. H. Auden, "At the End of the Quest, Victory," *New York Times Book Review*, 22 January 1956, 5; and Colin Wilson, *Tree* by Tolkien (Santa Barbara, Calif.: Capra Press, 1974), 7.

102. Quoted in T. A. Shippey, *The Road to Middle-earth* (Boston: Houghton Mifflin, 1983), 34.

103. Edmund Wilson, "Oo, Those Awful Orcs!" Nation 182 (14 April 1956): 314. On Wilson's leftism and minor retreat from it, see Paul Johnson, *Intellectuals* (New York: Harper and Row, 1988), 252–68.

104. "The Two Towers," *New Yorker*, 14 May 1955, 173.

105. Mark Roberts, "Adventure in English," *Essays in Criticism* 6 (October 1956): 459.

106. Robert H. Flood, C.S.B., "Hobbit Hoax? The Fellowship of the Ring," *Books on Trial* (February 1955).

107. W. H. Auden, "The Hero Is a Hobbit," *New York Times Book Review*, 31 October 1954.

108. Donald Barr, "Shadowy World of Men and Hobbits," *New York Times Book Review*, 1 May 1955, 4.

109. William Blissett, "The Despot of the Rings," *South Atlantic Quarterly* (Summer 1959): 451.

110. Louis J. Halle, "Flourishing Orcs," *Saturday Review*, 15 January 1955, 17–18.

111. Patricia Meyer Spacks, "Ethical Pattern in The Lord of The Rings," *Critique* 3 (1959): 41.

112. Michael Straight, "The Fantastic World of J. R. R. Tolkien," *New Republic*, 16 January 1956, 26.

113. Edward Wagenknecht, "'Ring' Joins Great Novels of the Year," *Chicago Sunday Tribune*, 26 December 1954.

114. Tolkien, *The Fellowship of the Ring*, 2nd ed. (Boston: Houghton Mifflin, 1993), 1, 6.

115. Carpenter, *Tolkien*, 223.

116. Quoted in ibid.

117. William Cater, "Lord of the Hobbits," *London Daily Express*, 22 November 1966.

118. Daphne Castell, "The Realms of Tolkien," *New Worlds*, November 1966, 143.

119. Joseph Mathewson, "The Hobbit Habit," *Esquire*, September 1966, 131.

120. Curtis, "Remembering Tolkien and Lewis," 430.

121. Plimmer, "The Man Who Understands Hobbits," 31. Charles Elliott, an editor for *Life*, complained that liking Tolkien was no longer good, as too many people had made it popular. "He has ceased to be a cult possession," Elliott seethed. See Charles Elliott, "Can American Kick The Hobbit?" *Life*, 24 February 1967, 10.

122. "J. R. R. Tolkien," *New York Times*, 3 September 1973, 18.

123. William Cater, "Lord of the Hobbits"; and "The Hobbit Habit," *Time*, 15 July 1966.

124. William E. Ratliff and Charles G. Flinn, "The Hobbit and the Hippie," *Modern Age* (Spring 1968): 142.

125. Philip Norman, "The Magic of Meeting the REAL Lord of the Rings," *London Daily Mail*, 13 December 2001, 13.

126. Quoted in Norman, "The Prevalence of Hobbits."

127. "The Hobbit Habit," *Time*, 51.

128. Plimmer, "The Man Who Understands Hobbits," 31.

129. "The Hobbit Habit," *Time*, 48.

130. CSK Notes, taken while reading mss. of SILMARILLION for JRRT in 1966, "Comment on Ainulindale," WCWC, Kilby Files, 3–9.

131. Quoted in Clyde S. Kilby, Tolkien and *The Silmarillion* (Wheaton, Ill.: Harold Shaw, 1976), 16.

132. Quoted in Norman, "The Prevalence of Hobbits." See also Donald Swann, *Swann's Way: A Life in Song* (London: Heinemann, 1991), 209.

133. Julian Dibbell, "J. R. R. Tolkien Still Feeds the Nerd Nation's Imagination: Lord of the Geeks," *Village Voice*, 6–12 June 2001.

134. Quoted in Ratliff and Flinn, "The Hobbit and the Hippie," 144.

135. "Tolkien Talking," *London Sunday Times*, 27 November 1966, 9.

136. Carpenter, ed., *Letters*, 412.

137. Dan Miller, "The Hobbit Cult: A Fantastic Ring," *Chicago Daily News*, 8–9 September 1973, 6.

138. J. R. R. Tolkien to William E. Ratliff, Seattle, Washington, 25 August 1967; copy of letter in possession of author.

139. Joy Hill, "Brief Account," 2 January 1972, Folder 7, Box 2, Series 5, in J. R. R. Tolkien Papers, Marquette University.

140. Joy Hill, "Brief Account," JRRT Papers; and Joy Hill, "Echoes of the Old Ringmaster," *London Times*, 10 December 1990, 16.

141. Quoted in "Letters Give Insight into Author Tolkien," *Coventry Evening Telegraph*, 12 December 2001, 6.

142. Quoted in Philip Norman, "Lord of the Flicks," *Show* 1 (January 1970), 29.

143. Henry Resnick, "An Interview with Tolkien," *Niekas* (Late Spring 1966): 42.

144. JRRT, Oxford, to Clyde Kilby, Wheaton, Illinois, 18 December 1965, in JRRT to Miscellaneous Correspondents, WCWC.

145. Kilby, *Tolkien and* The Silmarillion, 19.

146. William Cater, "Filial Duty," chapter in The Tolkien Scrapbook (Philadelphia: Running Press, 1978), 93. See, especially, Tolkien's last writings regarding *The Silmarillion* in *Morgoth's Ring: The Later Silmarillion, Part 1*, ed. Christopher Tolkien, *History of Middle-earth*, vol. 10 (Boston: Houghton Mifflin, 1993), and Tolkien, *The War of the Jewels: The Later Silmarillion*,

Part 2, ed. Christopher Tolkien, *History of Middle-earth*, vol. 11 (Boston: Houghton Mifflin, 1994).

147. Kilby, *Tolkien and* The Silmarillion, 33.

148. Christopher Tolkien, foreword to *The Book of Lost Tales, Part 1* (Boston: Houghton Mifflin, 1983), 7.

149. Sayer, "Recollections," 15.

150. Cater, "Filial Duty, 94; Raynor Unwin, "Early Days of Elder Days," in *Tolkien's Legendarium: Essays on* The History of Middle-earth (Westport, Conn.: Greenwood Press, 2000), 5–6; Betram Rota, London, to William Ready, Marquette, 10 January 1957, in MU, J. R. R. Tolkien, Acquisition File, 1957–59; and J. R. R. Tolkien to J. L. N O'Loughlin, 29 January 1943, in MU, JRRT COLLECTION, Series 7, Box 1, Folder 8.

151. A. N. Wilson, "Tolkien Was Not a Writer," *London Daily Telegraph*, 24 November 2001, 7.

152. Quoted in John and Priscilla Tolkien, *The Tolkien Family Album* (Boston: Houghton Mifflin, 1992), 58.

153. Mitgang, "Behind the Best Sellers: J. R. R. Tolkien," 48.

154. "Tolkien's Publisher Says 'Silmarillion' Will Be Released," *New York Times*, 4 September 1973, 31.

155. Charles E. Noad, "A Tower in Beleriand: A Talk by Guy Gavriel Kay," *Mythprint* (April 1989): 4.

156. Noad, "A Tower in Beleriand," 3–4. See also Tolkien, *Book of Lost Tales, Part 1*, 6.

157. Kilby, "Tolkien the Man" from TOLKIEN AND THE SILMARILLION, K23, WCWC, Kilby Files, 3–8. Christopher discusses the possibility of this narrative device in the foreword to Tolkien, *The Book of Lost Tales, Part 1*, 5–6.

158. "Tolkien's Publisher Says 'Silmarillion' Will Be Released," *New York Times*; and Robert Dahlin, "Houghton Mifflin's Fall Title by J. R. R. Tolkien to Excavate the Founding of Middle-earth," *Publisher's Weekly*, 14 February 1977, 59.

159. Christopher Tolkien, *The Silmarillion: A Brief Account of the Book and Its Making* (Boston: Houghton Mifflin, 1977), 4.

160. Cater, "We Talked of Love, Death, and Fairy Tales," 23.

161. On sales records, see "HM's 'The Silmarillion' Sets New Records," *Publishers Weekly*, 26 September 1977, 106–8.

162. Fuller, "A Superb Addition to Tolkien's Mythological Realm."

163. Joseph McLellan, "Frodo and the Cosmos," *Washington Post*, 4 September 1977.

164. Richard Brookhiser, "Kicking the Hobbit," *National Review*, 9 December 1977, 1439–40.

165. Charles Nicol, "The Invented Word," *Harper's* 255 (November 1977): 103.

166. Cheryl Forbes, "Answers about Middle-earth," *Christianity Today*, 7 October 1977, 30–31.

167. Timothy Foote, "Middle-earth Genesis," *Time*, 24 October 1977, 122.

168. L. J. Davis, "The Silmarillion," *New Republic*, 1 October 1977, 38–40.

169. Daniel Coogan, "Failing Fantasy, Tragic Fact," *America*, 5 November 1977, 315; "J. R. R. Tolkien: Mythbegotten," *Economist*, 17 September 1977, 141; and Margo Jefferson, "Fool's Gold," *Newsweek*, 24 October 1977, 114, 117.

170. Eric Korn, "Doing Things by Elves," *Times Literary Supplement*, 30 September 1977, 1097.

171. Robert M. Adams, "The Hobbit Habit," *New York Review of Books*, 24 November 1977, 22; Joy Gerville-Reache, "Tolkien's 'Silmarillion' Tests Fans," *Christian Science Monitor*, 21 September 1977; and Martha Spaulding, "The Silmarillion," *Atlantic Monthly*, October 1977, 105.

172. John Gardner, "The World of Tolkien," *New York Times Book Review*, 23 October 1977, 1, 39–40.

173. Quoted in "Tolkien Disney Rant," *Scottish Daily Record and Sunday Mail*, 5 July 2001.

174. Peter Conrad, "The Babbit," *New Statesmen*, 23 September 1977, 408–9.

175. Christopher did mention the negative criticism, though, in his foreword to Tolkien, *The Book of Lost Tales, Part 1*, 2.

176. On "Leaf by Niggle" being autobiographical, see Michael Foster, "Dr. Clyde S. Kilby Recalls the Inklings," 10 October 1980, JRRT MSS., Series 5, Box 1, Folder 23, Marquette University Archives. For one example of Tolkien's newfound wealth, he received $250,000 for the film rights to *The Lord of the Rings* in 1969. See John Ezard, "So, Would Tolkien Have Liked the Film?" *London Guardian*, 14 December 2001, 4.

177. William Cater, "Lord of the Hobbits," *London Daily Express*, 22 November 1966.

178. JRRT, to Robert Havard, 9 August 1968, in MU JRRT Collection, Series 7, Box 1, Folder 9.

179. Cater, "More and More People Are Getting the J. R. R. Tolkien Habit," 14.

180. Bernard Weinraub, "Cecil Beaton Knighted by Queen; A Racing Driver Is Also Honored," *New York Times*, 1 January 1972, 3.

Chapter 2

1. See, especially, Christopher Tolkien, ed., *The Lays of Beleriand*, 150–367; and J. R. R. Tolkien, *The Silmarillion* (Boston: Houghton Mifflin, 1977), 162–87. See also Swann, *Swann's Way*, 208.

2. Carpenter, ed., *Letters*, 420–21.

3. Tolkien, quoted in Harvey Breit, *New York Times Book Review*, 5 June 1955, 8.

4. Curtis, "Remembering Tolkien and Lewis," 429–30.

5. Carpenter, ed., *Letters*, 100.

6. See, for example, Resnick, "An Interview with Tolkien," 40.

7. Christopher Tolkien, *The Silmarillion: A Brief Account of the Book and Its Making*, 3; Christopher Tolkien, ed., *Morgoth's Ring*, viii–ix; Wayne G. Hammond and Christian Scull, "The History of Middle Earth: Review Article," VII 12 (1995): 105, 109; and Carpenter, ed., *Letters*, 216.

8. Clyde S. Kilby, *Tolkien and* The Silmarillion, 45.

9. Tolkien, *The Two Towers* (Boston: Houghton Mifflin, 1993), 321.

10. Ibid., 37.

11. Ibid., 321.

12. Kilby, *Tolkien and* The Silmarillion, 43.

13. Carpenter, ed., Letters, 79, 231, 252, 258; and Christopher Tolkien, *The Silmarillion: A Brief Account of The Book and Its Making*, 4.

14. Carpenter, ed., *Letters*, 231.

15. Quoted in Kilby, *Tolkien and* The Silmarillion, 13.

16. Carpenter, ed., *Letters*, 145, 253.

17. Hooper, ed., *The Letters of C. S. Lewis to Arthur Greeves*, 427.

18. Chesterton, *The Everlasting Man*, 111.

19. William Foster, "An Early History of the Hobbits [interview with Tolkien]," *Edinburgh Scotsman*, 5 February 1972.

20. Carpenter, ed., *Letters*, 21, 31.

21. Denys Gerrolt, *Now Read On* [interview with Tolkien]. Radio broadcast. London: BBC Radio 4, 1971.

22. Carpenter, ed., *Letters*, 278.

23. Ibid., 34.

24. See also, Christopher Tolkien, ed., *The Return of the Shadow: The History of the Lord of the Rings, Part 1* (Boston: Houghton Mifflin, 1988), 43–44.

25. Carpenter, ed., *Letters*, 216–17, lists a number of surprises Tolkien encountered while writing The Lord of the Rings.

26. Tolkien, *The Fellowship of the Ring*, 325.

27. Daphne Castell, "The Realms of Tolkien," 147; and J. R. R. Tolkien, *Unfinished Tales of Númenor and Middle-earth* (Boston: Houghton Mifflin, 1980), 401–2.

28. On their possible fates, see Tolkien, *Unfinished Tales*, 388–402. See also, Carpenter, ed., *Letters*, 231, 248, 277, 280, and 448. Tolkien offers yet another possibility concerning the Blue Wizards in his writings published posthumously. They might be, he argued, agitators against Sauron in the East of Mordor, perhaps "weakening and disarraying the forces of the East." The names he gave them were "Morinehtar and Rómestámo," meaning "Darkness-slayer and East-helper." See J. R. R. Tolkien, *The Peoples of Middleearth*, ed. Christopher Tolkien (Boston: Houghton Mifflin, 1996), 384–85.

29. Resnick, "An Interview with Tolkien," 41.

30. Plimmer, "The Man Who Understands Hobbits," 32.

31. [Anonymous], obituary of J. R. R. Tolkien, *London Times*, 3 September 1973; and Tolkien, "English and Welsh," 191–92. The belief that the London Times obituary of Tolkien was written by C. S. Lewis sometime before Lewis died in 1963, though widespread, has been dismissed by a number of scholars, and so I have not attributed the obituary to him. I am grateful to David Bratman for giving me his insight regarding this controversy.

32. Quoted in Carpenter, Tolkien, 101.

33. Foster, "An Early History of the Hobbits"; and William Cater, "Lord of the Hobbits."

34. [Anonymous], obituary of Tolkien, *London Times*, 3 September 1973.

35. William Cater, "More and More People Are Getting the J. R. R. Tolkien Habit," 14.

36. Foster, "An Early History of the Hobbits."

37. For an excellent explanation and list of particular linguistic influences on Tolkien's Middle-earth, see Carpenter, ed., *Letters*, 379–87.

38. Castell, "Realms of Tolkien," 149.

39. J. R. R. Tolkien, "A Secret Vice," in Christopher Tolkien, ed., *The Monsters and the Critics and Other Essays*, 210–11.

40. Norman, "The Prevalence of Hobbits," 98; Plimmer, "The Man Who Understands Hobbits," 32; and "Tolkien on Tolkien," *Diplomat* October 1966, 39.

41. Owen Barfield, *Poetic Diction: A Study in Meaning* (1928; Hanover: Wesleyan University Press, 1973); and obituary of Owen Barfield, *London Daily Telegraph*, 22 December 1997, 21.

42. Verlyn Flieger, *Splintered Light: Logos and Language in Tolkien's World* (Grand Rapids, Mich.: Wm. B. Eerdmans Publishing Co, 1983), 38.

43. Dick Plotz, "J. R. R. Tolkien Talks about the Discovery of Middle-earth, the Origins of Elvish," *Seventeen*, January 1967, 93.

44. Kilby, *Tolkien and* The Silmarillion, 47.

45. Ibid., 57; and J. R. R. Tolkien, Oxford, to Clyde Kilby, Wheaton, Illinois, 18 December 1965, WCWC, J. R. R. Tolkien to Misc. Correspondents. The translation from Anglo-Saxon to English is Tolkien's. See Kilby, unpublished chapter, "The Manuscript of THE SILMARILLION," p. 81, WCWC, Kilby Files, 1–12, TOLKIEN AND THE SILMARILLION.

46. Quoted in Carpenter, *Tolkien*, 64.

47. Carpenter, ed., *Letters*, 7–8.

48. See, J. R. R. Tolkien, *The Silmarillion*, 246–55.

49. Carpenter, ed., *Letters*, 78.

50. Ibid.

51. Tolkien, "On Fairy Stories," 135.

52. Christopher Tolkien, *The Silmarillion: A Brief Account of the Book and Its Making*, 3.

53. Carpenter, ed., *Letters*, 345.

54. For an excellent discussion of the evolutionary changes from the original *Book of Lost Tales*, Tolkien's original title for the Middle-earth mythology, and *The Silmarillion*, see Christina Scull, "The Development of Tolkien's Legendarium: Some Threads in the Tapestry of Middle-earth," in *Tolkien's Legendarium*, 7. See also Tolkien, *The Silmarillion*, 7–8; and Cater, "The Filial Duty of Christopher Tolkien," 92.

55. Quoted in Carpenter, *Tolkien*, 92. See also Lawlor, C. S. Lewis, 35.

56. Shippey, *The Road to Middle-earth*, 19.

57. Ibid., 22–42, 89.

58. See, for example, J. R. R. Tolkien, "Hobbits," *London Observer*, 20 February 1938; Carpenter, ed., *Letters*, 31–32, 87, 92, 159, 214, 354, 379–87; Paul H. Kocher, *A Reader's Guide to the Silmarillion* (Boston: Houghton Mifflin, 1980); and George Burke Johnson, "Poetry of J. R. R. Tolkien," in *The Tolkien Papers: Ten Papers Prepared for the Tolkien Festival at Mankato State College, October 28 and 29, 1966* (Mankato, Minn.: Mankato State College, 1967), 63–75. On various possible influences, a plethora of secondary

writings exists. See, for example, Shippey, *The Road to Middle-earth*, the whole thing; Joseph Pearce, *Tolkien: Man and Myth*, 15; Gary B. Herbert, "Tolkien's Tom Bombadil and the Platonic Ring of Gyges," *Extrapolation* 26 (Summer 1985): 152–59; James Obertino, "Moria and Hades: Underworld Journeys in Tolkien and Virgil," *Comparative Literature Studies* 30 (1993): 153–69; Jonathan B. Himes, "What J. R. R. Tolkien Really Did with the Sampo," *Mythlore* 22: 69–85; and C. W. Sullivan III, "Name and Lineage Patterns: Aragorn and Beowulf," *Extrapolation* (Fall 1984): 239–46.

59. Davenport, "Hobbits in Kentucky," A27.

60. Shippey, *The Road to Middle-Earth*, 223. Tolkien scholars and followers have arguably gone a bit overboard in their attempt to find every possible influence on their subject. While Tolkien drew upon a number of sources for his greater mythology, he made those sources his own, taking what he needed and, most importantly, sanctifying them by Christianizing them (Carpenter, ed., *Letters*, 212). Guesses as to influences, Tolkien thought, were a waste of time (Resnick, "An Interview with Tolkien,"2). Only he, and later his son Christopher, held "the key" to it all, he told an interviewer in the mid-1960s (Ibid., 38). Not only did Tolkien think that God directed the mythology and its formation, but Tolkien was intimately and intricately wrapped up in its creation. When a reviewer in 1937 labeled the mythology in an early version of *The Silmarillion* dark and Celtic, Tolkien responded, "They have bright colour, but are like a broken stained glass window reassembled without design." It would be hard to find a more apt description for the entire legendarium. Tolkien crafted it from his own life, his own readings, and, as he believed, from God's inspiration (Carpenter, ed., *Letters*, 26).

61. Carpenter, ed., *Letters*, 21.

62. Quoted in J. R. R. Tolkien, *The Lays of Beleriand*, 150–51.

63. "Tolkien and C. S. Lewis: An Interview with Walter Hooper," 192.

64. Hooper, ed., *The Letters of C. S. Lewis to Arthur Greeves*, 341.

65. W. H. Lewis, ed., *Letters of C. S. Lewis*, 376.

66. Ibid., 426.

67. Lawlor, *C. S. Lewis*, 40.

68. Carpenter, ed., *Letters*, 362.

69. Ibid., 350.

70. J. R. R. Tolkien, *The Monsters and the Critics and Other Essays*, 1.

71. Ibid., 3.

72. Carpenter, ed., *Letters*, 220.

73. Ibid., 216, 232–33, 310.

74. On Tolkien's reputation among scholars of Anglo-Saxon, see, for example, Eileen Battersby, "Lord of the Hobbits," *Irish Times*, 23 December 2000; Malcolm Godden, "From the Heroic," *London Times Literary Supplement*, 8 July 1983, 736; Matthew Beard, "Oxford Dons Call for Slaying of Beowulf," *London Daily Telegraph*, 22 June 1998; Tom Shippey, *J. R. R. Tolkien: Author of the Century* (Boston: Houghton Mifflin, 2001), xi; and Charles Moseley, "A Creature of Hobbit," *London Observer*, 8 October 2000.

75. Shippey, *The Road to Middle-earth*, 26.

76. Ibid., 37.

77. Seamus Heaney, *Beowulf* (New York: Farrar, Straus and Giroux, 2000), 11.

78. J. R. R. Tolkien, "The Monsters and the Critics," in Lewis E. Nicholson, ed., *An Anthology of Beowulf Criticism* (Notre Dame, Ind.: University of Notre Dame Press, 1963), 59. Michael O'Brien argues forcefully that whenever a dragon appears in Western literature, it represents some manifestation of the devil or his allies. Tolkien most likely would not disagree. See, Michael O'Brien, *A Landscape with Dragons: The Battle for Your Child's Mind* (San Francisco: Ignatius Press, 1998).

79. Tolkien, "The Monsters and the Critics," 66.

80. Ibid., 61.

81. Ibid.

82. Ibid., 62.

83. Ibid., 67.

84. Ibid., 78.

85. Ibid., 77.

86. Carpenter, ed., *Letters*, 56.

87. Romano Guardini, *The End of the Modern World* (Wilmington, Del.: ISI Books, 1998), 9.

88. Clement of Alexandria, "Miscellanies."

89. Sayer, "Recollections," 5.

90. Tolkien, "The Monsters and the Critics," 72.

91. Ibid., 73.

92. Ibid., 77.

93. Tolkien, "On Fairy-Stories," in Christopher Tolkien, ed., *The Monsters and the Critics and Other Essays*, 109.

94. Ibid., 130–31.

95. Ibid., 133.

96. Ibid., 135.

97. Ibid., 144.

98. Ibid., 140.

99. Ibid., 147.

100. Ibid., 146.

101. Ibid., 150; and "J. R. R. Tolkien Dead at 81; Wrote 'Lord of the Rings,'" *Time*, 17 September 1973, 101.

102. Wain, *Sprightly Running*, 182.

103. Carpenter, ed., *Letters*, 146.

104. Tolkien, "On Fairy-Stories," 153.

105. Ibid., 153.

106. C. S. Lewis, "Myth Became Fact," in *God in the Dock: Essays on Theology and Ethics*, ed. Walter Hooper (Grand Rapids, Mich.: Eerdman's, 1970), 66.

107. Tolkien, "On Fairy-Stories," 153.

108. Christopher Tolkien, *Morgoth's Ring*, 345.

109. Carpenter, ed., *Letters*, 307.

110. See, for example, Louis J. Halle, "History through the Mind's Eye," *Saturday Review*, 28 January 1956, 11–12; Daphne Castell, "Tolkien on Tolkien: Making of a Myth," *Christian Science Monitor*, 11 August 1966, 11.

111. Norman, "Lord of the Flicks," 29.

112. Tolkien, *The Fellowship of the Ring*, 6. See also Tolkien's interview with the Plimmers, "The Man Who Understands Hobbits," 32; and C. S. Lewis, "J. R. R. Tolkien," *London Times*, 3 September 1973.

113. CSL quoted in Tolkien, *Lays of Beleriand*, 151.

114. Carpenter, ed., *Letters*, 41, 121. See also, the reprint (and reedited version) of Tolkien's 1951 letter to Milton Waldman, in J. R. R. Tolkien, *The Silmarillion*, 2d ed. (Boston: Houghton Mifflin, 2001), xi–xii.

115. Carpenter, ed., *Letters*, 212.

116. Ibid., 283.

117. Resnick, "An Interview with Tolkien," 41. Tolkien told Clyde Kilby that he had never said this. See Kilby, *Tolkien and* The Silmarillion, 51.

118. Kilby, *Tolkien and* The Silmarillion, 51; Brace, "In the Footsteps of the Hobbits"; and Foster, "An Early History of the Hobbits."

119. Carpenter, ed., *Letters*, 144, 230–31. Despite Tolkien's rather strong views on the Arthurian legend, Guy Kay and Christopher Tolkien found an unfinished poem entitled "The Fall of Arthur," in Tolkien's files. See Noad, "A Tower in Beleriand," 3.

120. Cater, "We Talked of Love, Death, and Fairy Tales," 23.

121. Kilby, *Tolkien and* The Silmarillion, 43–44.

122. Ibid., 51; Norman, "The Prevalence of Hobbits," 98; and Tolkien interview with D. Gerrolt, BBC Radio 4, January 1971.

123. Shippey first made this point in *The Road to Middle-earth*, 77–78.

124. Ibid., 97, 223.

125. Tolkien, "On Fairy-Stories," 134. For Cooper's mixing of myth, history, and politics, see Bradley J. Birzer and John Willson, introduction to James Fenimore Cooper, *The American Democrat and Other Political Essays* (Washington, D.C.: Regnery, 2000).

126. Resnick, "An Interview with Tolkien," 41.

127. Christopher Dawson, *The Making of Europe: An Introduction to the History of European Unity* (1932; New York: Meridian, 1974), 169–201.

128. Carpenter, ed., *Letters*, 376.

129. See, for example, ibid., 223; and Carpenter, *Tolkien*, 222.

130. Quoted in Carpenter, *Tolkien*, 222.

131. Quoted in Barry Leighton, "Tolkien's Clue to The Lord of the Rings," *Bristol Western Daily Press*, 26 February 2002, 11.

132. John Emerich Edward Dalberg-Acton, *Essays in the History of Liberty* (Indianapolis, Ind.: Liberty Fund, 1986), 409–33.

133. Lewis, *God in the Dock*, 67.

134. Tolkien, "Mythopoeia," 100.

Chapter 3

1. Plimmer, "The Man Who Understands Hobbits," 35. See also "Tolkien on Tolkien," *Diplomat*, 39.

2. Carpenter, ed., *Letters*, 172.

3. Quoted in Kilby, "Mythic and Christian Elements in Tolkien," in John Warwick Montgomery, ed., *Myth, Allegory, and Gospel: An Interpretation of*

J. R. R. Tolkien, C. S. Lewis, G. K. Chesterton, and Charles Williams (Minneapolis: Bethany Fellowship, 1974), 141.

4. Quoted in Pearce, "Tolkien and the Catholic Literary Revival," in Pearce, ed., *Tolkien: A Celebration* (London: Fount, 1999), 103. On Sayer's close friendship to Tolkien, see "Letters, Book Proofs on the Block," *Toronto Sun*, 3 November 2001, 50. Tolkien wrote to Sayer: "You were extremely kind to me at a low ebb. And I believed your praise, somehow more than anyone else's."

5. Quoted in Pearce, *Tolkien: Man and Myth*, 194.

6. Tolkien, quoted in Ready, *The Tolkien Relation*, 51.

7. Sayer, "Recollections," 8.

8. Kilby, *Tolkien and* The Silmarillion, 53.

9. Sayer, "Recollections," 10.

10. Ibid., 13.

11. W. H. Lewis, *Friends and Brothers*, 185.

12. Kilby, *Tolkien and* The Silmarillion, 53; and Pearce, *Tolkien: Man and Myth*, 29.

13. Carpenter, ed., *Letters*, 340.

14. J. R. R. Tolkien, "Valedictory Address," in Christopher Tolkien, ed., *The Monsters and the Critics and Other Essays*, 225.

15. S.T.R.O. D'Ardenne, "The Man and the Scholar," in *J. R. R. Tolkien: Scholar and Storyteller: Essays in Memoriam*, ed. Mary Salu and Robert T. Farrell (Ithaca, N.Y.: Cornell University Press, 1979), 35.

16. J. R. R. Tolkien, "The Name Coventry," [letter to editor], February 1945 in MU JRRT Collection, Series 7, Box 1, Folder 8.

17. Lawlor, *C. S. Lewis*, 35, 40.

18. Quoted in Judith Priestman, *Tolkien: Life and Legend* (Oxford: Bodleian Library, 1992), 31.

19. William Cater, "The Filial Duty of Christopher Tolkien," 93.

20. Christopher Tolkien, quoted in Cater, "The Filial Duty of Christopher Tolkien," 93; and Christopher Tolkien, ed., *Morgoth's Ring: The Later Silmarillion, Part 1*, viii.

21. Carpenter, ed., *Letters*, 172.

22. See, for example, Priscilla Tolkien, "Memories," 12.

23. [Anonymous], obituary of JRRT in *London Times*, 11

24. Carpenter, ed., *Letters*, 54, 340, 353–54.

25. Ibid., 353–54. The letter does not specify in what way or ways Tolkien's children were straying.

26. For an excellent analysis of Newman's influence on Tolkien, see Pearce, "Tolkien and the Catholic Literary Revival," 105–15.

27. Carpenter, ed., *Letters*, 395.

28. Sayer, "Recollections," 14.

29. Carpenter, ed., *Letters*, 354.

30. Ibid., 416.

31. Ibid., 394.

32. Ibid., 66.

33. Ibid., 67.

34. See, for example, W. H. Lewis, *Friends and Brothers*, 203.

35. Sayer, "Recollections," 13–14.

36. Kilby, unpublished parts of chapter "Woodland Prisoner," p. 13, WCWC, Kilby Files, 3–8, "Tolkien the Man" from TOLKIEN AND THE SILMARILLION.

37. Carpenter, ed., *Letters*, 96, 394.

38. Quoted in Carpenter, *Tolkien*, 65.

39. Carpenter, ed., *Letters*, 339.

40. Ibid., 96.

41. Quoted in Carpenter, *The Inklings*, 51.

42. W. H. Lewis, *C. S. Lewis: A Biography* [unpublished], 251, in WCWC.

43. Quoted in Lawlor, *C. S. Lewis*, 41. See also Havard, "Philia: Jack at Ease," 226; and Bayley, "A Passionate Pilgrim."

44. W. H. Lewis, *C. S. Lewis: A Biography*, 232.

45. Lewis, *Surprised by Joy*, 209.

46. Pearce, *Tolkien: Man and Myth*, 69.

47. Quoted in Christopher Derrick, *C. S. Lewis and the Church of Rome* (San Francisco: Ignatius Press, 1981), 215. The original letter was destroyed and very few Lewis scholars take Derrick's claims at face value.

48. Carpenter, ed., *Letters*, 352.

49. Quoted in Carpenter, *The Inklings*, 51–52.

50. Christopher Mitchell, the director of the Wade Center at Wheaton College, first pointed this out to me and greatly tempered my thoughts. Subsequent conversations with Joseph Pearce and Andrew Cuneo have only strengthened my belief that scholars too readily exaggerate the rift between Tolkien and Lewis.

51. Quoted in Carpenter, *The Inklings*, 216.

52. A. N. Wilson, *C. S. Lewis*, xvii.

53. Quoted in ibid., 135.

54. Carpenter, ed., *Letters*, 341, 349; and Green and Hooper, *C. S. Lewis: A Biography*, 184. Clyde Kilby noted that the tension between Tolkien and Lewis began in 1940, but he offered no explanation as to why that year was important. See, Kilby, unpublished parts of the chapter "Woodland Prisoner," p. 12, WCWC, Kilby Files, 3–8, "Tolkien the Man," from TOLKIEN AND THE SILMARILLION.

55. Carpenter, ed., *Letters*, 349.

56. Nevill Coghill, "The Approach to English," in Jocelyn Gibb, ed., *Light on Lewis* (New York: Harcourt Brace, 1965), 63; and W. H. Lewis, *Letters of C. S. Lewis*, 481.

57. James Patrick, "J. R. R. Tolkien and the Literary Catholic Revival," *The Latin Mass* (Spring 1999): 86.

58. See, for example, Sayer, "Recollections," 14.

59. Quoted in Carpenter, *The Inklings*, 120–21. "Apparition" from Carpenter, ed., *Letters*, 341.

60. Daniel Grotta, *J. R. R. Tolkien: Architect of Middle Earth* (Philadelphia, Pa.: Courage Books, 1992), 94; and Carpenter, *The Inklings*, 73–100.

61. Tolkien, *The Fellowship of the Ring*, 278.

62. Tolkien, *The Silmarillion*, 15. See also Kilby, *Tolkien and* The Silmarillion, 59.

63. Tolkien, *The Silmarillion*, 15.

64. Carpenter, ed., *Letters*, 285.

65. Christopher Tolkien, ed., *Morgoth's Ring*, ix.

66. Tolkien, *The Silmarillion*, 255.

67. J. R. R. Tolkien, *The Lost Road and Other Writings: Language and Legend Before 'The Lord of the Rings,"* ed. Christopher Tolkien, *History of Middle-earth*, vol. 5 (Boston: Houghton Mifflin, 1987), 333; Kilby, *Tolkien and* The Silmarillion, 64–65; and Kilby, notes taken while reading mss. of *The Silmarillion*, 1966, WCWC Kilby Files, 3–9. Christopher Tolkien downplays the importance of the "Final Battle" in his father's mythology. See Christopher Tolkien, Oxford, to Darrell A. Martin, Wheaton, 26 January 1983, WCWC, Folder; JRRT to Miscellaneous Correspondents.

68. Carpenter, ed., *Letters*, 203–4.

69. Christopher Tolkien, ed., *Morgoth's Ring*, 341,

70. C. S. Lewis, *The Kilns*, to Warnie Lewis, 11 August 1940, WCWC, CSL Letters to Warnie Lewis, Letter Index 220.

71. Clyde Kilby, unpublished chapter, "The Manuscript of THE SILMARILLION," WCWC, Kilby Files, 1–12, TOLKIEN AND THE SILMARILLION.

72. Christopher Tolkien, ed., *Morgoth's Ring*, 303.

73. Ibid., 313.

74. Ibid., 316.

75. Carpenter, ed., *Letters*, 76.

76. Christopher Tolkien, ed., *Morgoth's Ring*, 318.

77. Ibid., 319.

78. Ibid., 322.

79. Ibid.

80. Kilby, *Tolkien and* The Silmarillion, 61–62.

81. Tolkien, *The Fellowship of the Ring*, 65.

82. Tolkien, *Unfinished Tales*, 326.

83. Tolkien, *The Fellowship of the Ring*, 255.

84. Carpenter, ed., *Letters*, 172.

85. Tolkien, *The Fellowship of the Ring*, 68–69.

86. Tolkien, *The Two Towers*, 324; and Castell, "The Realms of Tolkien," 151–52.

87. Carpenter, ed., *Letters*, 330.

88. Ibid., 191.

89. Tolkien, *The Two Towers*, 316.

90. Carpenter, ed., *Letters*, 326.

91. Ibid., 326.

92. Ibid., 355.

93. Ibid., 146.

94. Tolkien, *The Two Towers*, 284–85.

95. Tolkien, *The Fellowship of the Ring*, 208, 226.

96. Ibid., 210.

97. Carpenter, ed., *Letters*, 193.

98. Translation of Sam's prayer in J. R. R. Tolkien, "A Elbereth Gilthoniel," in Donald Swann, *The Road Goes Ever On: A Song Cycle* (Boston: Houghton Mifflin, 1967), 64.

99. Tolkien, *The Two Towers*, 338–39.

100. Carpenter, ed., *Letters*, 149.

101. Ibid., 387, 146.

102. Ibid., 387.

103. Ibid., 283.

104. Tolkien, *The Fellowship of the Ring*, 344.

105. Kilby, *Tolkien and* The Silmarillion, 59.

106. Carpenter, ed., *Letters*, 274–75.

107. Tolkien, *The Peoples of Middle-earth*, 404.

108. Tolkien, *The Return of the King* (Boston, Mass: Houghton Mifflin, 1993), 213.

109. Tolkien, *The Two Towers*, 29, 31.

110. Ibid., 92; and Tolkien, *The Return of the King*, 190–91.

111. Tolkien, *The Silmarillion*, 202–5, 207.

112. Tolkien, *Unfinished Tales*, 276.

113. Charles A. Coulombe, "The Lord of the Rings—A Catholic View," in Pearce, ed., *Tolkien: A Celebration*, 57.

114. Carpenter, ed., Letters, 53.

115. Sayer, "Recollections," 10.

116. Carpenter, ed., Letters, 338.

117. Carpenter, Tolkien, 143.

118. Carpenter, ed., Letters, 338.

119. Ibid., 99.

120. Ibid., 172.

121. Ibid., 49.

122. Ibid., 286.

123. Sayer, "Recollections," 11.

124. Christopher Tolkien, ed., *Morgoth's Ring*, 333.

125. W. H. Lewis, *Friends and Brothers*, 207.

126. Tolkien, *The Fellowship of the Ring*, 372.

127. Carpenter, ed., *Letters*, 407.

128. Tolkien to Kilby, ca. 1966, *Tolkien Letters*, WCWC.

129. Tolkien, *The Silmarillion*, 26.

130. Tolkien, *Unfinished Tales*, 393.

131. Christopher Tolkien, ed., *Morgoth's Ring*, 166.

132. Revelation 12:1 (New International Version).

133. Carpenter, ed., *Letters*, 400.

134. Wain, *Sprightly Running*,182.

135. Carpenter, ed., *Letters*, 413. See also Priscilla Tolkien, "Memories," 14.

136. Carpenter, ed., *Letters*, 128.

Chapter 4

1. Christopher Tolkien, ed., *Morgoth's Ring*, 400–2.

2. St. Augustine, *City of God* (Chicago: Encyclopaedia Britannica, 1952), 133.

3. Tolkien, *The Two Towers*, 40–1.

4. St. Augustine, *City of God*, 133.

5. Carpenter, ed., *Letters*, 76.

6. St. Augustine, *City of God*, 133–34.

7. Hugh of St. Victor, *De Sacramentis*, II.2.1-2. Ryan Freeburn provided me with this quote.

8. Patrick, "J. R. R. Tolkien and the Literary Catholic Revival," 85.

9. St. Paul aptly describes "The Body" in the twelfth chapter of both his letter to the Romans and his first to the Corinthians and in his letter to the Colossians (1:12–20). "For as in one body , and all the members do not have the same function," the Apostle wrote, "so we, though many, are one body in Christ, and individually members one of another." Gifts such as teaching or speaking "differ according to the grace given to us, let us use them." (RSV)

10. See especially, Tolkien, *The Silmarillion*, 252.

11. Carpenter, ed., *Letters*, 149.

12. Christopher Tolkien, ed., *Morgoth's Ring*, 345.

13. Carpenter, ed., *Letters*, 172.

14. This schema of priest, prophet, and king comes from an essay written by Barry Gordon and discussed by Clyde S. Kilby. Tolkien admitted to Kilby that the Gordon thesis worked, but had been unconscious on Tolkien's part. See Kilby, *Tolkien and* The Silmarillion, 55–56.

15. See Kilby, *Tolkien and* The Silmarillion, 55–56.

16. JRRT-CSK notes, taken while reading mss. of SILMARILLION for JRRT in 1966, "Summary of 'Kingship, Priesthood and Prophecy in THE LORD OF THE RINGS,' by Barry Gordon, Sr., Lecturer in Economics, U. of Newcastle, New South Wales." WCWC, Kilby Files, 3–9.

17. Carpenter, ed., *Letters*, 327.

18. Tolkien denied this interpretation in his *Letters*, 255.

19. J. R. R. Tolkien, "The Sea-Bell," in *The Tolkien Reader* (New York: Ballantine Books, 1966), 246–47.

20. Carpenter, ed., *Letters*, 105.

21. See Carpenter, ed., *Letters*, 105.

22. For an excellent analysis of Sam as hero, see Stratford Caldecott, "Over the Chasm of Fire: Christian Heroism in the *The Silmarillion* and *The Lord of the Rings*," in Pearce, ed., Tolkien: A Celebration, 29–32.

23. Tolkien, *The Fellowship of the Ring*, 53–55.

24. Quoted in Carpenter, *Tolkien*, 81.

25. St. John was Tolkien's patron saint. See Carpenter, *The Inklings*.

26. Tolkien, "Sir Gawain and the Green Knight," 75.

27. J. R. R. Tolkien, "The Homecoming of Beorhtnoth Beorhtelm's Son," *Essays and Studies* 6 (1953): 14.

28. Ibid., 14.

29. Tolkien, *The Two Towers*, 338–39.

30. Carpenter, ed., *Letters*, 105.

31. Ibid., 161.

32. Tolkien, *The Fellowship of the Ring*, 96.

33. Carpenter, ed., *Letters*, 105.

34. See, for example, ibid., 104.

35. Ibid., 179, 227. See also the reprint of the section of the letter not found in Carpenter's edition of Tolkien's letters in J. R. R. Tolkien, The End of the Third Age: The History of the Lord of the Rings Part Four, ed. Christopher Tolkien (Boston: Houghton Mifflin, 1998), 129–32.

36. Tolkien, *The Return of the King*, 378.

37. Christopher Tolkien, ed., *The End of the Third Age*, 117.

38. Ibid., 115.

39. Ibid., 125.

40. Ibid., 128.

41. For a while, Tolkien believed Gandalf may be an incarnate Valar rather than Maiar. See, for example, Kilby, the unpublished chapter "The Manuscript of *The Silmarillion*," p. 85-A, n. 225, WCWC, Kilby Files, 1–12. Tolkien also speculated, though dismissed the idea, that Gandalf may be an incarnate Manwë. See Tolkien, *Unfinished Tales*, 412–13.

42. Tolkien, *The Silmarillion*, 30–31.

43. Ibid., 31.

44. Tolkien, *Unfinished Tales*, 406.

45. Tolkien, *The Fellowship of the Ring*, 270.

46. Carpenter, ed., *Letters*, 280.

47. Ibid., 259.

48. St. Paul, First Letter to Timothy 6:6–8 (NEB).

49. Tolkien, *The Two Towers*, 106.

50. Book of Job 1:21 (NEB).

51. Tolkien, *The Return of the King*, 310; and Tolkien, *The Silmarillion*, 304.

52. Tolkien, *Unfinished Tales*, 408.

53. Tolkien, *The Fellowship of the Ring*, 344; See also "Flame Imperishable" in *The Silmarillion*, 15–16.

54. Tolkien, *Unfinished Tales*, 361.

55. Tolkien, *The Fellowship of the Ring*, 185.

56. Ibid., 371.

57. Ibid., 232.

58. Tolkien, *The Two Towers*, 195.

59. Ibid., 98.

60. Ibid., 98.

61. Carpenter, ed., *Letters*, 203.

62. Tolkien, *The Return of the King*, 249.

63. Ibid., 249, 275.

64. "Seeress's Prophecy," in *The Poetic Edda*, trans. Carolyne Larrington (Oxford, 1996), 12.2.

65. Carpenter, ed., *Letters*, 119.

66. *The Saga of the Volsungs: The Norse Epic of Sigurd the Dragon Slayer*, ed. and trans. Jesse L. Byock (London: Penguin, 1999), 38.

67. Several authors have commented on the similarities between Odin and Gandalf. See, for example, Majorie Burns, "Gandalf and Odin," in *Tolkien's Legendarium*, 219–31.

68. Carpenter, ed., *Letters*, 202–3.

69. Christopher Dawson, Religion and the Rise of Western Culture (New York: Image Books, 1991), 61.

70. Ibid., 62. See also "St. Boniface of Mainz," entry in *Butler's Lives of the Saints* (New York: P. J. Kenedy and Sons, 1962) II: 477–81; and Gerald J. Russello, ed., *Christianity and European Culture: Selections from the Work of Christopher Dawson* (Washington, D.C.: Catholic University of America Press, 1998), 39.

71. Dawson, *The Making of Europe*, 185.

72. Donald Swann, *The Road Goes Ever On: A Song Cycle* (Boston: Houghton Mifflin, 1967), vi; and Donald Swann, Swann's Way, 207.

73. Carpenter, ed., *Letters*, 376.

74. Tolkien, *Unfinished Tales*, 335.

75. Tolkien, *The Return of the King*, 152.

76. Tolkien, *The Fellowship of the Ring*, 261.

77. Ibid.

78. Tolkien, *The Return of the King*, 136.

79. Ibid., 150–51.

80. Ibid., 156.

81. Jane Chance, *Tolkien's Art: A Mythology for England*, rev. ed. (Lexington: University of Kentucky Press, 2001), 174–75. T. A. Shippey takes this further, noting that Tolkien's Theoden strongly resembles the historic Theodorid, a Gothic king, overwhelmed by foes at the Battle of the Catalaunian Plains. See Shippey, *The Road to Middle-earth*, 12.

82. Dawson, *Religion and the Rise of Western Culture*, 182.

83. Carpenter, ed., *Letters*, 206–7.

84. Tolkien, *The Return of the King*, 246.

85. Ibid., 246.

86. Ibid.

87. Ibid., 246–47.

88. Carpenter, ed., *Letters*, 160.

89. Ibid., 324.

90. Tolkien, *The Return of the King*, 250.

91. Christopher Tolkien, ed., *Morgoth's Ring*, 341.

92. Carpenter, ed., *Letters*, 286.

93. Tolkien, *The Return of the King*, 344.

94. Carpenter, ed., *Letters*, 267.

95. Ibid., 79.

96. Ibid.

97. Ibid., 232.

98. Ibid., 213, 232. See also Tolkien, *The Lost Road*.

99. Tolkien, *The Two Towers*, 271–73.

100. Ibid., 278.

101. Carpenter, ed., *Letters*, 241.

102. Tolkien, *The Two Towers*, 284.

103. Carpenter, ed., *Letters*, 178–9.

104. Gerrolt, 1971 BBC interview.

105. Russell Kirk, "Tolkien and Truth through Fantasy," *To the Point* (General Features Corporation), 29–30 June 1968.

106. Tolkien, *The Two Towers*, 244.

Chapter 5

1. Carpenter, *The Inklings*, 174.

2. Ibid., 174–75.

3. Clyde Kilby, unpublished parts of the chapter on Tolkien, Lewis, and Williams, p. 100, n. 32 WCWC, Kilby Files, 1–12, TOLKIEN AND THE SILMARILLION.

4. Carpenter, ed., *Letters*, 207.

5. Gospel of St. John 8:44 (Revised Standard Version).

6. Tolkien, *The Fellowship of the Ring*, 270, 278.

7. Ibid., 57.

8. See Kilby, *Tolkien and* The Silmarillion, unpublished chapter parts on Tolkien, Lewis, and Williams, p. 100, n. 32, in Kilby Files, 1–12, WCWC.

9. Quoted in Carpenter, *The Inklings*, 121.

10. Quoted in Michael Moorcock, *Wizardry and Wild Romance: A Study of Epic Fantasy* (London: Victor Gollancz, Ltd., 1987), 45. See also, Edward Power, "Michael Moorcock," Irish Times, 29 December 2001, 61.

11. Moorcock, *Wizardry and Wild Romance*, 125.

12. Ibid., 127. See also Anthony Gardner, "Literary Giant or Monstrous Myth?" *London Times*, 28 December 1991.

13. Christopher Tolkien, ed., *Morgoth's Ring*, 344.

14. Ursula K. Le Guin, "The Dark Tower and Other Stories by C. S. Lewis [book review]," *The New Republic*, 16 April 1977, 30.

15. See, for example, Peter Kreeft, *Back to Virtue: Traditional Moral Wisdom for Modern Moral Confusion* (San Francisco: Ignatius Press, 1992), 191.

16. Kilby, "Tolkien the Man" from TOLKIEN AND THE SILMARILLION, unpublished parts of the chapter "Woodland Prisoner," p. 13 in WCWC, Kilby Files, 3–8.

17. Carpenter, ed., *Letters*, 255.

18. Ibid., 41.

19. Russell Kirk, *Enemies of the Permanent Things: Observations of Abnormality in Literature and Politics* (Peru, Ill.: Sherwood Sugden, 1988), 113.

20. Carpenter, ed., *Letters*, 80.

21. Ibid., 24.

22. Tolkien, "Mythopoeia."

23. Tolkien, *The Fellowship of the Ring*, 281.

24. Tolkien, *The Silmarillion*, 141, 156.

25. Ibid., 141.

26. Ibid., 156.

27. Ibid., 73ff.

28. Tolkien, *TheReturn of the King*, 190; and Carpenter, ed., *Letters*, 195.

29. Tolkien labeled them "Goblins" in *The Hobbit*.

30. Carpenter, ed., *Letters*, 287. One should not, however, take this definitively, as Tolkien seems to have been unsure how to deal with the Orcs and their origins. See, for example, his late essays on why Orcs come from men rather than from Elves: "Orcs," in Christopher Tolkien, ed., *Morgoth's Ring*, 409–24.

31. Carpenter, ed., *Letters*, 178.

32. Tolkien, *The Silmarillion*, 50.

33. Carpenter, ed., *Letters*, 195.

34. J. R. R. Tolkien, *The Hobbit* (Boston: Houghton Mifflin, 1978), 60.

35. Carpenter, ed., *Letters*, 190.

36. Ibid., 90.

37. On the Orcs hating lembas, see Tolkien, *The Return of the King*, 190. On the Orcs eating man flesh, see Tolkien, *The Two Towers*, 49.

38. Tolkien, *The Silmarillion*, 43–44.

39. For the story of Isildur, see Tolkien, "The Disaster of the Gladden Fields," in *Unfinished Tales*, 283–300.

40. Christopher Tolkien, ed., *Morgoth's Ring*, 313.

41. Ibid., 346–47.

42. Ibid., 348.

43. Ibid., 334.

44. Ibid., 313ff.

45. On protection in the waters, see Tolkien, *Unfinished Tales*, 189.

46. Ibid., 174.

47. Tolkien, *The Silmarillion*, 259–61.

48. Ibid., 261–66.

49. Ibid., 266.

50. For the acquisition of silver and gold, see Tolkien, *Unfinished Tales*, 178.

51. Ibid., 200.

52. Tolkien, *The Silmarillion*, 267.

53. Ibid., 269–70; and Tolkien, *Unfinished Tales*, 233.

54. Tolkien, *The Silmarillion*, 270–72.

55. Voegelin, *Science, Politics, and Gnosticism: Two Essays* (Chicago: Regnery, 1968), 9.

56. Carpenter, ed., *Letters*, 243.

57. Tolkien, *The Silmarillion*, 272–74.

58. Ibid., 277.

59. Ibid., 278–79.

60. Ibid., 279.

61. Ibid., 276. "A Description of the Island of Númenor" is one such history book. It is reprinted in Tolkien, *Unfinished Tales*, 173–80.

62. Tolkien, *The Silmarillion*, 280–81.

63. Carpenter, ed., *Letters*, 186.

64. Ibid., 197–98, 361.

65. Ibid., 347.

66. Tolkien, *The Lost Road*, 67.

67. Tolkien, *Unfinished Tales*, 192.

68. Carpenter, ed., *Letters*, 206–7.

69. Tolkien, "On Fairy-Stories," in Christopher Tolkien, ed., *The Monsters and the Critics and Other Essays*, 114.

70. St. Luke, Acts of the Apostles, 8:9–24 (New Revised Standard).

71. Acts of the Apostles, 13:8–11.

72. Carpenter, ed., *Letters*, 199.

73. Tolkien, *The Fellowship of the Ring*, 377.

74. Tolkien, "On Fairy-Stories," 143.

75. Ibid.

76. Carpenter, ed., *Letters*, 200.

77. Ibid., 146.

78. Tolkien, *The Two Towers*, 100.

79. Tolkien, *The Fellowship of the Ring*, 58.

80. Carpenter, ed., *Letters*, 145.

81. Ibid., 146. See also *Letters*, 87–88.

82. Guardini, *Letters from Lake Como*, 43.

83. Ibid., 79.

84. Quoted in Michael D. Henry, "Voegelin and Heidegger as Critics of Modernity," *Modern Age* 43 (Spring 2001): 125.

85. Tolkien, *The Two Towers*, 172.

86. Carpenter, ed., *Letters*, 151–52.

87. Tolkien, *The Fellowship of the Ring*, 63.

88. Ibid., 56.

89. Ibid., 63.

90. Ibid., 42.

91. Ibid., 71.

92. Carpenter, ed., *Letters*, 153–54.

93. Christopher Tolkien, ed., *Morgoth's Ring*, 396–97.

94. Tolkien, *The Fellowship of the Ring*, 68.

95. Tolkien, *The Peoples of Middle-earth*, 409–21.

96. Carpenter, ed., *Letters*, 344, 419.

97. J. R. R. Tolkien, "The New Shadow," in *The Peoples of Middle-earth*, ed. Christopher Tolkien, *History of Middle-earth*, vol. 12 (Boston: Houghton Mifflin, 1996), 411.

98. Tolkien, *The Return of the King*, 155.

Chapter 6

1. Andrew Rissik, review of Tom Shippey, *J. R. R. Tolkien: Author of the Century*, in the *London Guardian*, 2 September 2000.

2. Roz Kaveney, "The Ring Recycled," *New Statesmen and Society*, 27 December 1991, 47.

3. Greere quoted in Paul Goodman, "Is This Really the Century's Greatest Book?" *London Telegraph*, 25 January 1997.

4. Kirk, *Enemies of the Permanent Things*, 124.

5. Harvey Breitt, "Oxford Calling," *New York Times Book Review*, 5 June 1955, 8.

6. Carpenter, ed., *Letters*, 87–88, 115.

7. Ibid., 102.

8. Ibid., 165.

9. Kilby, *Tolkien and* The Silmarillion, 10.

10. Foster, "Dr. Clyde S. Kilby Recalls the Inklings," JRRT Series 5, Box 1, Folder 23, p. 11, *Tolkien Papers*, Marquette University Archives.

11. Sayer, "Recollections," 8.

12. George Sayer, liner notes to *J. R. R. Tolkien Reads and Sings His Lord of the Rings* (Caedmon CDL5 1478).

13. Carpenter, ed., *Letters*, 349.

14. Kilby, *Tolkien and* The Silmarillion, 25.

15. Carpenter, ed., *Letters*, 220.

16. Ibid., 321.

17. Ibid., 420; and Sayer, "Recollections," 6.

18. Tolkien, *The Silmarillion*, 76.

19. Tolkien, *The Two Towers*, 68.

20. Ibid., 160.

21. Ibid., 172.

22. Lawlor, *C. S. Lewis*, 7.

23. For the numbers, see R. J. Rummel, *Death by Government* (New Brunswick, N.J.: Transaction Press, 1994); and Stephane Courtois et al., *Black Book of Communism: Crimes, Terror, Repression* (Cambridge, Mass.: Harvard University Press, 1999). For a fine analysis of the century and its crimes, see Robert Conquest, *Reflections on a Ravaged Century* (New York: W. W. Norton, 2000). The numbers Mao killed are currently in dispute, with some scholars arguing he may have killed, directly and indirectly, 65 million Chinese. See *Black Book of Communism*, 4.

24. Tolkien, *The Two Towers*, 239.

25. Grotta, *J. R. R. Tolkien: Architect of Middle Earth*, 52–53. Tolkien acknowledges as much in Carpenter, ed., *Letters*, 303, but stressed that William Morris's novels also provided an influence.

26. C. S. Lewis, *On Stories and Other Essays on Literature* (New York: Harcourt Brace Jovanovich, 1988), 88. Shippey has continued this argumentation in his excellent *J. R. R. Tolkien: Author of the Century*.

27. Tolkien, *The Fellowship of the Ring*, 7.

28. Carpenter, ed., *Letters*, 55–56.

29. Ibid., 93.

30. Ibid., 111.

31. Fred Inglis, "Gentility and Powerlessness: Tolkien and the New Class," in Robert Giddings, ed., *J. R. R. Tolkien, This Far Land* (Totowa, N.J.: Barnes & Noble Books, 1984), 40.

32. Nick Farrell, "Italian Fascists Take Bilbo Baggins and Gandalf Hostage," *London Sunday Telegraph*, 26 March 2000; and Frances Kennedy, "Fascists Take Heart from Hobbit Revival," *London Independent*, 18 January 2002, 12.

33. W. H. Lewis, ed., *Letters of C. S. Lewis*, 176.

34. Carpenter, ed., *Letters*, 110.

35. For penetrating analysis of the communist attack on Christianity, see Whittaker Chambers, *Witness* (Washington, D.C.: Regnery, 1952), especially pages 3–22.

36. Carpenter, ed., *Letters*, 95. For a clear analysis of Franco and the Spanish Civil

War, affirming Campbell's and Tolkien's views, see Paul Johnson, *Modern Times: From the Twenties to the Nineties* (New York: Harper Collins, 1991), 323–40.

37. Carpenter, ed., *Letters*, 89.

38. Ibid., 65.

39. Ibid.

40. Christopher Dawson, *The Judgment of the Nations* (New York: Sheed and Ward, 1942), 3.

41. Ted Flynn, *Thunder of Justice* (Sterling, Va.: MaxKol, 1993), 8.

42. Patrick Curry, *Defending Middle-earth: Tolkien, Myth, and Modernity* (Edinburgh: Floris Books, 1997), 24.

43. Michal Semin to the author, 13 November 2000.

44. Alan Philps, "Young Russians Seek Refuge in Tolkien's Middle Earth," *London Telegraph*, 12 February 1997.

45. Tolkien, "English and Welsh," in Christopher Tolkien, ed., *The Monsters and the Critics and Other Essays*, 182.

46. C. S. Lewis, *That Hideous Strength* (New York: Macmillan, 1946), 295.

47. Carpenter, ed., Letters, 107.

48. Ibid., 246.

49. Edith, Tolkien's wife, stated her dislike for the Labour Party. Tolkien made no comment, but merely listened. Most likely, he agreed with her. See Sayer, "Recollections," 15. John Wain, the youngest member of the Inklings, wrote that the Inklings "took for granted that a Labour government was the enemy of everything they stood for." See Wain, *Sprightly Running*, 181.

50. Carpenter, ed., *Letters*, 354.

51. Ibid., 63.

52. Walter Hooper, ed., *They Stand Together: The Letters of C. S. Lewis and Arthur Greeves, 1914–1963* (New York: Macmillan, 1979), 363–64.

53. Quoted in Carpenter, *Tolkien*, 124–25.

54. Sayer, liner notes to *J. R. R. Tolkien Reads and Sings His The Lord of the Rings*.

55. Guy Davenport, "J. R. R. Tolkien, RIP," *National Review*, 28 September 1973, 1043.

56. Pearce, *Tolkien: Man and Myth*, 153–181; and Colin Wilson, *Tree by Tolkien*.

57. Hilaire Belloc, *The Servile State* (1912; Indianapolis, Ind.: Liberty Fund, 1977), 39.

58. For the best examination of republican thought throughout Western history,

see Paul Rahe, *Republics: Ancient and Modern* (Chapel Hill, N.C.: University of North Carolina Press, 1992).

59. Hilaire Belloc, "The Modern Man," in Who Owns America?: *A New Declaration of Independence*, ed. *Herbert Agar and Allen Tate* (Wilmington, Del.: ISI Books, 1999), 434.

60. Dawson, *The Judgment of Nations*, 7.

61. Tolkien, *The Fellowship of the Ring*, 10.

62. Carpenter, ed., *Letters*, 250.

63. Lewis, *On Stories*, 85.

64. Carpenter, ed., *Letters*, 241.

65. See, J. R. R. Tolkien, "The Quest for Erebor," in *Unfinished Tales*, 321–36.

66. Tolkien, *The Fellowship of the Ring*, 14.

67. Ibid., 18.

68. Ibid., 18–19.

69. Ibid., 19.

70. Ibid., 108.

71. Ibid., 188–89.

72. Tolkien, *The Return of the King*, 303.

73. This may very well have stemmed from Aquinas's writings, favorable toward Christian kingship. See Thomas Aquinas, *Summa Contra Gentiles*, Book 1.

74. Coulombe, "The Lord of the Rings—A Catholic View," 56.

75. Henry Resnik, "The Hobbit-Forming World of J. R. R. Tolkien," *Saturday Evening Post*, 2 July 1966, 94.

76. Quoted in Carpenter, *Tolkien*, 225–26.

77. Tolkien, "Mythopoeia," 100.

Conclusion

1. John Dichtl, Bloomington, Indiana, to author, Hillsdale, Michigan, 30 June 2000. E-mail in possession of author. Because of the continuing eco-terrorism associated with E.L.F., Elf Lore, the Tolkien-inspired environmental group, has since changed its name to "Lothlorien."

2. Harold Bloom, introduction to *Modern Critical Interpretations: J. R. R.*

Tolkien's The Lord of the Rings (Philadelphia, Pa.: Chelsea House Publishers, 2000), 1. See Bloom's similar statement in his introduction to *Modern Critical Views: J. R. R. Tolkien* (Philadelphia, Pa.: Chelsea House, 2000), 2.

3. Bloom, introduction to *Modern Critical Interpretations: J. R. R. Tolkien's* The Lord of the Rings, 1–2. For the best account and summation of the myriad of Tolkien critics, see Patrick Curry's insightful and witty essay, "Tolkien and His Critics: A Critique," in Thomas Honegger, ed., *Root and Branch: Approaches towards Understanding Tolkien* (Zurich: Walking Tree Publishers, 1999), 81–148.

4. Hannah Mcgill, "Youth Culture Risks Picking up a Filthy Hobbit," *The Scotsman*, 3 November 2000, 5.

5. J. R. R. Tolkien, "The New Shadow," in *The Peoples of Middle-earth*, 413.

6. Guardini, *Letters from Lake Como*, 10.

7. Tolkien, *The Hobbit*, 105; and Tolkien, *The Fellowship of the Ring*, 270.

8. Patrick Curry discusses the Czech Radegast in *Defending Middle-earth*, 114.

9. Tolkien, *The Silmarillion*, 2d ed., 300; and Tolkien, *Unfinished Tales*, 406.

10. Tolkien, *The Silmarillion*, 302. On him becoming enamored with creation, see Tolkien, *Unfinished Tales*, 407.

11. Tolkien, *The Fellowship of the Ring*, 272.

12. Edward Rothstein, "Flaming Swords and Wizards' Orbs," *New York Times Book Review*, 8 December 1996, 60.

13. George R. R. Martin, introduction to Karen Haber, ed., *Meditations on Middle-earth* (New York: St. Martin's Press, 2001), 3.

14. Harry Turtledove, "The Ring and I," in *Meditations on Middle-earth*, 69. See also Edmund Fuller, "Catnip for Hobbit Lovers," *Wall Street Journal*, 24 July 1984.

15. Jane Yolen, introduction to Martin H. Greenberg, *After the King: Stories in Honor of J. R. R. Tolkien* (New York: Tor, 1992), ix.

16. Quoted in Douglas A. Anderson, "Tolkien after All These Years," in *Meditations on Middle-earth*, 139–40.

17. *The Lord of the Rings* was first published in Russia in 1982. Prior to that, one had to find it on "samizdat—fuzzy carbon copies of a typed translation. The Kremlin also suspected that Tolkien's evil land of Mordor was really Russia and his brutish orcs were a slander against the noble proletariat." (Philps, "Young Russians Seek Refuge in Tolkien's Middle Earth," *London Telegraph* (electronic version), 12 February 1997.) The communists were, of course, right to be suspicious of the trilogy. Tolkien loathed them.

18. Helen Womack, "Teenage Elves, Goblins Frolic in Gorky Park," *Moscow Times*, 10 January 1998.

19. Ibid.

20. Philps, "Young Russians Seek Refuge."

21. Craig Nelson, "Kazakhstan Crackdown on Human Hobbits Middle Earth and Former Soviet Republic in Collision of Cultures," *London Sunday Telegraph*, 26 August 2001, 27.

22. Patrick Cockburn, "Police Get Tough with the Hobbit-Lovers of Kazakhstan," *London Independent on Sunday*, 29 July 2001, 18; and "Dressing Up Gets Dressing Down in Russia," *Ottawa Citizen*, 24 February 2002, C16.

23. Daniel Foggo, "Lord of the Rings Films 'Will Force Tolkien Family into Hiding,'" *London Sunday Telegraph*, 7 January 2001, 11. See also Christopher Wilson, "As the Fantasy World of the Lord of the Rings Is Brought to Life on the Big Screen, the Author's Family Has Bitterly Condemned the Project: The Sad Legacy of Tolkien's Fable," *London Express*, 12 October 2001, 37; and David Gates and Devin Gordon, "One Ring to Lure Them All," *Newsweek*, 29 January 2001, 60.

24. Janet Hunter, "Meet Bilbo, the 'New' Harry Potter," *Ottawa Citizen*, 28 July 2001, J1.

25. Ibid.

26. None of this is to suggest that Jackson's vision is better than Tolkien's vision. Indeed, Jackson's vision leaves much to be desired. Several chapters as well as characters are simply missing from Jackson's narrative. This analysis simply considers Jackson's use of religious themes.

27. Shippey, *The Road to Middle-earth*, 178–79.

28. Russell Kirk, *The Politics of Prudence* (Bryn Mawr, Pa.: ISI Books, 1993).

29. Marcus T. Cicero, *On the Republic* 3:22.

30. St. Paul's Letter to the Romans 1:20 (RSV).

31. Pope John Paul II, "Incarnation Inspires Christian Genius," *L'Osservatore Romano* (Vatican City), 4 December 1996.

32. T. S. Eliot, *Christianity and Culture* (San Diego: Harvest, 1976), 50.

33. St. Paul's Letter to the Philippians 4:8 (RSV)

34. For the importance of each, see Joseph Pearce, *Literary Converts: Spiritual Inspiration in an Age of Unbelief* (San Francisco: Ignatius Press, 1999).

35. Tolkien, *The Fellowship of the Ring*, 60.

36. Quoted in Pearce, *Tolkien: Man and Myth*, 35.

37. Tolkien, *The Two Towers*, 155.

38. Tolkien, *The Return of the King*, 199.

39. Carpenter, ed., *Letters*, 400.

Bibliography

Archival Sources

Wade Collection, Marion Wade Center, Wheaton College, Wheaton, Illinois [WCWC].

J. R. R. Tolkien Archives, Marquette University Library, Milwaukee, Wisconsin [MU JRRT].

Works by J. R. R. Tolkien and/or Christopher Tolkien

Tolkien, Christopher, ed. *The Saga of King Heidrek*. London: Thomas Nelson, 1960.

_____. *The Silmarillion: A Brief Account of the Book and Its Making*. Boston: Houghton Mifflin, 1977.

Tolkien, J. R. R. "The Adventures of Tom Bombadil." In *The Tolkien Reader*, 189–251. New York: Ballantine, 1966.

_____. "Beowulf: The Monsters and the Critics." In *An Anthology of Beowulf Criticism*. Edited by Lewis E. Nicholson, 51–103. Notre Dame, Ind.: University of Notre Dame Press, 1963.

_____. *The Book of Lost Tales, Part One*. Vol. 1, *History of Middle-Earth*. Edited by Christopher Tolkien. Boston: Houghton Mifflin, 1983.

_____. *The Book of Lost Tales, Part Two*. Vol. 2, *History of Mid-*

dle-Earth. Edited by Christopher Tolkien. Boston: Houghton Mifflin, 1984.

————. "Chaucer as Philologist: The Reeve's Tale." *Transactions of the Philological Society* (1934): 1–70.

————. "English and Welsh." In *The Monsters and the Critics and Other Essays,* edited by Christopher Tolkien, 162–97. Boston: Houghton Mifflin, 1983.

————. "Enquiry into the Communication of Thought." *Vinyar Tengwar,* no. 39 (1998): 21–34.

————. *The Fellowship of the Ring.* 2nd ed. Boston: Houghton Mifflin, 1993.

————. *Finn and Hengest: The Fragment and the Episode.* Edited by Alan Bliss. Boston: Houghton Mifflin, 1983.

————. *"The Homecoming of Beorhtnoth Beorhthelm's Son."* Essays and Studies 6 (1953): 1–18.

————. *The Hobbit,* or, *There and Back Again.* Boston: Houghton Mifflin, 1997.

————. "Inram." *Time and Tide,* 3 December 1955, 1561.

————. "The Lay of Aotrou and Itrou." *Welsh Review* 4, no. (1945): 254–66.

————. *The Lays of Beleriand.* Vol. 3, *History of Middle-Earth.* Edited by Christopher Tolkien. Boston: Houghton Mifflin, 1985.

————. *The Letters of J. R. R. Tolkien.* Edited by Humphrey Carpenter. Boston: Houghton Mifflin, 1981.

————. *The Lost Road and Other Writings: Language and Legend before 'The Lord of the Rings.'* Vol. 5, *History of Middle-Earth.* Edited by Christopher Tolkien. Boston: Houghton Mifflin, 1987.

————. *The Monsters and the Critics and Other Essays.* Edited by Christopher Tolkien. Boston: Houghton Mifflin, 1983.

_____. *Morgoth's Ring: The Later Silmarillion*. Vol. 10, *History of Middle-Earth*. Edited by Christopher Tolkien. Boston: Houghton Mifflin, 1993.

_____. "The Name 'Nodens.'" *Report on the Excavation of the Prehistoric, Roman, and Post Roman Site in Lydney Park, Cloucestershire* (1932): 132–37.

_____. "The Oxford English School." *Oxford Magazine*, 29 May 1930, 778–82.

_____. "On Fairy-Stories." In *The Monsters and the Critics and Other Essays*, edited by Christopher Tolkien, 109–61. Boston: Houghton Mifflin, 1983.

_____. "On Translating Beowulf." In *The Monsters and the Critics and Other Essays*, edited by Christopher Tolkien, 49-71. Boston: Houghton Mifflin, 1983.

_____. *The Peoples of Middle-Earth*. Vol. 12, *History of Middle-Earth*. Edited by Christopher Tolkien. Boston: Houghton Mifflin, 1996.

_____. *Pictures by J. R. R. Tolkien*. Edited by Christopher Tolkien. Boston: Houghton Mifflin, 1992.

_____. Preface to *The Ancrene Riwle*, by M. B. Salu. LondonBurns and Oates, 1955.

_____. *The Return of the King*. Boston: Houghton Mifflin, 1993.

_____. *The Return of the Shadow: The History of The Lord of the Rings, Part One*. Vol. 6, *History of Middle-Earth*. Edited by Christopher Tolkien. Boston: Houghton Mifflin, 1988.

_____. "The Rivers and Beacon-Hills of Gondor." *Vinyar Tengwar*, no. 42 (2001): 5–31.

_____. *Sauron Defeated: The End of the Third Age: The History of The Lord of the Rings, Part Four*. Vol. 9, *History of Middle-Earth*. Edited by Christopher Tolkien. Boston: Houghton Mifflin, 1992.

_____. "A Secret Vice." In *The Monsters and the Critics and Other Essays*, edited by Christopher Tolkien, 198–223. Boston: Houghton Mifflin, 1983.

_____. *The Shaping of Middle-Earth: The Quenta, the Ambarkanta, and the Annals, Together with the Earliest 'Silmarillion' and the First Map*. Vol. 4, *History of Middle-Earth*. Edited by Christopher Tolkien. Boston: Houghton Mifflin, 1986.

_____. *Smith of Wootton Major and Farmer Giles of Ham*. New York: Nelson, 1976.

_____. "Sigelwara Land, Part I." *Medium Aevum* 1 (1932): 183–96.

_____. "Sigelwara Land, Part II." *Medium Aevum* 3 (1934): 95–111.

_____. "Sir Gawain and the Green Knight." In *The Monsters and the Critics and Other Essays*, edited by Christopher Tolkien, 72–108. Boston: Houghton Mifflin, 1983.

_____. *The Silmarillion*. 1st American ed. Edited by Christopher Tolkien. Boston: Houghton Mifflin, 1977.

_____. *The Silmarillion*. 2nd ed. Edited by Christopher Tolkien. Boston: Houghton Mifflin, 2001.

_____. *The Tolkien Reader*. New York: Ballantine Books, 1966.

_____. *The Treason of Isengard: The History of The Lord of the Rings, Part Two*. Vol. 7, *History of Middle-Earth*. Edited by Chritopher Tolkien. Boston: Houghton Mifflin, 1989.

_____. *Tree and Leaf: Including the Poem Mythopoeia*. Boston: Houghton Mifflin, 1989.

_____. *The Two Towers*. Boston: Houghton Mifflin, 1993.

_____. *Unfinished Tales of Númenor and Middle-Earth*. Edited by Christopher Tolkien. Boston: Houghton Mifflin, 1980.

_____. *The War of the Ring: The History of The Lord of the Rings, Part Three*. Vol. 8, *History of Middle-Earth*. Edited by Christopher Tolkien. Boston: Houghton Mifflin, 1990.

_____. "Valedictory Address to the University of Oxford." In *The Monsters and the Critics and Other Essays*, edited by Christopher Tolkien, 224–40. Boston: Houghton Mifflin, 1983.

Tolkien, J. R. R., E. V. Gordon, and Norman Davis. *Sir Gawain and the Green Knight*. 2nd ed. Oxford: Clarendon Press, 1967.

Interviews, Quotes, Misc. Primary Sources

Brace, Keith. "In the Footsteps of the Hobbits." *Birmingham Post*, 25 May 1968.

_____. "Tolkien Dismissed Idea of a Deeper Meaning." *Birmingham Post*, 27 November 2001, 11.

Breit, Harvey. "Oxford Calling." *New York Times Book Review*, 5 June 1955, 8.

Carpenter, Humphrey. "J. R. R. Tolkien: Our Brief Encounter." *London Sunday Times*, 25 November 2001.

_____, ed. *The Letters of J. R. R. Tolkien*. Boston: Houghton Mifflin, 1981.

Castell, Daphne. "The Realms of Tolkien." *New Worlds*, November 1966.

_____. "Tolkien on Tolkien: Making of a Myth." *Christian Science Monitor*, 11 August 1966, 11.

Cater, William. "The Filial Duty of Christopher Tolkien." In *The Tolkien Scrapbook*, edited by Alida Becker, 90–95. Philadelphia: Running Press, 1978.

_____. "Lord of the Hobbits." *London Daily Express*, 22 November 1966.

_____. "More and More People Are Getting the J. R. R. Tolkien Habit." *Los Angeles Times*, 9 April 1972, 14, 18.

_____. "We Talked of Love, Death, and Fairy Tales." *London*

Daily Telegraph, 29 November 2001, 23.

Ezard, John. "Light Going." *Manchester Guardian*, 8 January 1972, 9.

_____. "So, Would Tolkien Have Liked the Film?" *London Guardian*, 14 December 2001, 4.

_____. "Tolkien's World." *Manchester Guardian*, 22 January 1972, 19.

Foster, William. "An Early History of the Hobbits." *Edinburgh Scotsman*, 5 February 1972.

Gerrolt, Dennis. "J. R. R. Tolkien: Middle England to Middle-Earth." *Birmingham Post*, 29 December 2001, 45.

_____. *Now Read On*. Radio Broadcast. London: BBC Radio 4, 1971.

"Letters Give Insight into Author Tolkien Family Man." *Coventry Evening Telegraph*, 12 December 2001, 6.

"Letters Reveal Tolkien as a Grouchy Hobbit." *Independent* (London), 2 November 2001, 11.

Norman, Philip. "The Magic of Meeting the Real Lord of the Rings." *London Daily Mail*, 13 December 2001, 13.

Plimmer, Charlotte, and Denis Plimmer. "The Man Who Understands Hobbits." *London Daily Telegraph Magazine*, 22 March 1968, 31–32, 35.

Resnick, Henry. "The Hobbit-Forming World of J. R. R. Tolkien." *Saturday Evening Post*, 2 July 1966.

_____. "An Interview with Tolkien." *Niekas* (late spring 1966): 37–43.

"Tolkien Disney Rant." *Scottish Dail Record and Sunday Mail*, 5 July 2001, 27.

"Tolkien Talking." *London Sunday Times*, 27 November 1966, 9.

Tolkien, J. R. R. "Hobbits." *London Observer*, 20 February 1938, 9.

_____. "Letter to Deborah Webster, 25 October 1958." In *J. R. R. Tolkien*. Edited by Deborah Webster Rogers and Ivor A. Rogers, 125–26. Boston: Twayne, 1970.

_____. "Tolkien on Tolkien." *Diplomat* (October 1966): 39.

Memoirs Regarding Tolkien

Anonymous. "Professor J. R. R. Tolkien: Creator of Hobbits and Inventor of a New Mythology [London Times Obit, 3 September 1973]." In *J. R. R. Tolkien, Scholar and Storyteller: Essays in Memoriam*, edited by Mary Salu and Robert T. Farrell, 11–15. Ithaca, N.Y.: Cornell University Press, 1979.

Burchfield, Robert. "My Hero," *Independent Magazine*, 4 March 1989.

Como, James T., ed. *C. S. Lewis at the Breakfast Table and Other Reminiscences*. New York: Collier, 1979.

Curtis, Anthony. "Hobbits and Heroes." *London Sunday Telegraph*, 10 November 1963, 16.

_____. "Remembering Tolkien and Lewis." *British Book News*, June 1977, 429–30.

Hill, Joy. "Echoes of the Old Ringmaster." *The London Times*, 10 December 1990, 16.

Hooper, Walter. "The Other Oxford Movement." In *Tolkien: A Celebration*, edited by Joseph Pearce, 183–90. London: Fount, 1999.

Kilby, Clyde S. *Tolkien and the Silmarillion*. Wheaton, Ill.: Harold Shaw Publishers, 1976.

Lawlor, John. *C. S. Lewis: Memories and Reflections*. Dallas, Tex.: Spence, 1998.

Lewis, C. S. *All My Road before Me: The Diary of C. S. Lewis, 1922–1927*. San Diego, Calif.: Harcourt Brace Jovanovich, 1991.

_____. *Surprised by Joy: The Shape of My Early Life*. New York: Harcourt Brace and Company, 1955.

Lewis, Warren Hamilton. *Brothers and Friends: The Diaries of Major Warren Hamilton Lewis*. San Francisco, Calif.: Harper and Row, 1982.

_____, ed. *Letters of C. S. Lewis*. New York: Harcourt, Brace, and World, 1982.

Murray, Robert. "J. R. R. Tolkien and the Art of the Parable." In *Tolkien: A Celebration*, edited by Joseph Pearce, 40–52. London: Fount, 1999.

Pearce, Joseph. "Tolkien and C. S. Lewis: An Interview with Walter Hooper." In *Tolkien: A Celebration*, edited by Joseph Pearce, 190–98. London: Fount, 1999.

Sayer, George. "Recollections of J. R. R. Tolkien." In *Tolkien: A Celebration*, edited by Joseph Pearce. London: Fount, 1999.

Tolkien, John and Priscilla Tolkien. *The Tolkien Family Album*. Boston: Houghton Mifflin, 1992.

Tolkien, Michael. "J. R. R. Tolkien—the Wizard Father." *London Sunday Telegraph*, 9 September 1973.

Tolkien, Priscilla. "Memories of J. R. R. Tolkien in His Centenary Year." *The Brown Book* (December 1992): 12–14.

Wain, John. *Sprightly Running: Part of an Autobiography*. New York: St. Martin's, 1962.

Secondary Writings

Acton, John Emerich Edward Dalberg. *Essays in the History of Liberty*. Indianapolis, Ind.: Liberty Fund, 1986.

Aldrich, Kevin. "The Sense of Time in Tolkien's The Lord of the Rings." In *Tolkien: A Celebration*, edited by Joseph Pearce, 86–101. London: Fount, 1999.

Anderson, Douglas A. "Christopher Tolkien: A Bibliography." In *Tolkien's Legendarium: Essays on the History of Middle-Earth*, edited by Verlyn Flieger and Carl F. Hostetter. Westport, Conn.: Greenwood Press, 2000.

_____. "Tolkien after All These Years." In *Meditations on Middle-Earth*, edited by Karen Haber. New York: St. Martin's, 2001.

Anderson, Poul. Introduction to *Awakening the Elves*, edited by Karen Haber. New York: St. Martin's, 2001.

"Baptists Hail Lord of the Rings." *Calgary Herald*, 29 December 2001, 9.

Barbour, Brian. "Lewis and Cambridge." *Modern Philology* 96 (May 1999): 439–84.

Belloc, Hilaire. *The Servile State*. Indianapolis, Ind.: Liberty Fund, 1977.

Birzer, Bradley J. "The Christian Gifts of J. R. R. Tolkien." *New Oxford Review* (November 2001): 25–29.

Birzer, Bradley J., and John Willson. Introduction to James Fenimore Cooper, *The American Democrat and Other Political Essays*. Washington, D.C.: Regnery, 2000.

Bloom, Harold, ed. *J. R. R. Tolkien*. Philadelphia: Chelsea House Publishers, 2000.

_____, ed. *J. R. R. Tolkien's The Lord of the Rings*. Philadelphia: Chelsea House Publishers, 2000.

Boffetti, Jason. "Tolkien's Catholic Imagination." *Crisis* (November 2001): 34–40.

Boniface, St. *The Letters of Saint Boniface*. Translated by Ephraim Emerton. New York: Columbia University, 2000.

"Books of the Century." *Christianity Today* (24 April 2000): 92–93.

Bratman, David. "The Literary Value of the History of Middle-Earth." In *Tolkien's Legendarium: Essays on the History of*

Middle-Earth, edited by Verlyn Flieger and Carl F. Hostetter. Westport, Conn.: Greenwood Press, 2000.

Breit, Harvey. "Oxford Calling." *New York Times Book Review*, 5 June 1955, 8.

Bruner, Kurt, and Jim Ware. *Finding God in The Lord of the Rings*. Wheaton, Ill.: Tyndale, 2001.

Burns, Marjorie. "Gandalf and Odin." In *Tolkien's Legendarium: Essays on the History of Middle-Earth*, edited by Verlyn Flieger and Carl F. Hostetter. Westport, Conn.: Greenwood Press, 2000.

Butler, Robert W., and John Mark Eberhart. "Women Left at Ring Side: Female Sex Had Little Influence on Tolkien's Work." *Calgary Herald*, 28 December 2001, D10.

Byock, Jesse L., ed. *The Saga of the Volsungs*. London: Penguin, 1999.

Caldecott, Stratford. "Over the Chasm of Fire: Christian Heroism in the Silmarillion and The Lord of the Rings." In *Tolkien: A Celebration*, edited by Joseph Pearce, 17–33. London: Fount, 1999.

Card, Orson Scott. "How Tolkien Means." In *Meditations on Middle-Earth*, edited by Karen Haber. New York: St. Martin's, 2001.

Carney, Brian M. "The Battle of the Books." *Wall Street Journal*, 30 November 2001.

Carpenter, Humphrey. *The Inklings: C. S. Lewis, J. R. R. Tolkien, Charles Williams, and Their Friends*. 1st American ed. Boston Houghton Mifflin, 1979.

————. *J. R. R. Tolkien: A Biography*. Boston: Houghton Mifflin, 1977.

Carvajal, Doreen. "Marketing Plan: Taking God out of the Narnia Tales." *New York International Herald Tribune*, 5 June 2001, 15.

Chance, Jane. *Tolkien's Art: A Mythology for England*. Lexington: University of Kentucky Press, 2001.

Chesterton, G. K. *The Everlasting Man*. San Francisco: Ignatius, 1993.

————. *G. K. Chesterton: Collected Works.* Vol. III. San Francisco: Ignatius, 1990.

————. *Orthodoxy.* Colorado Springs, Colo.: Shaw, 1994.

Christopher, Joe. "Tolkien's Lyric Poetry." In *Tolkien's Legendarium: Essays on the History of Middle-Earth,* edited by Verlyn Flieger and Carl F. Hostetter. Westport, Conn.: Greenwood Press, 2000.

Clausen, Christopher. "Lord of the Rings and the Ballad of the White Horse." *South Atlantic Bulletin* 39 (May 1974): 10–16.

"Colin Hardie." *London Times,* 20 October 1998.

Conrad, Peter. "The Babbit." *New Statesman,* 23 September 1977, 408–9.

Cooperman, Stanley. "The Two Towers." *Nation* (17 September 1955): 251.

Crabbe, Katharyn W. *J. R. R. Tolkien.* New York: F. Ungar, 1981.

Crumm, David. "The Spirit of Fantasy." *Detroit Free Press,* 14 May 2001.

Curry, Patrick. *Defending Middle-Earth: Tolkien, Myth and Modernity.* Edinburgh: Floris Books, 1997.

————. "Modernity in Middle-Earth." In *Tolkien: A Celebration,* edited by Joseph Pearce, 34–39. London: Fount, 1999.

————. "Tolkien and His Critics: A Critique." In *Root andBranch: Approaches Towards Understanding Tolkien,* edited by Thomas Honegger, 81–148. Zurich: Walking Tree, 1999.

Coulombe, Charles A. "The Lord of the Rings—a Catholic View." In *Tolkien: A Celebration,* edited by Joseph Pearce, 53–66. London: Fount, 1999.

Dahlin, Robert. "Houghton Mifflin's Fall Title by J. R. R. Tolkien to Excavate the Founding of Middle-Earth." *Publisher's Weekly* (14 February 1977): 59.

Davenport, Guy. "Hobbits in Kentucky." *New York Times,* 23 February 1979, A27.

_____. "J. R. R. Tolkien, RIP." *National Review* (28 September 1973): 1042–43.

Davis, Erik. "The Fellowship of the Ring." *Wired* (October 2001): 120–32.

Dawson, Christopher. *Christianity and the New Age*. Manchester, N.H.: Sophia Institute Press, 1985.

_____. *The Judgment of Nations*. New York: Sheed and Ward, 1942.

_____. *Progress and Religion: An Historical Inquiry*. Washington, D.C.: Catholic University of America Press, 2001.

_____. *Religion and the Rise of Western Culture*. New York: Image, 1991.

Day, David. *Tolkien's Ring*. New York: Barnes and Noble, 1999.

De Lint, Charles. "The Tales Goes Ever On." In *Meditations on Middle-Earth*, edited by Karen Haber. New York: St. Martin's, 2001.

Del Ray, Lester. "A Report on J. R. R. Tolkien." *Worlds of Fantasy* 1, no. 1 (1968): 84–85.

Derrick, Christopher. *C. S. Lewis and the Church of Rome*. San Francisco: Ignatius Press, 1981.

Dibbell, Julian. "J. R. R. Tolkien Still Feeds the Nerd Nation's Imagination: Lord of the Geeks." *Village Voice*, 6–12 June 2001.

Doyle, John S. "Debating the Century's Best Reads." *World Press Review* (April 1997): 44–45.

"Dressing Up Gets Dressing Down in Russia." *Ottawa Citizen*, 24 February 2002, C16.

Duane, Diane. "The Longest Sunday." In *Meditations on Middle-Earth*, edited by Karen Haber. New York: St. Martin's, 2001.

Duriez, Colin, and David Porter. *The Inklings Handbook*. St. Louis, Mo.: Chalice Press, 2001.

Duriez, Colin. *Tolkien and The Lord of the Rings: A Guide to Middle-earth*. Mahwah, N.J.: Hidden Spring, 2001.

Edwardes, Charlotte, and Daniel Foggo. "Jk Vs Jrr: The Film Adaptations of Harry Potter and The Lord of the Rings Should Set Box Office Records." *London Sunday Telegraph*, 11 November 2001, 20.

Eliot, T. S. *Christianity and Culture*. San Diego: Harvest, 1976.

Ernst, Trent. "Three Ring Circus." *Vancouver Sun*, 20 January 2001.

"Eucastrophe." *Time* (17 September 1973): 101.

Evans, Robley. *J. R. R. Tolkien*. New York: Crowell, 1972.

"Families at War: Discord of the Rings for Tolkiens." *London Independent*, 2 December 2001, 9.

Fairburn, Elwin. "J. R. R. Tolkien: A Mythology for England." In *Tolkien: A Celebration*, edited by Joseph Pearce, 73–85. London: Fount, 1999.

Farrell, Robert T., and Mary Salu. *J. R. R. Tolkien, Scholar and Storyteller : Essays in Memoriam*. Ithaca, N.Y.: Cornell University Press, 1979.

Feist, Raymond. "Our Grandfather: Meditation on J. R. R. Tolkien." In *Meditations on Middle-Earth*, edited by Karen Haber. New York: St. Martin's, 2001.

"The Fellowship of the Ring." *New Yorker* (13 November 1954): 218–19.

Fisher, Jude. *The Lord of the Rings: The Fellowship of the Rings: Visual Companion*. Boston: Houghton Mifflin, 2001.

Flieger, Verlyn. "The Footsteps of Aelfwine." In *Tolkien's Legendarium: Essays on the History of Middle-Earth*, edited by Verlyn Flieger and Carl F. Hostetter. Westport, Conn.: Greenwood Press, 2000.

_____. *A Question of Time: J. R. R. Tolkien's Road to Faerie*. Kent, Ohio: Kent State University Press, 1997.

_____. *Splintered Light: Logos and Language in Tolkien's World*. Grand Rapids, Mich.: Eerdmans, 1983.

Flieger, Verlyn, and Carl F. Hostetter, eds. *Tolkien's Legendarium:*

Essays on the History of Middle-Earth. Westport, Conn.: Green-wood Press, 2000.

Flood, Robert H. "Hobbit Hoax? The Fellowship of the Ring." *Books on Trial* (February 1955).

Flynn, Ted. *Thunder of Justice*. Sterling, Va.: MaxKol, 1993.

Foggo, Daniel. "Lord of the Rings Films 'Will Force Tolkien Family into Hiding.'" *London Sunday Telegraph*, 7 January 2001.

Forbes, Cheryl. "Answers About Middle-Earth." *Christianity Today* (7 October 1977): 30–31.

Foster, Robert. *The Complete Guide to Middle-Earth*. New York: Del Ray, 1979.

Fraser, Lindsey. *Conversations with J. K. Rowling*. New York: Scholastic, Inc., 2001.

Friesner, Esther M. "If You Give a Girl a Hobbit." In *Meditations on Middle-Earth*, edited by Karen Haber. New York: St. Martin's, 2001.

Fuller, Edmund. "Catnip for Hobbit Lovers." *Wall Street Journal*, 24 July 1984.

_____. *Myth, Allegory, and Gospel: An Interpretation of J. R. R. Tolkien, C. S. Lewis, G. K. Chesterton [and] Charles Williams*. Minneapolis: Bethany Fellowship, 1974.

_____. "A Superb Addition to Tolkien's Mythological Realm." *Wall Street Journal*, 19 September 1977.

Gardner, Anthony. "Literary Giant or Montrous Myth?" *London Times*, 28 December 1991.

Garth, John. "Tolkien Fantasy Was Born in Trenches of the Somme." *London Evening Standard*, 13 December 2001, 22.

Gaslin, Glenn. "The Language of the Elves: Many of the World's Languages Are Dying out, but Soon a New One Will Surge to Prominence, a Tongue with Ancient Roots and a Big Hollywood Budget." *Vancouver Sun*, 14 July 2001, H3.

Gerville-Reache. "Tolkien's 'Silmarillion' Tests Fans." *Christian Science Monitor*, 21 September 1977.

Giddings, Robert, and Elizabeth Holland. *J. R. R. Tolkien : The Shores of Middle-Earth*. London: Junction Books, 1981.

Gilson, Christopher. "Gnomish Is Sindarin: The Conceptual Evolution of an Elvish Lanuguage." In *Tolkien's Legendarium: Essays on the History of Middle-Earth*, edited by Verlyn Flieger and Carl F. Hostetter. Westport, Conn.: Greenwood Press, 2000.

Gilson, Etienne. *The Spirit of Medieval Philosophy*. Notre Dame, Ind.: University of Notre Dame Press, 1991.

Goldstein, Lisa. "The Mythmaker." In *Meditations on Middle-Earth*, edited by Karen Haber. New York: St. Martin's, 2001.

Green, Roger Lancelyn, and Walter Hooper. *C. S. Lewis: A Biography*. San Diego: Harcourt Brace, 1994.

Greenberg, Martin H., ed. *After the King: Stories in Honor of J. R. R. Tolkien*. New York: Tor, 1992.

Gresham, Douglas H. *Lenten Lands*. New York: MacMillan, 1988.

Greydanus, Steven D. "From Book to Film." *Catholic World Report* (December 2001): 44–47.

Gritten, David. "Why Frodo May Be More Than a Match for Harry." *London Daily Telegraph*, 6 January 2001, 8.

Grotta, Daniel. *The Biography of J. R. R. Tolkien: Architect of Middle-Earth*. Philadelphia: Running Press, 1992.

Guardini, Romano. *The End of the Modern World* (Wilmington, Del.: ISI Books, 1998),

_____. *Letters from Lake Como: Explorations in Technology and the Human Race*. Translated by George Bromiley. Grand Rapids, Mich.: Eerdmans, 1994.

Gunton, Colin. "A Far-Off Gleam of the Gospel: Salvation in Tolkien's The Lord of the Rings." In *Tolkien: A Celebration*, edited by

Joseph Pearce, 124–40. London: Fount, 1999.

Haber, Karen. *Meditations on Middle-Earth*. New York: St. Martin's, 2001.

Halle, Louis J. "Flourishing Orcs." *Saturday Review* (15 January 1955): 17–18.

————. "History through the Mind's Eye." *Saturday Review* (28 January 1956): 11–12.

Hammond, Wayne G. "'A Continuing and Evolving Creation': Dis-tractions in the Later History of Middle-Earth." In *Tolkien's Legendarium: Essays on the History of Middle-Earth*, edited by Verlyn Flieger and Carl F. Hostetter. Westport, Conn.: Greenwood Press, 2000.

————. *J. R. R. Tolkien: A Descriptive Biography*. New Castle, Del.: Oak Knoll Books, 1993.

Hammond, Wayne G., and Christian Scull. "The History of Middle Earth: Review Article." *VII* 12 (1995): 105–10.

————. *J. R. R. Tolkien : Artist & Illustrator*. Boston: Houghton Mifflin, 1995.

Heinen, Tom. "Rings a Catholic Journey." *London Free Press*, 29 December 2001, F7.

Helms, Randel. *Tolkien and the Silmarils*. Boston: Houghton Mifflin, 1981.

Henry, Michael D. "Voegelin and Heidegger as Critics of Modernity." *Modern Age* 43, no. 2 (2001): 118–27.

Herbert, Gary B. "Tolkien's Tom Bombadil and the Platonic Ring of Gyges." *Extrapolation* 26 (1985): 152–59.

Hillegas, Mark Robert. *Shadows of Imagination; the Fantasies of C. S. Lewis, J. R. R. Tolkien, and Charles Williams*. Carbondale, Ill.: Southern Illinois University Press, 1969.

Himes, Jonathan B. "What Did J. R. R. Tolkien Really Do with the Sampo?" *Mythlore* 22, no. 4 (2000): 69–85.

"A History Lesson for Harry Potter." *London Daily Mail*, 12 November 2001, 26–27.

Hobb, Robin. "A Bar and a Quest." In *Meditations on Middle-Earth*, edited by Karen Haber. New York: St. Martin's, 2001.

Hume, Stephen. "Fantasy Casts Welcome Spell in Age of Uncertainty." *Vancouver Sun*, 9 November 2001, F2.

Hurdling, Glenn. "'The Radical Distinction': A Conversation with Tim and Greg Hildebrandt." In *Meditations on Middle-Earth*, edited by Karen Haber. New York: St. Martin's, 2001.

Isaacs, Neil D., and Rose A. Zimbardo, eds. *Tolkien and the Critics: Essays on J. R. R. Tolkien's The Lord of the Rings*. Notre Dame, Ind.: University of Notre Dame Press, 1968.

"J. R. R. Tolkien Dead at 81; Wrote 'Lord of the Rings.'" *New York Times*, 3 September 1973, 18.

Jeffery, Richard. "Root and Tree: The Growth of Tolkien's Writings." In *Tolkien: A Celebration*, edited by Joseph Pearce, 141–55. London: Fount, 1999.

John Paul II, Pope. "Incarnation Inspires Christian Genius." *L'Osservatore Romano* (Vatican City). 4 December 1996.

Johnson, George Burke. "Poetry of J. R. R. Tolkien." In *The Tolkien Papers: Ten Papers Prepared for the Tolkien Festival at Mankato State College, October 28 and 29, 1966*, 63–75. Mankato, Minn.: Mankato State College, 1967.

Johnson, Judith Anne. *J. R. R. Tolkien: Six Decades of Criticism*. Bibliographies and Indexes in World Literature, No. 6. Westport, Conn.: Greenwood Press, 1986.

Judge, Mark Gauvreau. "One Ring to Rule Them All." *Soujourners* (November/December 1996): 50, 53.

Kaveney, Roz. "The Ring Recycled." *New Statesman and Society*, 27 December 1992, 47.

Kennedy, Frances. "Fascists Take Heart From Hobbit Revival." *Independent*, 18 January 2002, 12.

Kilby, Clyde S. "Mythic and Christian Elements in Tolkien." In *Myth, Allegory, and Gospel: An Interpretation of J. R. R. Tolkien, C. S. Lewis, G. K. Chesterton, Charles Williams*, edited by John Warwick Montgomery, 119–43. Minneapolis, Minn.: Bethany Fellowship, 1974.

Kirk, Russell. "Contemporary Literature." *National Review* (22 November 1974): 1359.

————. *Enemies of the Permanent Things: Observations of Abnormity in Literature and Politics*. New Rochelle, N.Y.: Arlington House, 1969.

————. "The Great Mysterious Incorporation of the Human Race." In *Permanent Things: Toward the Recovery of a More Human Scale at the End of the Twentieth Century*, edited by Andrew A. Tadie and Michael H. Macdonald, 1–13. Grand Rapids, Mich.: Eerdmans, 1995.

————. *Prospects for Conservatives*. Chicago: Gateway, 1956.

————. "Tolkien and Truth Through Fantasy," *To the Point* (General Features Corporation), 29/30 June 1968.

Knight, Gareth. *The Magical World of the Inklings : J. R. R. Tolkien, C. S. Lewis, Charles Williams, Owen Barfield*. Shaftesbury, U.K.: Element, 1990.

Kocher, Paul Harold. *A Reader's Guide to the Silmarillion*. Boston: Houghton Mifflin, 1980.

————. *Master of Middle-Earth: The Fiction of J. R. R. Tolkien*. Boston: Houghton Mifflin, 1972.

Kopff, E. Christian. *The Devil Knows Latin: Why America Needs the Classical Tradition*. Wilmington, Del.: ISI Books, 1999.

Kreeft, Peter. *Back to Virtue: Traditional Moral Wisdom for Modern Moral Confusion*. San Francisco: Ignatius Press, 1992.

_____. "Wartime Wisdom in The Lord of the Rings." *St. Austin Review*, January 2002, 4–11.

_____. "The Wonders of the Silmarillion." In *Shadows of Imagination*, ed. Mark R. Hillegas, 161–78. Carbondale, Ill.: Southern Illinois Press, 1979.

Kuitenbrouwer, Peter. "Tolkien Tale Is Magic for Harpercollins." *National Post*, 12 December 2001, FP6.

Lacey, Liam. "The Most Colossal Movie Production Ever Embarked On." *Toronto Globe and Mail*, 15 May 2001.

Laing, Andrew. "At Loss over a Blockbuster: J. R. R. Tolkien's Lord of the Rings Is Coming to the Big Screen." *Glasgow Herald*, 28 November 2001, 17.

Lawhead, Stephen R. "J. R. R. Tolkien: Master of Middle-Earth." In *Tolkien: A Celebration*, ed. Joseph Pearce, 156–71. London: Fount, 1999.

Lawson, Jim. "A Pipe-Smoking Hobbit from the Shire." *Pipes* (2002): 16–20.

Le Guin, Ursula K. "The Dark Tower and Other Stories by C. S. Lewis." *New Republic* (16 April 1977): 29–30.

_____. "Rhythmic Pattern in The Lord of the Rings." In *Meditations on Middle-Earth*, edited by Karen Haber. New York: St. Martin's, 2001.

Leighton, Barry. "Tolkien's Clue to Lord of the Rings." *Bristol Western Daily Press*, 26 February 2002, 11.

Lewis, C. S. *That Hideous Strength*. New York: Macmillan, 1946.

Little, T. E. *The Fantasts: Studies in J. R. R. Tolkien, Lewis Carroll, Mervyn Peake, Nikolay Gogol, and Kenneth Grahame*. Amersham, England: Avebury, 1984.

Lutz, Donald, ed. Preface to *Colonial Origins of the American Constitution*. Indianapolis, Ind.: Liberty Fund, 1998.

Manlove, C. N. *Modern Fantasy: Five Stories.* Cambridge: Cambridge University Press, 1975.

Markos, Louis A. "Myth Matters." *Christianity Today* (23 April 2001): 32–39.

Martin, George. Introduction to *Meditations on Middle-Earth*, edited by Karen Haber. New York: St. Martin's, 2001.

Martinez, Michael. *Visualizing Middle-Earth.* Philadelphia: Xlibris, 2000.

Mathews, Anna Wilde. "New Line Cinema Gives 'Rings' Trilogy a Big Push on Web for Obsessive Fans." *Wall Street Journal*, 10 January 2001, B1.

Mcgill, Hannah. "Youth Culture Risks Picking up a Filthy Hobbit." *Scotsman*, 3 November 2000, 5.

McGrath, Sean. "The Passion According to Tolkien." In *Tolkien: A Celebration*, edited by Joseph Pearce, 172–82. London: Fount, 1999.

McLellan, Joseph. "Frodo and the Cosmos." *Washington Post*, 4 September 1977.

Miller, Dan. "The Hobbit Cult: A Fantastic Ring." *Chicago Daily News*, 8–9 September 1973, 5–6.

Mitgang, Herbert. "Behind the Best Sellers: J. R. R. Tolkien." *New York Times*, 2 October 1977, 48.

Moorcock, Michael. *Wizardry and Wild Romance: A Study in Epic-Fantasy.* London: Victor Gollancz, 1987.

Moseley, C. W. R. D. *J. R. R. Tolkien.* Plymouth, U.K.: Northcote House & British Council, 1997.

Moseley, Charles. "A Creature of Hobbit." *London Observer*, 8 October 2000.

Neimark, Anne E., and Brad Weinman. *Myth Maker : J. R. R. Tolkien.* San Diego: Harcourt Brace & Co., 1996.

"Nibelungenlied." In *Medieval Epics*, edited by Helen M. Mustard, 217–254. New York: Modern Library, 1998.

Nicol, Charles. "The Reinvented World." *Harper's* 255 (November 1977): 95–103.

Noad, Charles E. "On the Construction of 'The Silmarillion.'" In *Tolkien's Legendarium: Essays on the History of Middle-Earth*, edited by Verlyn Flieger and Carl F. Hostetter. Westport, Conn.: Greenwood Press, 2000.

Noble, Thomas F. X., and Thomas Head, eds. *Soldiers of Christ/: Saints and Saints' Lives from Late Antiquity and the Early Middle Ages*. University Park, Pa.: Penn State University, 1995.

Norman, Philip. "The Magic of Meeting the Real Lord of the Rings." *London Daily Mail*, 13 December 2001, 13.

"Notes on People." *New York Times*, 4 October 1977, 32.

Obertino, James. "Moria and Hades: Underworld Journeys in Tolkien and Virgil." *Comparative Literature Studies* 30, no. 2 (1993): 153–69.

O'Brien, Michael. *A Landscape with Dragons: The Battle for Your Child's Mind*. San Francisco: Ignatius Press, 1998.

———. "Restoring the Sense of Wonder." *Catholic World Report* (December 2001): 39–43.

O'Hehir, Andrew. "The Book of the Century." *Salon* (4 June 2001).

Partridge, Brenda. "No Sex Please—We're Hobbits: The Construction of Female Sexuality in The Lord of the Rings." In *J. R. R. Tolkien: This Far Land*, edited by Robert R. Giddings, 179–97. Totowa, N.J.: Barnes and Noble, 1984.

Patrick, James. "J. R. R. Tolkien and the Literary Catholic Revival." *Latin Mass* (spring 1999): 82–86.

Pearce, Joseph. *Literary Converts: Spiritual Inspiration in an Age of Unbelief*. San Francisco: Ignatius, 2000.

_____, ed. *Tolkien: A Celebration*. London: Fount, 1999.

_____. "Tolkien and the Catholic Literary Revival." In *Tolkien: A Celebration*, edited by Joseph Pearce, 102–23. London: Fount, 1999.

_____. *Tolkien: Man and Myth*. San Francisco: Ignatius Press, 1998.

_____. "True Myth: The Catholicism of The Lord of the Rings." *Catholic World Report* (December 2001): 34–38.

Person, James E., Jr. *Russell Kirk: A Critical Biography of a Conservative Mind*. Lanham, Md.: Madison Books, 1999.

Plimmer, Charlotte, and Denis Plimmer. "The Man Who Understands Hobbits." *London Daily Telegraph Magazine* (22 March 1968): 31–32, 35.

Power, Edward. "Michael Moorcock." *Irish Times*, 29 December 2001, 61.

Pratchett, Terry. "Cult Classic." In *Meditations on Middle-Earth*, edited by Karen Haber. New York: St. Martin's, 2001.

Priestman, Judith. *Tolkien: Life and Legend*. Oxford: Bodleian Library [1992].

Purtill, Richard L. *J. R. R. Tolkien: Myth, Morality, and Religion*. 1st ed. San Francisco: Harper & Row, 1984.

_____. *Lord of the Elves and Eldils; Fantasy and Philosophy in C. S. Lewis and J. R. R. Tolkien*. Grand Rapids, Mich.: Zondervan, 1974.

Rahe, Paul. *Republics: Ancient and Modern*. Chapel Hill, N.C.: University of North Carolina Press, 1992.

Rateliff, John D. "The Lost Road, the Dark Tower, and the Notion Club Papers: Tolkien and Lewis's Time Travel Triad." In *Tolkien's Legenarium: Essays on the History of Middle-Earth*, ed. Verlyn Flieger and Carl F. Hostetter. Westport, Conn.: Greenwood Press, 2000.

Ratliff, William E., and Charles G. Flinn. "The Hobbit and the Hippie." *Modern Age* (spring 1968): 142–46.

Reuter, Madalynne. "Hm's 'The Silmarillion' Sets New Record." *Publishers Weekly* (26 September 1977): 106–8.

Reynolds, Barbara. "Memories of C. S. Lewis in Cambridge." *Chesterton Review* 17 (1991): 378–84.

Robson, John. "The Lion, the Witch, and the Whatever." *Ottawa Citizen*, 6 June 2001, A18.

Rossi, Lee D. *The Politics of Fantasy, C. S. Lewis and J. R. R. Tolkien.* Studies in Speculative Fiction, No. 10. Ann Arbor, Mich.: UMI Research Press, 1984.

Rothstein, Edward. "Flaming Swords and Wizards' Orbs." *New York Times Book Review*, 8 December 1996, 60–61.

Russello, Gerald J., ed. *Christianity and European Culture: Selections from the Work of Christopher Dawson.* Washington, D.C.: Catholic University Press of America, 1998.

Sale, Roger. *Modern Heroism: Essays on D. H. Lawrence, William Empson, & J. R. R. Tolkien.* Berkeley, Calif.: University of California Press, 1973.

Sayer, George. Liner notes to *J. R. R. Tolkien Reads and Sings His Lord of the Rings.* Caedmon CDL5 1478.

Schall, James V. "On the Reality of Fantasy." *Crisis* (March 1992): 42–44.

Scripps Howard News Service. "Observers Question How Tolkien Will Translate to Film." *Evansville Courier & Press*, 4 August 2001.

Scull, Christina. "The Development of Tolkien's Legendarium: Some Threads in the Tapestry of Middle-Earth." In *Tolkien's Legendarium: Essays on the History of Middle-Earth*, edited by Verlyn Flieger and Carl F. Hostetter. Westport, Conn.: Greenwood Press, 2000.

Shippey, T. A., ed. *Leaves from the Tree: J. R. R. Tolkien's Shorter Fiction.* London: The Tolkien Society, 1991.

_____. *The Road to Middle-Earth.* Boston: Houghton Mifflin, 1983.

_____. *J. R. R. Tolkien: Author of the Century*. Boston: Hougton Mifflin, 2001.

_____. "Why the Critics Must Recognize Lord of the Rings as a Classic." *London Daily Telegraph*, 2 January 2002.

Sibley, Brian. *The Lord of the Rings: Official Movie Guide*. Boston: Houghton Mifflin, 2001.

Smith, Alan. "A Shire Pleasure." *Pipes* (2001): 20–24.

Smith, Arden R. "Certhas, Skirditaila, Fupark: A Feigned History of Runic." In *Tolkien's Legendarium: Essays on the History of Middle-Earth*, edited by Verlyn Flieger and Carl F. Hostetter. Westport, Conn.: Greenwood Press, 2000.

Soukup, Daniel. "Middle-Earth—A Fundamentally Catholic World?" *St. Austin Review* (January 2002): 18–21.

Spacks, Patricia Meyer. "Ethical Pattern in The Lord of the Rings." *Critique* 3 (1959): 30–42.

Spencer, Stewart, and Barry Millington, eds. *Selected Letters of Richard Wagner*. New York: W.W. Norton, 1988.

Stanton, Michael N. *Hobbits, Elves, and Wizards: Exploring the Wonders and Worlds of J. R. R. Tolkien's The Lord of the Rings*. New York: St. Martins, 2001.

Stanwick, Michael. "A Changeling Returns." In *Meditations on Middle-Earth*, edited by Karen Haber. New York: St. Martin's, 2001.

Stevens, David, Carol D. Stevens, and Roger C. Schlobin. *J. R. R. Tolkien—the Art of the Myth-Maker*. Rev. ed. San Bernardi no, Calif.: R. Reginald, 1993.

Stewart, Douglas J. "The Hobbit War." *Nation* (9 October 1967): 332–34.

Stimpson, Catharine R. *J. R. R. Tolkien*. New York: Columbia University Press, 1969.

Straight, Michael. "The Fantastic World of Professor Tolkien." *New Republic* (16 January 1956): 24–26.

Sullivan, C. W. "Name and Lineage Patterns: Aragorn and Beowulf." *Extrapolation* 25 (1984): 239–46.

Swann, Donald. *Swann's Way: A Life in Song.* London: Heinemann, 1991.

Taylor, D. J. "The Lion, the Witch, and the Boardroom." *London Independent*, 7 June 2001, 1.

_____. "The Secret Life of J. R. R. Tolkien: The Lord of the Rings Is the Product of a Magnificent Imagination." *London Independent*, 21 November 2001, 7.

Taylor, J. E. A. *The Tolkien Companion.* New York: Grammercy, 2000.

Thomas, Paul Edmund. "Some of Tolkien's Narrators." In *Tolkien's Legendarium: Essays on the History of Middle-Earth*, edited by Verlyn Flieger and Carl F. Hostetter. Westport, Conn.: Greenwood Press, 2000.

Timmons, Daniel. "Sub-Creator and Creator: Tolkien and the Design of the One." *St. Austin Reiew* (January 2002): 12–14.

Todd, Douglas. "The Christian Roots of the Rings." *Vancouver Sun*, 14 December 2001, A23.

"Tolkien Letters, Book Proofs on the Block." *Toronto Sun*, 3 November 2001, 50.

"Tolkien's Enduring Legacy." *Irish News*, 24 December 2001, 41.

"Tolkien's Publisher Says 'Silmarillion' Will Be Released." *New York Times*, 4 September 1973, 31.

"Tolkiens in Family Feud over Film." *Toronto Sun*, 3 December 2001, 39.

Turner, Jenny. "The Lure of the Rings." *London Sunday Telegraph*, 25 November 2001, 1.

_____. "Reasons for Liking Tolkien." *London Review of Books*, 15 November 2001.

Turtledove, Harry. "The Ring and I." In *Meditations on Middle-Earth*, edited by Karen Haber. New York: St. Martin's, 2001.

"The Two Towers." *New Yorker* (14 May 1955): 170, 173.

Unwin, Rayner. "Early Days of Elder Days." In *Tolkien's Legendarium: Essays on the History of Middle-Earth,* edited by Verlyn Flieger and Carl F. Hostetter. Westport, Conn.: Greenwood Press, 2000.

Urang, Gunnar. *Shadows of Heaven: Religion and Fantasy in the Writing of C. S. Lewis, Charles Williams, and J. R. R. Tolkien.* Philadelphia: Pilgrim Press, 1971.

Voegelin, Eric. *Science, Politics, and Gnosticism: Two Essays.* Chicago: Regnery, 1968.

Wagenknect, Edward. "'Ring' Joins Great Novels of the Year." *Sunday Tribune,* 26 December 1954.

Wagner, Richard. *The Ring of the Nibelung.* New York: W.W. Norton, 1976.

Ware, Jim. "Stories within Stories: Finding God in 'The Lord of the Rings.'" *Focus on the Family* (December 2001): 9–11.

Weigel, George. "John Paul II and the Crisis of Humanism." *First Things* 98 (December 1999): 31–36.

Weinraub, Bernard. "Cecil Beaton Knighted by Queen; a Racing Driver Is Also Honored." *New York Times,* 1 January 1972, 3.

West, John G., Jr. "The Lord of the Rings as a Defence of the Freedoms of Western Civilization." *St. Austin Review* (January 2002): 15–17.

West, Richard C. "Turin's Ofermod: An Old English Theme in the Development of the Story of Turin." In *Tolkien's Legendarium: Essays on the History of Middle-Earth,* edited by Verlyn Flieger and Carl F. Hostetter. Westport, Conn.: Greenwood Press, 2000.

Williams, Lynn. "Tolkien Is Still Fantastic, 100 Years after His Birth." *St. Louis Post-Dispatch,* January 12 1992, 1C.

Wilson, A. N. "'Tolkien Was Not a Writer' What Is the Secret of The Lord of the Rings' Appeal?" *London Daily Telegraph*, 24 November 2001, 7.

Wilson, Christopher. "As the Fantasy World of The Lord of the Rings Is Brought to Life on the Big Screen, the Author's Family Has Bitterly Condemned the Project: The Sad Legacy of Tolkien's Fable." *London Express*, 12 October 2001, 37.

Wilson, Colin. *Tree by Tolkien*. Santa Barbara, Calif.: Capra Press, 1974.

Wilson, Edmund. "Oo, Those Awful Orcs." *Nation* 182 (14 April 1956): 312–14.

Windling, Terry. "On Tolkien and Fairy-Stories." In *Meditations on Middle-Earth*, edited by Karen Haber. New York: St. Martin's, 2001.

Wynne, Patrick, and Carl F. Hostetter. "Three Elvish Verse Modes: Ann-Thennath, Minlamad Thent/Estent, and Linnod." In *Tolkien's Legendarium: Essays on the History of Middle-Earth*, edited by Verlyn Flieger and Carl F. Hostetter. Westport, Conn.: Greenwood Press, 2000.

Yolen, Jane. Introduction to *After the King: Stories in Honor of J. R. R. Tolkien*, edited by Martin H. Greenberg. New York: Tor, 1992.

Index